GHOSTS OF EVEREST

THE AUTHORIZED STORY
OF THE SEARCH FOR MALLORY & IRVINE

JOCHEN HEMMLEB, LARRY A. JOHNSON
& ERIC R. SIMONSON

*Of the expedition team that found
Mallory on Everest*

As told to WILLIAM W. NOTHDURFT

PAN BOOKS

First published 1999 by The Mountaineers Books, Seattle, Washington, USA

First published in Great Britain 1999 by Macmillan

This edition published 2000 by Pan Books
an imprint of Macmillan Publishers Ltd
25 Eccleston Place London SW1W 9NF
Basingstoke and Oxford
Associated companies throughout the world
www.macmillan.com

ISBN 0 330 39379 0

3 5 7 9 8 6 4 2

Typeset by SX Composing DTP, Rayleigh, Essex
Printed and bound in Great Britain by Mackays of Chatham plc, Chatham, Kent

Editor-in-Chief: Margaret Foster
Edited by Kris Fulsaas
Historical Photo Research: Margaret K. Sullivan
Production Director: Helen Cherullo
Cover Design by Jennifer LaRock Shontz

Photographers and Picture Sources: We gratefully acknowledge all those who provided
pictures for use in this book. We have made every attempt to trace copyright holders and
gain permission for such use and apologize for any errors or omissions.

A CIP catalogue record for this book is available from the British Library.

CONTENTS

Jochen Hemmleb is The Mallory & Irvine Research Expedition Team Historian.

Born in 1971, he is recognized as one of the world authorities on Mount Everest's North Ridge and the history of mountaineering in the region. An active mountaineer, he has climbed extensively in the European Alps and East Africa, and has travelled widely in Europe, Africa and New Zealand. He is at present studying at the University of Frankfurt in Germany.

Larry A. Johnson is The Mallory & Irvine Research Expedition Team Co-ordinator.

Born in 1946, he is a former Director of Stackpole Books, an independent publisher of non-fiction books. Larry is active in climbing in the Eastern United States, the Rockies, the Yosemite, and in the Cascades. He became acquainted with Hemmleb's research on the Mallory/Irvine mystery and helped Simonson and Hemmleb to co-ordinate the expedition.

Eric R. Simonson is The Mallory & Irvine Research Expedition Leader.

Born in 1956, he has been a professional guide since 1973 and has personally conducted over seventy expeditions around the world, including over twenty in the Himalayas. He is one of the most respected expedition organizers in the world and took the lead in organizing the entire expedition, bringing together an expert team of high altitude climbers.

William E. Nothdurft is a renowned consultant, author, and travel writer.

The author of several books and countless articles, he has written books for President Bill Clinton, Vice-President Al Gore, and Mount Everest pioneer and adventurer Jim Whittaker. He lives in Seattle, Washington.

ACKNOWLEDGMENTS

The 1999 Mallory & Irvine Research Expedition would not have been successful without the hard work and support of many individuals, organizations, and companies in the United States, Britain, Nepal, China, and Tibet.

For their pioneering work into the mystery of Mallory and Irvine, we are indebted to Tom Holzel and Audrey Salkeld.

For their expert mountaineering skills, team spirit, and enthusiasm for this project, we thank the entire expedition team and the Sherpa, who took this dream into the real world and became a part of a historic event.

For her hard work in helping to manage and organize every phase of the expedition and well beyond, we are indebted to Erin Copland.

We thank our media partners: Chuck Gottschalk, Peter Potterfield, and Anya Zolotusky at MountainZone.com; Liesl Clark, David Breashears, and Paula Apsell at WGBH/NOVA; Graham Hoyland, Peter Firstbrook, and Kate Slattery at the BBC; Nate Simmons, Lisa Raleigh, and Penn Newhart at Backbone Media.

For their special assistance during the course of the expedition, we thank old friends and new, including: Mr. Ying Daoshui at China-Tibet Mountaineering Association; Liu Feng, Zhao Lin Lin, and Renchin Phinjo, our Everest 1999 Rongbuk Liaison Officers; Xu Chuan, interpreter; Sonam Gyalpo and Ang Jangbo of Great Escapes Trekking in Kathmandu.

For their invaluable expertise and assistance with the artifacts: Schelleen Scott and Heather Macdonald; Larry Huntington, Dan Mann, and Charlie Peck of the American Foundation for International Mountaineering, Exploration, and Research; Patricia Blankenship and Lynn Anderson of the Washington State Historical Museum; archaeologist Dr. Rick Reanier; coroner Donald T. Reay, M.D.

Clare Millikan and John Mallory and their families.

For making this book into a reality and this event into an engaging, authentic story: writer Bill Nothdurft along with Margaret Foster, Art Freeman, and the staff at The Mountaineers Books.

In addition:

Jochen Hemmleb would like to thank Larry Johnson for his unrelenting support and loyalty, and Eric Simonson for organizing and leading the expedition to a successful conclusion. The following individuals helped in the course of the research for this book: Dr. Gerhard Bax, Gay Blanchard at Barnard Castle School, Russell Brice, the late Mal Duff, Kiyoshi Furuno, Harry Hett, Maohai Huang, Tim Macartney-Snape, Colin Monteath, Sandra Noel, Joanna Scadden at the Royal Geographical Society, Marc Small, Mike Smith, Julie Summers at the Sandy Irvine Trust, Swiss Airphoto & Survey,

Jon Tinker, Brad Washburn, Thomas Wetter, and Professor Zhou Zheng. And finally, he wishes to thank his family and friends for their love and support over the years.

Larry Johnson would like to thank Jochen Hemmleb for the inspiration to become involved in this grand adventure and Eric Simonson who made the expedition happen. No less important, his wife, Dottie, who has stood by with love and support, and his children for their help and encouragement.

Eric Simonson would like to thank his parents, Hal and Carolyn Simonson, and his friends, clients, and fellow guides for their ongoing support and encouragement.

LIST OF ILLUSTRATIONS

SECTION ONE

The 1924 British Everest Expedition. (© *John Noel Photographic Collection*)

John Noel with his cine camera on the North Col, 1922. (© *John Noel Photographic Collection*)

The first summit team in 1922. (*Photo by John Noel. Courtesy Mountain Camera Archive*)

Mallory and Irvine departing from the North Col, June 6, 1924. (*Photo by Noel Odell. © Royal Geographical Society, London*)

Mallory's note to Odell. (© *John Cleare/Mountain Camera*)

Mallory's note to Noel. (© *John Noel Photographic Collection*)

Noel Ewart Odell. (© *John Noel Photographic Collection*)

Edward Felix Norton. (© *John Noel Photographic Collection*)

Pony train on the approach to Everest, 1924. (© *John Noel Photographic Collection*)

Camp II on the East Rongbuk Glacier, 1924. (*Photo by Bentley Beetham. © Royal Geographical Society, London*)

Sandy Irvine at Everest Base Camp, 1924. (*Photo by Bentley Beetham. © Royal Geographical Society, London*)

Geoffrey Bruce. (© *John Noel Photographic Collection*)

Theodore Howard Somervell. (© *John Noel Photographic Collection*)

Norton at 28,000 feet (8,530 m). (*Photo by T. H. Somervell. © Royal Geographical Society, London/Print courtesy Mountain Camera Archive*)

Irvine with his modified oxygen apparatus. (*Photo by Noel Odell. © Royal Geographical Society, London*)

The ice chimney on the North Col in 1924. (© *John Noel Photographic Collection*)

SECTION TWO

The 1999 Mallory & Irvine Research Expedition. (*Photo by Schelleen Scott*)

Graham Hoyland. (*Photo by Jochen Hemmleb*)

Larry Johnson. (*Photo by William J. Schwartz*)

The Sherpa team. (*Photo by Tap Richards*)

'The trough' on the East Rongbuk Glacier, above Camp II. (*Photo by Andy Politz*)

Rongbuk Base Camp, 1999. (*Photo by Schelleen Scott*)

Puja ceremony at Base Camp. (*Photo by Jake Norton*)

1999 summit route with critical features and sites. (*Photo © Galen Rowell/Mountain Light Photography*)

Dave Hahn approaching the summit of Everest, May 17, 1999. (*Photo by Conrad Anker*)

George Mallory and the summit of Everest. (*Photo by Jake Norton*)

Altimeter; matchbox and tin of meat lozenges; Mallory's wristwatch; letters and handkerchief in which they were wrapped; notes found in Mallory's pocket; spare left glove and a section of climbing rope; Mallory's pocketknife; Mallory's goggles. (*All photos by Jim Fagiolo. © Mallory & Irvine Research Expedition*).

Camp VI. (*Photo by Jake Norton*)

FOREWORD

When Sir Edmund Hillary and Tenzing Norgay made the successful ascent of Mount Everest in 1953, I had mixed feelings. I rejoiced at their success—it seemed especially timely, a gift to the young Queen Elizabeth on her coronation. But I wondered whether people would now forget my father, George Mallory, who had disappeared, along with his young companion Andrew Irvine, during the final summit attempt of the pioneering 1924 British Everest Expedition.

My father chose "Sandy" Irvine as his partner for the summit attempt rather than another expedition member, Noel Odell, who was a more experienced climber. In large part, I think this decision was made because Irvine had worked tirelessly for weeks to perfect the oxygen apparatus upon which their chances of success would depend. In the end, of course, it was Odell's sighting of the two climbers as they ascended an escarpment high on the final summit ridge and then continued upward into the mist, that created much of the drama and controversy over whether the two reached the summit.

My father and expedition leader Edward Norton were deeply pained by the loss of seven porters in an avalanche during the 1922 expedition, and they were determined to take no undue risk on the 1924 expedition—for their porters or for themselves. As to whether my father and Andrew Irvine made the summit before they disappeared, Norton later wrote my mother from base camp, "I put it at an even money chance. They were unaccountably late at the point where they were last seen and yet had time to get to the top without serious risk. They had apparently surmounted the most serious obstacle." Perhaps my father's judgment was clouded by altitude. Perhaps turning back sooner would have saved them.

Four days before my father's summit attempt, Norton and another expedition member, Howard Somervell, climbed to more than 28,000 feet on Everest's North Face, a historic achievement. But who, except avid students of climbing history, remembers Norton or Somervell, or Captain Noel, who brought back amazingly fine photographs of that precipitous, icy world? Who remembers the later attempts by Shipton, Smythe, and Longland?

Yet the mystery of what happened to my father and his young companion on June 8, 1924, continues to fascinate people, nearly three-quarters of a century later. Everest has been climbed now by hundreds of people—men, women, experts, novices. It has been climbed by solo climbers. It has been climbed by George Mallory II, Mallory's grandson and my nephew. It has been climbed with and without oxygen, and by a number of different routes. But still the image of these two early adventurers, with their primitive equipment and sturdy but poorly insulated clothing, working their way up that icy pyramid into the unknown, stirs imaginations of those who dream of adventure the world over.

The remarkable discovery of my father's body in the spring of 1999, which this book chronicles, at first left me feeling very little beyond a mild annoyance that his resting place had been disturbed. It seemed to me that his spirit was far from his body. Gradually, though, as I actually spoke with the climbers who found him, as I experienced their reverence for this man and their sense of his being at peace with the mountain, an old feeling began to resurface: had he turned back earlier, he might have survived instead of lying there, broken on that cold ledge, and I would have grown up to know a wonderful man as my father. Later, when Mallory & Irvine Research Expedition leader Eric Simonson visited me in Berkeley, and showed the objects found on my father's body to members of our family, I was able to touch the goggles found in his pocket—the same goggles, perhaps, my father had shown me when I was eight years old. The climbers also found letters from family and friends in his pocket. What they did not find, however, was a picture of my mother. I have a childhood memory of being told that he carried such a picture to place on the summit. Did the fact that it was missing mean he had, indeed, experienced the joy of knowing he had reached the world's highest point before he died? The mystery remains—perhaps it is more interesting that way!

I have not been much of a student of climbing literature, except for the books of a few people I knew, like Geoffrey Young or Wilfred Noyce, and a few books about my father. Reading about climbing only makes me wish I could be there myself. But as a historian, this book really interests me—it is a compelling, step-by-step account of both the 1924 climb and the 1999 expedition's ascent and discovery of my father's body. I hope it will find many readers.

Clare Millikan
née Frances Clare Leigh-Mallory
Santa Rosa, California
August 1999

A NOTE TO READERS

When three people decide to write a book together, the first practical problem they face is, "Who's telling the story?" What's more, this is more than just our story; it incorporates the best of extensive interviews with other expedition team members as well—Dave Hahn, Jake Norton, Andy Politz, Tap Richards, and our expedition doctor, Lee Meyers.

In the end, we chose to tell our story to Seattle-based author Bill Nothdurft, and let him tell it to you.

Jochen Hemmleb
Larry A. Johnson
Eric R. Simonson

PROLOGUE

LAST ATTEMPT

I can't see myself coming down defeated . . .
GEORGE MALLORY

For three-quarters of a century, this is all that has been known with any certainty:

Just after dawn on the morning of June 6, two members of the 1924 British Everest Expedition, George Leigh Mallory and Andrew Comyn Irvine, crawled out of their simple canvas tent on the North Col, a wind-savaged, 23,180-foot- (7,066-m-) high saddle of snow, ice, and rock between the hulking mass of Everest itself and its lesser northern peak, Changtse, and took the first steps in what would become a climb into history.

They were not alone on that brilliant but bitter-cold morning. Two of their colleagues, Noel Ewart Odell and John de Vere Hazard, had prepared them a hearty breakfast of fried sardines, biscuits, tea, and hot chocolate, which, Odell would later complain, they "hardly did justice to."[1] In another tent draped with sleeping bags to keep it dark, Colonel Edward Felix Norton, the expedition leader, utterly snow-blind and in excruciating pain after an unsuccessful summit attempt two days earlier, awaited help down to Advance Base Camp, some 1,700 feet (500 m) below the col.

The men said little to each other. There was little need. They all knew the situation was critical. It had been more than two months since they had walked out of Darjeeling, India, toward Tibet, and more than a month since they had arrived at their Base Camp at the terminal moraine of the main Rongbuk Glacier, on the Tibetan plain to the north. Twice in that preceding month, they had tried to push higher on the mountain—once as far as Camp III at the base of the North Col, once to Camp IV on the col itself—and twice, miserable weather and mishaps drove them all the way back down to Base Camp. Finally, in the first few days of June, the expedition team succeeded in establishing two higher camps, Camp V at 25,300 feet (7,710 m) and Camp VI at 27,000 feet (8,230 m)[2] but two attempts to reach Everest's 29,029-foot (8,848-m) summit had failed. They were running out of supplies and Sherpa support. Many of their native porters were too sick to climb, and the expedition team itself had been whittled down to a few hardy souls. Most of all, they were running out of time. In a matter of days, perhaps even hours, the annual monsoon would sweep up from the humid Indian subcontinent to the south and bury the high Himalaya under wave upon wave of snowstorms.

Mallory had seen it all before. Twice. The 1924 Everest expedition was in fact the third British attempt in four years. The English had failed to be the first to reach either the North or South Pole, and were now determined that "the Third Pole," Everest, would be theirs. Spurred on by a well-publicized talk by Himalaya explorer Captain John Noel, who had made a clandestine foray into Tibet in 1913, a first expedition was organized for 1921, primarily as a reconnaissance trip into the unmapped Tibetan territory north and east of Everest. Yet the lure of the summit had been strong even before the expedition team left England and Mallory had complained that the composition of the team was inadequate to that task. Except for Mallory's friend and climbing partner Guy Bullock, most of the other expedition members drawn from the Alpine Club's "old-boy network" were just that: old, and generally unfit for climbing at high altitude. Indeed, one expedition member died on just the approach walk.

After weeks of reconnaissance, Mallory sighted a route to the summit from the northeast. A last-minute summit attempt was mounted, but the climbers could get no higher than the North Col before appalling weather forced them down. Ill-equipped and ill-prepared—"I doubt if any big mountain venture has ever been made with a smaller margin of strength,"[3] Mallory wrote—it was a historic achievement nonetheless.

Even before the 1921 expedition team returned from Tibet, officials in London had begun planning another expedition for the next year. This time there were several experienced climbers involved besides Mallory. On that expedition, the first summit team established a Camp V at 25,000 feet (7,620 m), but only reached 26,700 feet (8,130 m)[4] before exhaustion and illness turned them back. A second team, using oxygen, succeeded in establishing a fifth camp at 25,500 feet (7,770 m), but trouble with the oxygen apparatus forced that team to retreat from a height of 27,500 feet (8,380 m).[5] Finally, Mallory led a third attempt on the peak, but this effort failed even to reach the

North Col; an avalanche on the snow slope above Advance Base Camp killed seven of their porters, and the expedition was over.

Now, on this promising June morning, as Mallory and Irvine struggled into their primitive, unreliable, and brutally heavy oxygen apparatus, Noel Odell snapped their picture. In it, Irvine, a strapping young man only twenty-two years old, stands calmly with his hands in his pockets, his head tilted slightly as he watches Mallory fuss with his oxygen mask. Mallory, while certainly the finest English mountaineer of his day, is at age thirty-eight getting "a bit long in the tooth" for Himalaya expeditions. Yet he is driven, almost to the point of obsession, by this mountain and is determined to conquer it, for himself and for his country. This will be the third and last attempt to reach the summit during this expedition. If he fusses with the oxygen device, therefore, it is understandable: everything must be perfect. They have run out of chances. If they are to become the first human beings to reach the highest point on earth, they must succeed on this attempt. It is do or die.

Moments after Odell took the picture, at 8:40 A.M., Mallory and Irvine, accompanied by eight Tibetan porters carrying provisions, blankets, and additional oxygen cylinders, set off up the North Ridge toward Camp V. A little more than eight hours later, four of the porters returned to Camp IV with a note from Mallory: "There is no wind here and things look hopeful."[6] The next morning, the two climbers and the remaining four porters pushed higher to Camp VI. At the same time, Odell and two other porters headed up from the North Col to Camp V to support the summit team should they require assistance on their descent. Odell climbed without supplemental oxygen; he was no fan of the experimental and controversial apparatus and, in any event, the oxygen set he had used on an earlier occasion appeared to give him little benefit.[7]

With Mallory and Irvine established at Camp VI, their remaining four porters descended, carrying with them two notes from Mallory scribbled in pencil on the torn-out pages of a small notebook. One was addressed to Captain John Noel, the expedition cinematographer who would attempt to film the summit assault from Camp III at the base of the North Col:

Dear Noel,
We'll probably start early to-morrow (8th) in order to have clear weather. It won't be too early to start looking for us either crossing the rock band under the pyramid or going up skyline at 8.0 P.M.
Yours ever,
G. Mallory[8]

The "8.0 P.M." was obviously an error; Mallory meant 8:00 A.M. The "rock band" refers to a belt of gray limestone that girdles the summit pyramid and ends in a prominent out-cropping on the Northeast Ridge called the "Second Step."

The other note was addressed to Odell. Ever the English gentleman, Mallory apologized for the condition in which they'd left Camp V; asked him to bring up to Camp VI a compass Mallory had, with characteristic forgetfulness, left behind at Camp V; instructed him to descend the next day to the North Col, as he planned to do the same thing and there was insufficient room at VI for the three of them anyway if he didn't; and filled Odell in on their oxygen use:

Dear Odell,

We're awfully sorry to have left things in such a mess—our Unna Cooker rolled down the slope at the last moment. Be sure of getting back to IV to-morrow in time to evacuate by dark, as I hope to. In the tent I must have left a compass—for the Lord's sake rescue it: we are here without. To here on 90 atmospheres for the two days—so we'll probably go on two cylinders—but it's a bloody load for climbing. Perfect weather for the job!

Yours ever,

G. Mallory

Having sent his ailing porters down with the others, Odell spent the night alone at Camp V. The North Ridge of Everest is notoriously windy, pummeled by gales even in good weather, but this night was relatively calm and the morning dawned clear.

Though Camp VI was only some 2,000 feet below the summit, Mallory and Irvine faced a series of daunting hurdles when they began climbing the next morning: a crumbly "Yellow Band" of steeply rising, scree-strewn limestone slabs; a nearly vertical 100-foot wall of harder rock called the "First Step"; a dicey and exposed ridge walk; the 100-foot "Second Step," far more difficult than the first and described as like "the sharp bow of a battle cruiser"; then a broad, gently rising plateau leading to the snow-covered summit pyramid itself. If they attained the summit, they then faced perhaps the most daunting hurdle of all: descending safely in what would almost certainly be a state of extreme exhaustion.

Mallory and Irvine would have been well on their way by the time Odell pulled on his boots at 8:00 A.M., shouldered a rucksack stuffed with the errant compass and additional provisions for the summit team, and began climbing toward the Northeast Ridge and Camp VI. Odell, a geologist, had achieved a remarkable level of acclimatization to the thin air of Everest's upper reaches (one-third as much oxygen as at sea level), was clear-headed and strong, and planned to spend the morning exploring the geology of the mountain's northern face. By midmorning he noticed the weather had begun to change: "rolling banks of mist began to form and sweep from the westward across the great face of the mountain."[9] He was not worried for the climbers above him, he later wrote, because "There were indications . . . that this mist might chiefly be confined to the lower half of the mountain, as on looking up one could see a certain luminosity that might mean comparatively clear conditions about its upper half."[10]

In no particular hurry to get to Camp VI, Odell wandered happily about the mountainside, a scientist at work. At one point, he scrambled to the top of a rock outcropping to take a look around. Then,

at 12:50, just after I had emerged from a state of jubilation at finding the first definite fossils on Everest, there was a sudden clearing of the atmosphere, and the entire summit ridge and final peak of Everest were unveiled. My eyes became fixed on one tiny black spot silhouetted on a small snow-crest beneath a rock-step in the ridge; the black spot moved. Another black spot became apparent and moved up the snow to join the other on the crest. The first then approached the great rock-step and shortly emerged at the top; the second did likewise. Then the whole fascinating vision vanished, enveloped in cloud once more. There was but one explanation. It was Mallory and his companion moving, as I could see even at that great distance, with considerable alacrity, realising doubtless that they had none too many hours of daylight to reach the summit from their present position and return to Camp VI by nightfall. The place on the ridge referred to is the prominent rock-step at a very short distance from the base of the final pyramid.[11]

Concluding that his colleagues were now perhaps three hours from the summit, Odell climbed up to Camp VI to make it ready should they need it upon what was now certain to be a late return. As he reached the camp, a snow squall blew up and he ducked into the two-man tent for shelter, finding it strewn with food scraps, clothing, the climbers' sleeping bags, oxygen cylinders, and spare parts of oxygen apparatus.

Concerned that the camp, perched on a ledge and backed by a small crag, might be difficult to find in the swirling snow, Odell left the tent and scrambled another 200 feet up the mountain, whistling and yodeling as he went, to guide Mallory and Irvine back to the safety of their tent. After taking shelter behind a rock from the wind and driving snow, however, he realized that it was still too early for the climbers to be returning from the summit and that his calls were pointless. As he arrived back at Camp VI, the squall ended as suddenly as it had started and the snow that had fallen simply evaporated in the dry, cold air and brilliant sunshine. At 4:30 P.M., leaving behind Mallory's compass and the extra food he had brought for them, Odell descended to Camp IV, as Mallory's note the day before had instructed him.

When he arrived, glissading part of the way down the snow slope to speed his descent, Hazard greeted him with hot soup and tea: "What a two days it had been. . . . A period of intensive experiences, alike romantic, aesthetic, and scientific in interest, these each in their various appeals enabling one to forget even the extremity of upward toil inherently involved, and ever at intervals carrying one's thoughts to that resolute pair who might at any instant appear returning with news of final conquest."[12]

But they did not appear.

Odell was not deeply concerned. After all, they had been late on their ascent; it was only reasonable that they would be late descending and that, like as not, they would shelter in one of the higher camps. The night was clear and Odell and Hazard stayed up watching for signs of movement—or flares of distress.

But they saw nothing.

Peering through binoculars at the tents at Camps V and VI the next morning, Odell and Hazard could detect no sign of movement. At noon, Odell once again began to climb, accompanied by two reluctant porters. It was a heroic performance. The man had been in what climbers today call "the Death Zone" for days. He had climbed and carried loads repeatedly during that time. And now he was at it again, struggling against the vicious western crosswind that made life so miserable on the North Ridge. When they reached Camp V at day's end, Odell found it exactly as he had left it two days before, empty and untouched. As darkness approached, "fleeting glimpses of stormy sunset could at intervals be seen through the flying scud, and as the night closed in on us the wind and the cold increased."[13]

The next morning, the porters refused to go higher. He sent them back down and once again climbed alone toward Camp VI. He carried a spare oxygen set from Camp V but, as before, seemed to receive no benefit from it. Like Camp V, Camp VI was as he had left it, except that the unrelenting wind had collapsed one of the tent poles. Ditching the oxygen set, he immediately began climbing toward the summit along the route he thought Mallory and Irvine would have taken. After another two hours in the fierce wind and bitter cold, he had found nothing. Thinking to himself that "this upper part of Everest must be indeed the remotest and most inhospitable spot on earth, but at no time more emphatically and impressively than when a darkened atmosphere hides its features and a gale races over its cruel face,"[14] he finally relented and returned to Camp VI. He laid the climbers' sleeping bags out on a snow slope in a pre-arranged signal to Hazard, below, signifying he had found no one, then began the arduous descent to the North Col. He glanced back over his shoulder at the summit: "It seemed to look down with cold indifference on me, mere puny man, and howl derision in wind-gusts at my petition to yield up its secret—the mystery of my friends."[15]

Mallory and Irvine had vanished.

Their disappearance created one of the most enduring and puzzling mysteries in exploration and mountaineering history. Did they reach the summit? Did they do it together? If they did, what became of them? Did they, singly or roped together, their guards down after their historic effort, make one false step on the descent and tumble through the gathering darkness to their deaths? Or were they, exhausted and oxygenless (as their cylinders would have been long since empty), forced to spend a night that never ended on the rooftop of the world?

In the months, years, and finally decades since their disappearance, theories have been proposed, debated, and debunked; calculations have been made of their possible departure time from Camp VI, climbing speed, and oxygen use rate; speculations have been raised about the characters of the two climbers and how they might have responded to a range of potential summit crises; tantalizing new clues have from time to time been discovered. The net result? Three-quarters of a century after their disappearance, the world knew little more about the fate of these two Everest pioneers than it did on June 21, 1924, when *The Times* of London published expedition leader Norton's terse telegraphed announcement:

"Mallory and Irvine killed on last attempt"[16]

CHAPTER 1

THE DETECTIVE AND THE MYSTERY

I cannot tell you how it possesses me . . .
GEORGE MALLORY

Jochen Hemmleb opens his eyes and waits for the world to come into focus.

He unzips his sleeping bag, rolls over on to the carpeted floor of his one-room apartment on the southern edge of Frankfurt, Germany, and stands.

Hemmleb owns a bed, but it is currently occupied. In neat piles laid out across the bedspread—as well as on the floor, desk, table, floor-to-ceiling shelves, and almost every other horizontal surface in the apartment—are dozens of old photographs, maps, and books. He is not a collector of antiquities. He is, in a sense, a detective.

On this morning, June 2, 1998, he makes a cup of tea with lemon, picks his way across the floor to his desk, powers up his laptop, and receives an e-mail message that will change his life and the history of Everest mountaineering as well.

Jochen Hemmleb is tall and slightly stoop-shouldered, as if he were always carrying a climbing rucksack. He has a strikingly open face, an almost musical voice, and a warm, rather mischievous smile that contrasts sharply with intense blue eyes—eyes that telegraph a seriousness of purpose and maturity far beyond his years. A twenty-six-year-old student at Johann Wolfgang Goethe University completing his final thesis in geology, he is also one of the world's experts on the history of Everest expeditions. Indeed, only a few of the documents stacked about his apartment have to do with his geology thesis; all the rest are about Everest.

Hemmleb has, in fact, one of the largest and most meticulously analyzed and archived private collections of Everest documents in the world. There is no feature of the mountain that he has not virtually committed to memory, no expedition to climb it that he has not scrutinized down to the last detail. But one task possesses him above all others: unraveling the mystery of the disappearance of Mallory and Irvine during the final days of the 1924 British Everest Expedition. The detective has been on this particular case for more than a decade.

He is no armchair mountaineering historian; Hemmleb has been a climber himself since he was a small boy. It is a passion passed down to him by his father. Rudolf Hemmleb was fifty-seven when Jochen was born. He had been a climber for much of his life, but the three children of his first marriage did not share their father's passion and he had to wait for the only son of his second marriage, Jochen, born August 13, 1971, to find a kindred soul. The two of them started climbing together when Jochen was only ten years old and his father nearly sixty-nine. His passion rekindled, the elder Hemmleb climbed until he was well into his seventies.

Jochen never stopped. By the age of eleven, he had climbed his first 10,000-foot (3,000-m) mountain in the Italian Alps. At fourteen, he climbed his first 13,000-foot (4,000-m) mountain, the

Zermatter Breithorn in Switzerland. By 1998, he had summited some forty-five 13,000-foot (4,000-m) peaks in the Alps and also climbed in South America, East Africa, and New Zealand.

For Hemmleb, mountaineering was both his salvation and his curse: "Climbing, and the intensity of my enthusiasm for it, which I did not hide, made me an outsider as a schoolboy. It made me different at an age when most boys are only interested in fitting in. Still, it was how I found myself, and the truth was that part of me rather liked not fitting in. As I have grown older, that sense of being different because of climbing, of being outside the mainstream, has persisted, but the wealth of experience I gain from climbing—the impressions, the adventure, the insights—is always proving to me that it is worth it."

It is the sheer intensity of experience that is the great attraction of mountaineering, Hemmleb explains: "During a couple of hours of climbing, you can experience more than you would in a week elsewhere. Your senses are completely alert when you're climbing—hearing, breathing, smelling everything—and you begin to get a glimpse of how deep the feeling of being alive can really become."

As for the dangers inherent in mountaineering, Hemmleb is philosophical: "I don't think climbers climb to risk death; I think they climb to prove to themselves that they are not already dead."

Passion has a price, however; Hemmleb has learned, as other climbers have learned before him, that establishing and maintaining meaningful intimate relationships is difficult. "To an extent," he says, "a part of me is always getting ready to leave again, and that is difficult for a partner to live with."

At the same time, Hemmleb marvels at the depth of his

relationships with his climbing partners: "When you know you have to rely on another person for your own safety, and he upon you, you learn a level of trust that simply doesn't exist very often in the normal world. Climbers are an odd combination of opposite characteristics: individualists who have to rely on one another. The bonds of friendship and trust you develop are profound."

It was on Christmas Day 1987 that the then sixteen-year-old Hemmleb's general interest in climbing and the history of Everest expeditions snapped into focus. His parents gave him a newly published book on the disappearance of Mallory and Irvine during the pioneering but ill-fated 1924 British expedition.[1] In a sense, he's never put it down. "I had read about them before, but for some reason now I was hooked," he recalls. "I felt that there was a possibility this mystery could be resolved, and that it was something I myself might be able to do."

There are those, including some of his friends, who think Hemmleb is obsessed with Mallory and Irvine. He confesses to being drawn to unsolved mysteries—real ones, and especially those that have to do with exploration—the kind where there is a story within the story that you can sense but that is not yet known or understood: "In the world of exploration and mountaineering, the question of what happened to Mallory and Irvine was the greatest mystery yet to be resolved. I wanted to know what happened; I wanted to solve the mystery. So yes, if that is obsession, I plead guilty."

If Hemmleb is obsessed with Mallory and Irvine, he is in good company. For three-quarters of a century, every climber to approach Everest has felt their presence. Many have reached its summit and looked for evidence of their passing. It is almost as if they half expect that, through some trick of magical realism, the two will simply step out of the mists of the mountain on which they disappeared so long ago.

In George Leigh Mallory's case at least, you can almost believe it possible. Mallory had reached almost mythical status even before he disappeared. A veteran of Britain's two previous Everest expeditions, he was, by all accounts, a climber of exceptional grace and strength even as a young man. His closest friend, the mountaineering pioneer Geoffrey Winthrop Young, was in awe of Mallory's fluidity: "His movement in climbing was entirely his own. It contradicted all theory. He would set his foot high against any angle of smooth surface, fold his shoulder to his knee, and flow upward and upright again on an impetuous curve. Whatever may have happened unseen the while between him and the cliff . . . the look, and indeed the result, were always the same—a continuous undulating movement so rapid and so powerful that one felt the rock must yield, or disintegrate."[2]

Another climbing partner, Harry Tyndale, said of Mallory: "In watching George at work one was conscious not so much of physical strength as of suppleness and balance; so rhythmical and harmonious was his progress in any steep place . . . that his movements appeared almost serpentine in their smoothness."[3]

Sir Francis Younghusband, the first chairman of the joint Royal Geographical Society/Alpine Club Everest Committee, describing the process by which the 1921 reconnaissance expedition members were selected, says simply: ". . . one name was immediately mentioned by the Alpine Club members, and that name was Mallory. There was no question in their mind that he was the finest climber they had."[4]

But as Younghusband himself noted, despite his renown, Mallory did not fit the mountaineer stereotype: "He was then a man of thirty-three, slim and supple if not broad and beefy ... . certainly good-looking, with a sensitive, cultivated air ... [but] no one who had not seen him on a mountain would have remarked anything very special in him."[5] Yet when he climbed into eternity on that June day in 1924, he ascended to the zenith of mountaineering legend for the rest of the twentieth century. Quite simply, Mallory was Everest.

Andrew Irvine, in contrast, was a novice. Born to an affluent family on April 8, 1902, in Birkenhead, just across the Mersey from Liverpool, he attended Shrewsbury School as a boy and then went up to Merton College, Oxford, in 1922. Inevitably called "Sandy" because of his blond hair, he distinguished himself immediately in rowing, becoming Captain of Boats. At twenty-one, when he was selected to join the 1924 Everest expedition, he had grown tall, handsome, square-jawed, and broad-shouldered. Though he had participated in a university-sponsored expedition to Spitzbergen, a frigid Norwegian archipelago in the high Arctic, done some skiing in the Alps, and a bit of climbing in North Wales, he was otherwise inexperienced—"Our Experiment," the 1924 expedition leader called him.[6]

Mallory and Irvine could hardly have been less alike, and yet the two became friends quickly, sharing a shipboard dinner table as they steamed east to India, gradually drawing closer through the course of the expedition: the priest and his acolyte.

There was about both men, as there is about many climbers, an irresistible idealism, an almost childlike innocence. Irvine's diaries reveal an uncomplicated young man of almost unshakable good humor eager to "get a whack at" the mountain.[7] Throughout the expedition, his diaries reveal him to be eager, hard-working, committed to the task before them, and devoted to Mallory.

Mallory was a far more complex character. Born on June 18, 1886, in Mobberley, Cheshire, he was the first son of the rector of the parish and, by all accounts, "climbed everything that it was at all possible to climb"—trees, downspouts and roof lines, the roof of the church, cliffs at the seaside.[8] He attended Winchester College, distinguished himself primarily in sports, and caught the eye of a young tutor, R. L. G. Irving, who introduced him to climbing and eventually took young Mallory and one or two of his classmates climbing in the Alps.

From the beginning, it was clear climbing meant more to Mallory than simply "a ripping good day in the hills." After summiting Mont Blanc, he wrote, "It is impossible to make any who have never experienced it realize what that thrill means. It proceeds partly from a legitimate joy and pride in life."[9]

After Winchester, Mallory went on to Magdalen College, Cambridge, where he was a middling student and, like Irvine at Oxford some years later, became Captain of Boats for Magdalen. But it seems clear that it was his informal education in the company of Cambridge's young intellectuals that most shaped his character during these years. He joined the left-leaning Fabian Society and counted the poet Rupert Brooke and several younger members of the "Bloomsbury Group," including Lytton Strachey and the artist Duncan Grant, among his friends. Stunningly handsome but not quite their intellectual equal, Mallory nonetheless gained the respect of this notoriously flamboyant crowd because of his principled idealism. Describing one heated philosophical debate, a longtime friend said, "[George] would not budge from his position that it might and must be necessary to alter the letter of principles to suit fresh facts . . . but that the spirit informing them would remain the same. There was a right, and if you wanted you could find it, and it was supremely important."[10] Though they kidded him for both his idealism and prudishness, his friends remained close and loyal to him long after he left school, became a teacher at Charterhouse School, and married the lovely and intelligent Ruth Turner, the daughter of an architect in Godalming, south of London, where Charterhouse was located.

This passion for clarity, for what is right and good, this striving for certainty, is something Jochen Hemmleb understands. He sees it in most climbers, and he sees it in himself. "Difficult and dangerous as it may sometimes be," he explains, "there is a purity and simplicity inherent in climbing. I think the reason mountaineering has become popular in recent years is that climbing feeds an emotional need: a climb has a beginning, a middle, and an end. It has a clear purpose—getting to the summit and dealing with the intricacies of the route and the sense of exposure—and it has a clear outcome—you reach the summit or you do not. It is not vague or uncertain or equivocal, like so much of modern life. And it is more than just a physical challenge; it is an intellectual and emotional challenge as well. You reach a high point not just topographically but emotionally. Nothing epitomizes the idea of accomplishment and the satisfaction one gets from it better than climbing to the top of a mountain."

*

Between 1987 and 1993, Jochen Hemmleb quietly built his Everest archive, collecting magazine articles, newspaper accounts, climbing journals, books, and expedition reports, and corresponding with climbers. "There were plenty of occasions," he recalls, "when I willingly cut back on food and other expenses in order to be able to afford some early expedition report from a rare book dealer."

Then, in late 1994, Hemmleb learned that the year before, the British climber Jon Tinker[11] had found a new and shorter route from Camp VI on Everest's North Face to the Second Step on the mountain's Northeast Ridge. "That gave me the idea that Mallory and Irvine might have used a different approach to the summit ridge than historians had previously assumed. The more I thought about this, the more I realized it was time for me to begin making contributions of my own to the debate. The irony is that I have since disproved my own original theory, but that was the beginning nonetheless. I wrote and circulated my first research paper and realized I had moved from being a student of the Mallory and Irvine mystery to its detective."

It was not a mystery without clues. The first clue, of course, was that 1924 expedition member Noel Odell had actually seen Mallory and Irvine surmount the Second Step, just 800 feet (250 m) from the summit, at 12:50 P.M. on the day they disappeared. Or had he? He was unequivocal in his first dispatch from Tibet, but after he returned to England, where a largely uninformed debate raged as to what had happened to the disappeared climbers, he became less certain whether he had seen them on the Second Step or the much lower First Step. Which account was right?

Then, in 1933, another unsuccessful British expedition

found Andrew Irvine's ice ax at 27,760 feet (8,460 m), a few hundred feet down the crest of the Northeast Ridge from the First Step. Many people concluded that the ice ax marked the spot of a fatal fall, perhaps after dark as the benighted climbers descended. But had it been dropped, or simply placed there? On the way up or on the way down?

In 1960, a Chinese expedition was rumored to have found a wooden tent pole and length of rope on the slabs of the North Face below the Second Step during a reportedly successful summit bid. If the rumor was true, it could only have been left by Mallory and Irvine; no subsequent expedition had left equipment behind that high. But given China's reluctance to communicate with the West in 1960, it was never clear where, precisely, the Chinese expedition had found the artifacts. Indeed, for many years western climbers were skeptical about whether the Chinese had summited at all. (See "No Matter of Doubt—The 1960 Chinese Ascent of the North Ridge" in Appendix 1, Everest North Side: Resolved and Unresolved Mysteries.)

In 1979, Wang Hongbao, a Chinese climber helping a Japanese reconnaissance expedition on the North Face, indicated to Japanese climber Yoshinori Hasegawa that four years earlier on another Chinese expedition, he had found an "English dead" at 26,575 feet (8,100 m) just a short walk from the 1975 expedition's Camp VI.[12] By means of hand signals, Wang, who did not speak Japanese, made it clear that the clothes on the body were very old and disintegrated when touched. But Hasegawa learned no more; Wang died in an avalanche the next day. Irvine's ice ax had been found above, but in the general vicinity of the presumed location of Camp VI. Had Wang found Irvine?

In 1991, American commercial expedition leader Eric Simonson had stumbled across an old oxygen bottle just below the First Step. He didn't think much of it at the time, but later it occurred to him that it might have belonged to one of the early British expeditions. Had it been left behind by Mallory and Irvine in 1924?

Far from clarifying the mystery, this accumulation of clues only deepened it. Hemmleb studied the historical accounts and contemporary theories to determine which pieces of the Mallory and Irvine puzzle were relevant, how—or even whether—they fit together, and what story they told. But the pieces didn't fit.

"Finally, I came to believe that little was to be gained from reviewing and revising the old material, and more was to be gained by looking for new information and taking a fresh look at old data in that context. I had, after all, been studying for some years to be a geologist, so I decided to take the scientific approach: start from ground zero. I looked at the old raw data without its accompanying interpretations, just as if no work had been done on it before, and tried to find out whether I could gain a new perspective that way."

More importantly, Hemmleb began to shift his attention from picking apart historical accounts to poring over photographs taken by previous expeditions and comparing them with the most detailed maps available of the North Face and Northeast Ridge. He was, in the vocabulary of climbers, searching for a new route.

In the fall of 1997 and the spring of 1998, Hemmleb published the findings of this new research on the Internet website EverestNews.com. Immediately, a lively debate began in the website's forum section, and a number of people contacted him by e-mail. He was gratified by the response, but few of the contacts were from other historians.

Then, on June 2, 1998, Hemmleb received an e-mail from someone who, like him, had been studying North Face expeditions for years and had been "particularly interested in the British prewar expeditions." The e-mail was from an American named Larry Johnson. "I gave him a rather standard response," Hemmleb recalls, "and for some reason mentioned that I hoped someday to make a trip to Everest to search for Mallory and Irvine. Then I thought nothing more about it."

In early 1998, Larry Johnson was the marketing director of a small, independent publisher of nonfiction books based in Pennsylvania. A then fifty-one-year-old self-confessed "armchair historian" of the Mallory and Irvine mystery, he had been connected to the Internet for only a few weeks when a friend mentioned EverestNews.com and he found Hemmleb's research papers.

Like Hemmleb, and for that matter Mallory, Johnson had gotten involved in climbing early. "Back in 1959, when I was only twelve, I read a book by James Ramsey Ullman called *Third Man on the Mountain*, a 35-cent pocket book about a fictional mountain guide on a mountain modeled after the Matterhorn. Somehow, I was attracted to climbing—which was pretty amazing when you consider that in those days I was so afraid of heights you couldn't get me up a 5-foot stepladder."

With some friends, Johnson formed a climbing club and they slowly "learned the ropes." Before long, the concentration and exhilaration of technical climbing overcame his fear of heights. "Over the years," he explains, "I've climbed both rock and ice, mostly in the east. But I've also climbed in Wyoming's Grand Tetons and independently summited both Mount Rainier and Mount Adams in the Cascades."

It was while he was still in high school that Johnson read another Ullman book, *Tiger of the Snows*, a biography of Tenzing Norgay, the Sherpa who summited Everest with Edmund Hillary in 1953. "That's when I first learned the story of Mallory and Irvine, and it captivated me completely. Here I was, a kid living basically in the middle of a famous Civil War battlefield in Gettysburg, Pennsylvania, and I became fascinated by this small piece of history that had occurred halfway around the world. I don't know whether it was something about the late Victorians and the way they sought out adventure, but I was drawn to it; from then on, I studied everything about that period I could get my hands on."

Johnson kept at the Mallory and Irvine mystery even as he began his career in publishing and started a family. "I drifted away from it from time to time over the years, but I kept coming back; I couldn't let it go. When I finally stumbled upon Jochen's work on the Internet, I realized it was completely new and incredibly thorough and detailed. I really felt I had to respond."

Johnson's June 2, 1998, e-mail to Jochen Hemmleb was the first in what immediately became a daily exchange. By the time the week was out, they were exploring the possibility of joining a commercial expedition to Everest's North Face to conduct a search the next year, the seventy-fifth anniversary of the 1924

British Everest Expedition and the disappearance of Mallory and Irvine.

Hemmleb already had what he hoped was an ace in the hole. A few months before the fateful June 2 e-mail from Johnson, Hemmleb had learned from the eminent Everest historian Audrey Salkeld that British Broadcasting Corporation film producer Graham Hoyland, an Everest climber himself, was trying to persuade the BBC to support an expedition to create a documentary film to coincide with the seventy-fifth anniversary. Hoyland's interest in the Mallory and Irvine mystery was more than just professional: the grandnephew of another 1924 Everest expedition veteran, T. H. Somervell, he wanted to recover the camera his granduncle had lent George Mallory on summit day.

Hoyland had in mind piggybacking his search on a 1999 expedition to Everest's north side that was being organized by Russell Brice of Himalayan Experience, a commercial expedition organizer, and he invited Hemmleb to participate in his proposed project. But for a college student and climber who was not exactly a household name, finding sponsors to cover the cost of participating would be no small challenge. Nonetheless, Hemmleb stayed in contact with Hoyland and a relationship grew. Only a few weeks after Hemmleb had first been contacted by Johnson, all three were talking about a joint expedition.

Though he was certain of Graham Hoyland's personal commitment, by July 1998 Hemmleb began to have misgivings about whether the BBC itself was committed to mounting an expedition. Hoyland was being circumspect about who the other expedition members might be and vague about the degree to which the BBC actually supported the idea. The fact that he was adamant that Johnson and Hemmleb not mention the BBC in their fund-raising efforts suggested to Johnson and Hemmleb that Hoyland did not yet have the BBC's approval for his proposal. In an e-mail to Johnson, Hemmleb wrote, "As far as I can see it at the moment, there is still a great deal of uncertainty concerning the members of the BBC project. Sometimes I find myself contemplating the idea of rigging up a separate team and going independently."

A few days later, that was exactly what they began doing.

CHAPTER 2

MORE LIKE WAR THAN ADVENTURE

*It would look rather grim to see others, without me, engaged in
conquering the summit.*
GEORGE MALLORY

In conversation, Eric Simonson's intense eyes tend to squint off
to a point somewhere in the far distance that perhaps only he
can see. They are not the eyes of a dreamer; he is not intent
upon some remote interior landscape. They are the eyes of a
worrier; they give the impression that there is no moment when
some part of him, some significant part, is not working out the
details of a problem, going through a checklist, thinking
through implications of actions that may have only indirect
relation to the events at hand.

He is a big man—6 feet, 4 inches tall—with a chiseled
Scandinavian face and the kind of shoulders that make him
instinctively turn slightly sideways when he passes through a
doorway. His languid, loping gait is an artifact of his height, not
a reflection of his manner; in fact, Simonson seems perpetually
coiled, barely contained. His hands give him away; they are
restless, as if they live a life independent of the rest of him. They
are in direct communication with whatever it is his distant eyes
see. However at ease the rest of him may seem to be, the eyes

and hands betray him as fully occupied. He is a born expedition organizer. The eyes see the big picture, the hands wrestle with the details. Everything else is just so much background noise.

In the spring of 1998, when Simonson's company, International Mountain Guides, sent out its 1999 expedition brochure, Simonson himself, then age forty-three, had been a mountain guide for twenty-six years and had led some seventy expeditions throughout the world. When he and his partners, Phil Ershler and George Dunn, founded IMG in 1981, they divided up the major expedition zones of the world. Simonson got the Himalaya, and that was just fine with him. By 1998, he'd been there more than twenty times and to Everest six times, along with several of the region's other 26,250-foot (8,000-m) peaks.

On the very day that Jochen Hemmleb had written Larry Johnson about his growing uncertainty about whether the BBC—as distinct from Graham Hoyland—was serious about a Mallory and Irvine research expedition, Johnson, at home in Gettysburg, was leafing through IMG's 1999 expedition brochure when something caught his eye. Simonson was offering a commercial expedition to the north side of Everest that would explicitly not be a summit climb, but would take clients up to 26,250 feet (8,000 m)—an idea that had been suggested to Simonson by clients themselves. More than a trek but less than a summit bid, it would also be far less expensive.

Johnson realized that 26,250 feet (8,000 m) might well be sufficient to reach what Hemmleb believed was the best area for finding the remains of Andrew Irvine and, perhaps, Somervell's camera. What's more, the price, $12,000, was substantially less than the $15,000 that Hoyland told Hemmleb the New Zealand expedition organizer, Russell Brice (both a competitor and friend of Simonson's), would charge the BBC for a trip to just Base Camp.[1]

That same day, July 7, Johnson wrote Simonson and described their proposed research expedition.

Eric Simonson was born almost literally in the shadow of Washington's Mount Rainier, the hulking 14,410-foot (4,392-m) dormant volcano that dominates the skyline of Seattle and Tacoma. In 1965, when he was ten years old, Simonson's father took him to Tacoma's Pacific Lutheran University to see *Americans on Everest*, the film of the first successful American expedition two years earlier. Mountaineering legends Jim Whittaker, Tom Hornbein, Lute Jerstad, and Dick Emerson spoke, and the young Simonson was hooked for life on Everest and Everest history.

He took to mountaineering himself at an unusually early age, climbing Mount Rainier for the first time at the age of fifteen and completing his first formal mountaineering training course at sixteen. In a confession that eerily echoes the youthful exploits of George Mallory himself, Simonson says, "I climbed everything I could find as a kid—trees, buildings, you name it. By my mid-teens, I'd climbed most of the tall buildings and bridges around Tacoma, rappelling off of them in the dark." An Eagle Scout and avid backpacker, Simonson climbed widely in the Cascade and Olympic mountain ranges of Washington throughout high school.

"My parents were also inveterate travelers and my father was a professor. During one of his sabbaticals, when I was a junior in high school, we spent a year in Scotland and traveled throughout the British Isles, Scandinavia, and France; I was bitten by the travel bug at an early age." When they returned, Simonson didn't bother to go back to high school; he enrolled in a junior college instead and, after a year, transferred to Carleton College in Minnesota. In 1977, he entered the University of Washington to earn a master's degree in geology.

In 1973, at the age of eighteen, Simonson became a guide for Rainier Mountaineering, Inc., founded by Everest pioneer Jim Whittaker's twin brother, Lou.

At the end of his freshman year at Carleton, Simonson participated in an epic forty-one-day traverse of Mount McKinley, and in 1976 he began leading McKinley expeditions himself. In 1997, after 25 years with RMI, Simonson got his own permit from the park service to guide on Rainier's east side with his new company, Mount Rainier Alpine Guides. Earlier, in 1981, he founded International Mountain Guides with George Dunn and Phil Ershler. Over the years, Simonson has summited Mount Rainier 260 times and McKinley sixteen times, participated in seven Everest expeditions (summiting in 1991), and climbed in India, Nepal, Tibet, Antarctica, Russia, Tajikistan, South America, and Africa.

"I'm convinced that creating an expedition company was my destiny. In another era, I probably would have been a ship captain or a general in charge of a military campaign somewhere in the steppes of Asia. I love the challenge of organizing and leading expeditions, and it's a job with tremendous variety; I'm a businessman, I'm a logistics organizer, I'm leading expeditions and traveling, I'm working and communicating with all kinds of people. I can't imagine another occupation that would give me that kind of job satisfaction."

While mountaineering and technical rock climbing—and climbing guide services—have grown dramatically in recent years, the number of experienced Himalaya guides is still small. Within this elite group, Eric Simonson has become the most experienced Himalaya expedition organizer in the United States, and possibly the world.

Two days after Johnson wrote to him, Simonson responded with interest, mentioning his own fascination with Everest expedition history. Within a week he, Johnson, and Hemmleb were discussing the logistical, personnel, and financial details of a formal Mallory & Irvine Research Expedition.

To their delight, the BBC's Graham Hoyland seemed to be pleased by Simonson's participation as well. In mid-July, Hoyland sent word that a joint BBC2–Discovery Channel coproduction of a search film looked promising. Johnson and Hemmleb, not sensing the message between the lines—that the BBC still hadn't approved the idea—took this as encouraging news.

As marketing director for a publisher of outdoor guidebooks, Johnson had long attended the Outdoor Retailer trade show held twice a year in Salt Lake City, both representing his company and developing relationships with the hundreds of manufacturers and retailers of outdoor equipment that set up displays at the show. Johnson knew that if he and Hemmleb could work quickly to produce a marketing proposal for the expedition, the August 1998 Outdoor Retailer show would be the ideal opportunity to prospect for sponsors. In early August, proposal in hand, Johnson was off to Salt Lake.

In his spare moments, he prowled the aisles of the Salt Palace convention center and managed to set up preliminary discussions with several potential sponsors. It wasn't an easy job: "Obviously, sponsors are interested in supporting an expedition like this only insofar as it increases the visibility of their products, so filming and broadcasting is what matters most to them," Johnson explains. "But Graham had prohibited us from mentioning the BBC's name, which put me in the position of only being able to make broad hints about the thing that mattered most to the sponsors. It didn't help our credibility any, and I suppose it should have warned us about the genuineness of the BBC's commitment."

It was the meeting with Simonson, however, that had the greatest effect on the expedition's planning, and eventually its outcome. Simonson was all business: "I told Larry, 'Look, you don't want to just buy a couple of slots on a commercial expedition where the main focus is going to be getting clients up to the summit'," Simonson recalls, "'you need to have a dedicated expedition for this project.'"

He also disabused Johnson of the idea that it would be a bargain. "Putting a search team high on the mountain was going to be almost as expensive as putting somebody on the summit; you'd need almost the same amount of oxygen, support, and logistics. It was going to be serious money, on the order of $200,000 to $300,000, and it would require a major fund-raising effort."

If this gave Johnson pause, he didn't show it. "The great thing about not knowing what you're doing," he remembers with amusement, "is that you don't know something's impossible."

*

It was a sentiment that would have resonated nicely in Victorian England at the turn of the century. That same naïve belief in the doability of things had made Great Britain the preeminent nation of explorers in the nineteenth and early twentieth centuries and, not incidentally, the world's premier imperial power. If the tiny island nation could claim, almost without hyperbole, that "the sun never sets on the British Empire," the reason was not solely or even principally its military might. The real reason was that the British seemed, as a people, simply unable to resist a blank spot on a map. Just as vitally, they seemed incapable of thinking it would be anything but great sport to fill in that blank. Often unprepared for the dangers they would encounter, expeditions sallied forth to every remote corner of the globe-ending in tragedy as often as success, and sometimes both.

It was in 1852 that the Survey of India identified "Peak XV" as the world's highest mountain. In 1865, the Royal Geographical Society, with classic imperial arrogance, named the peak "Mount Everest," after Sir George Everest, the Surveyor General for India. Everest the man was opposed to having Everest the mountain named after him, believing mountains should keep their local names, but the Society did so anyway, the year before he died.[2]

British mountaineering historian Audrey Salkeld suspects that the first discussion about scaling the mountain occurred some forty years later, in 1893, when a vigorous young officer in the crack 5th Gurkha Rifles, Charles Granville Bruce, suggested it to Francis Younghusband, then political officer at Chitral in the extreme western reaches of the Himalaya. "He was a great romantic and an adventurous traveler himself,"

Salkeld says. "Some years earlier, Younghusband had made an astonishing journey from Peking across the Gobi Desert and the Karakoram mountains to Rawalpindi, and on the way had stood atop a high pass and had seen a peak of such appalling height that it had taken his breath away. That was K2. If Everest were higher than that, what a formidable objective it would be!"[3] Both the Nepalese and Tibetan frontiers, of course, were closed at the time, and while a handful of exploratory missions, including John Noel's clandestine one, had gotten close, no westerner had yet reached the mountain when the outbreak of World War I put the idea of an expedition on the back burner.

By the time the subject came up again, Younghusband would be in a position to do something about the matter of Everest.

Only a few days after the August trade show at which he and Larry Johnson had met, Simonson learned that a major telecommunications company was interested in sponsoring an expedition that could showcase its equipment. Within two weeks, Simonson had produced a far more comprehensive proposal than the brief "talking piece" Johnson and Hemmleb had drafted, and had sent it off on behalf of the expedition.

Johnson was quick to recognize that a not-so-subtle shift was underway. He e-mailed Hemmleb, "I think he did a great job, but the control of the expedition seems to be changing hands, from ours to Eric's. Are you comfortable with that?" A few hours later, the German wrote back, "With Eric, the expedition's control is in the best hands. I absolutely don't have a problem with it."

The next day, the expedition got its first media commitment: *Climbing* magazine commissioned a major article on the search, and Johnson and Simonson at last had a source of visibility they could talk about with potential equipment sponsors.

Hemmleb remembers this period with a combination of awe and embarrassment: "It was as if our expedition was meant to be. Everything was coming together so quickly and so well."

He was, of course, wrong.

For one thing, Simonson, though interested, actually had yet to commit to the project. He had been invited to join a spring 1999 expedition to the south side of Everest being organized by the Boston Museum of Science's Brad Washburn, the dean of mountain cartography and photography. Compared to the Johnson/Hemmleb project, it appeared far more certain and professional. But by mid-October it was still not clear whether the Washburn expedition would happen. "It was with huge trepidation that I finally committed myself to Jochen and Larry's project, because I knew what a royal pain in the butt it was going to be to make it happen. I knew I'd have to expend a lot of personal capital to raise the money we'd need."

While he was waiting for the telecommunications company proposal to grind through its review process, Simonson talked the Seattle-based Internet site MountainZone.com, perhaps the preeminent mountaineering website in the world, into backing the Mallory & Irvine Research Expedition with significant funding and "cybercasting" the entire expedition. But this would be "last money in"—that is, it was contingent upon the expedition raising other funding first. That was the bad news. The good news was that, in MountainZone.com, the expedition had another powerful media partner and, thus, a better chance of interesting other potential sponsors for whom product visibility was critical.

Meanwhile, as the summer sped into fall, it emerged that the BBC's involvement was far less certain than Hemmleb and Johnson had believed. Part of their misperception was due to the alternately encouraging and cautioning messages they were receiving from Graham Hoyland, but part of it was due to the very nature of noncommercial television production itself. British Everest filmmaker Matt Dickinson, whom the BBC had initially told Hemmleb would participate in the project, has described this world succinctly, if somewhat brutally: "Television is a dirty business. To survive in it, you have to be part weasel, part python, and part wolf. To succeed in it, you have to be 99.9 percent great white shark. The capacity for bald-faced lying also comes in handy. . . ."[4]

It seems clear now that Graham Hoyland, who had been trying for more than a year to get his employers to see the importance of the seventy-fifth anniversary of Mallory and Irvine's disappearance—they were British, after all—was fighting an uphill battle. For whatever reason, perhaps simply bureaucratic ineptitude, the BBC wasn't "getting it." Since his interest was personal as well as professional, Hoyland was hedging his bets—pursuing a BBC production on the one hand, and keeping his chances alive with Hemmleb, Johnson, and Simonson on the other.

Then, in October, BBC Travel and Adventure Features series editor Peter Firstbrook took Hoyland's bait at last. Firstbrook, in turn, faxed Simonson a letter on October 21 saying that the BBC had decided to mount an expedition of its own and that it was in discussions with another expedition leader, Simonson's friend Russell Brice, to organize it.[5] The letter was utterly silent on the subject of Hemmleb, Johnson, and Simonson's lengthy discussions with Graham Hoyland about a joint expedition or, for that matter, the contract that Firstbrook had offered Hemmleb—a contract under which, for the exclusive right to use his Mallory and Irvine research, Hemmleb was offered £500 (not even enough to get him to Kathmandu, let alone Everest) with a vague promise of additional compensation later on, budget permitting.

A day later, it became clear that Hoyland had never disclosed his discussions with the American expedition to Firstbrook. Responding to an angry message from Hemmleb about the October 21 letter, Firstbrook disclaimed any responsibility, saying that Hoyland had only sent him the details of the American expedition a week earlier.

Hemmleb now was caught in a dilemma. On the one hand, he had a firm, if plainly insulting, contract offer from the BBC. On the other, he had a friendly but as yet unfunded opportunity with Johnson and Simonson. And here Johnson's almost paternal loyalty to Hemmleb really shone; Johnson encouraged Hemmleb to do what he felt was best for him, since the new work that made a search for Mallory and Irvine possible had been Hemmleb's alone (indeed, later, when expedition funds were short, he offered to cut his own trip to Everest if it would jeopardize Hemmleb's).

In the end, Hemmleb rejected the BBC offer and threw his lot in with Johnson and Simonson. "They had always been consistent in their statements," he explains. "I could never be certain of that with the BBC."

Through all of this, Simonson remained almost unnaturally calm and determined. Something inside told him that, its claims notwithstanding, the BBC's plans were not as firmly set as they were suggesting. He and Johnson decided to call their bluff: "We told them they could do whatever they wanted because we were going ahead with or without them," he recalls. "The choice was either to join us or to compete with us. It was brinkmanship. Our position was that it was foolish to send two underfunded expeditions to compete on the mountain, and that what made sense was to pool resources and put together one well-funded, well-supported expedition dedicated to one goal."

His instincts were right. In fact, the BBC still had not finalized its expedition and film production arrangements. It had found a production and funding partner, WGBH/Boston's NOVA series, but no deal had yet been signed. Bringing NOVA in created a power shift; the BBC needed them and that gave NOVA a great deal of influence over how the expedition would be structured. NOVA was quick to note that Simonson's expedition would be totally dedicated to the search, while the BBC's arrangement with Brice was still to piggyback on to a summit climb with climbers uncommitted to the search. More-over, Simonson had put together a roster of exceptional climbers to conduct the search high on the mountain. "I suspect," Simonson says with no small amusement, "that NOVA said they'd participate but that they wanted the American expedition to be the focus; that put Firstbrook in the awkward position of having to join us after all."

Negotiations continued through November and December 1998, and finally, at the winter Outdoor Retailer trade show in Salt Lake City, Simonson, on behalf of Johnson and Hemmleb, signed a formal Draft Letter of Agreement with the BBC for expedition funding (NOVA's funding would be passed through the BBC, though the agreement between the BBC and NOVA was not signed until after the expedition was over). In all of this, the real loser was Simonson's friend Russell Brice, whom the BBC had led to believe would run the expedition. Their dithering cost him financially. Notes Simonson: "Russell is the *crème de la crème* of expedition organizers, a good man and an excellent mountaineer; he deserved better treatment than he received at the BBC's hands."

Hemmleb, Johnson, and Simonson were struck by how little the world had changed in three-quarters of a century. Even in 1921, when the British began organizing their first expedition to the mountain, it soon became clear that in addition to the usual requirements—solid leadership, experienced climbers, thorough planning, and strong logistical support—Everest expeditions required two other things that were at least as important: media and money—with the former necessary to obtain the latter. The relationship between the two competing objectives of an expedition, raising money and visibility on the one hand, and achieving scientific and mountaineering objectives on the other, has always tended to be rather less than salubrious.

To raise money for the 1921 reconnaissance expedition, the organizers planned to rely on private subscriptions. Members of the Alpine Club quickly raised £3,000, no small sum in those days, but the Fellows of the Royal Geographical Society, of which there were many more, struggled to match that figure. Both King George V and the Prince of Wales made modest contributions and Lord Reading, the Viceroy of India, gave 750 rupees. To make up the rest of the estimated £10,000 budget for the 1921 reconnaissance and a follow-up 1922 summit attempt, the Everest Committee sold its media rights. *The Times of London* and *The Philadelphia Ledger* got exclusive rights to expedition telegrams for Britain and the United States, respectively, and the magazine *The Graphic* got the photo exclusive.[6]

Three years later, despite the fact that, in essence, Britain's honor was now at stake, the third Everest expedition (and the second summit attempt) found fund-raising more difficult than it had expected. Although Everest Committee chairman Sir Francis Younghusband wrote that "among the public generally there is a distinctly firmer determination to prosecute the project than there was when the idea was first mooted," apparently that determination did not extend to the public's pocketbook. A combined appeal by the presidents of the Alpine Club and Royal Geographical Society to the general public raised a whopping £10.[7]

It was Himalaya pioneer and 1922 expedition veteran Captain John Noel who ultimately bankrolled the 1924 expedition. Noel, an accomplished photographer and film-maker as well as mountaineer, had made a movie of the unsuccessful 1922 expedition, which he screened throughout Britain, though it was not a commercial success. Still, he was convinced of the commercial possibilities of an Everest expedition film and managed to persuade sufficient numbers of the rich and famous that he was right. He raised enough money to offer the Everest Committee a deal they could not, and did not, refuse: for the exclusive film and still photo rights to the expedition, Noel's new company, Explorer Films, Ltd., would pay the committee a princely £8,000—enough to fund the entire expedition. In fact, the offer was worth fully £10,000 to the expedition, since it would eliminate a £2,000 line item in the budget earmarked to cover photographic expenses. What's more, to keep "the buzz" going in the public, Noel even designed special "postage stamps" for expedition postcards.[8]

With Mallory & Irvine Research Expedition funding coming together at last, Eric Simonson turned his attention to forming the expedition team. His criteria were simple: he wanted seasoned high-altitude climbers who were even-tempered under pressure and would keep the expedition's common goals always in mind. His preference was for guides, rather than free agents, because they were trained to look out for the welfare of the others on a climb, a characteristic Simonson had learned was critical in Everest's dangerously unpredictable conditions.

His first choice was Dave Hahn, thirty-seven, a close friend and professional high-altitude guide who worked often for Simonson. Hahn had been a senior guide at Mount Rainier for more than a decade; held the record for the most summits (fourteen) of Mount Vinson in Antarctica, where he worked every winter as a guide for Adventure Network; had led expeditions to McKinley and in the Himalaya; and had summited Everest by the Northeast Ridge route in 1994.

On Hahn's recommendation, Simonson also invited Conrad Anker, thirty-six, one of the nation's leading all-around alpinists and technical rock climbers, with whom Hahn worked in Antarctica. Anker had not been at extreme high altitudes before, but was known to be an exceptionally strong climber.

Simonson summited Everest in 1991 with Andy Politz,

thirty-nine, a mountain guide for some fifteen years who had traveled and climbed widely throughout the world. Writer, photographer, mountaineer, sailor, boat-builder, carpenter, and teacher, Politz was the expedition's renaissance man and the only member of the climbing team who was married and had children.

The climbing team's "youngsters" were Tap Richards and Jake Norton, both twenty-five. They had each worked as guides for eight years; participated in or led expeditions in Alaska, South America, and Nepal; and summited Everest's neighboring peak Cho Oyu in Tibet.

As expedition doctor, Simonson chose Lee Meyers, a specialist in emergency medicine who had climbed widely in Alaska, Ecuador, Canada, Peru, and Antarctica and had summited McKinley, Aconcagua, and Mount Vinson.

Jochen Hemmleb would also join the expedition as its historical advisor, but to save the expedition money, Larry Johnson would wait to join a commercial trek Simonson was organizing to the expedition's base camp.

Both WGBH/NOVA and the BBC, of course, also sent expedition members. WGBH/NOVA assigned the project to producer Liesl Clark and hired climber and freelance cameraman Thom Pollard to accompany the climbing team in the search for Mallory and Irvine.

In addition to series editor Peter Firstbrook, the BBC had promised to have two experienced high-altitude climber/filmmakers on their team: BBC producer Graham Hoyland, who had summited Everest from the south side in 1993 and was the chief advocate of an expedition within the BBC, and freelance filmmaker Matt Dickinson, who had summited from the north side in 1996. Indeed, to accommodate Dickinson, who was on a book tour for his chronicle of the disastrous 1996 Everest climbing season, Simonson set back the expedition's departure date.

Then, at the last minute, the BBC announced that Dickinson was not coming after all and would be replaced by Ned Johnston, a cameraman who had been on Everest with Dickinson in 1996 but had no high-altitude experience. Simonson's expedition plan had depended upon having two teams of four climbers capable of going high into the so-called "Death Zone" to search for Mallory and Irvine. With Dickinson gone (and Hoyland later to drop out due to illness), that plan was blown, limiting the expedition's capacity to one team of six, two teams of three climbers being too small to provide the necessary backup support. "It wasn't until much later," Simonson remembers, "that I learned from Graham why Dickinson dropped off the roster. It seems Firstbrook had demanded that both Dickinson and Hoyland sign an agreement not to write a book about the expedition, because Firstbrook wanted to do one himself (indeed, he arrived at Base Camp with the manuscript already in progress). Matt, a published author, refused and Firstbrook apparently forced him off the team."

Ultimately, the high-altitude camera work was handled by one of Simonson's own climbers, Dave Hahn, who had shot a lot of video in the past at altitude, and Hahn was put under contract to the BBC.

The machinations involved in the selection of the British members of the expedition echoed the minor intrigues that marked the British Everest expeditions of the 1920s, in which the matter of choosing members of the expedition party had as much to do with who one was as what skills one had. In those days, most Himalaya explorers had gained their experience as officers in the frontier campaigns along India's northern borders. It only followed as a matter of course that the Imperial "old-boy network" would determine in large part who went on the expeditions, especially the first expedition in 1921. This essential fact of military life, combined with the personnel requirements of the surveying and scientific objectives of the 1921 expedition, made it little wonder that there were only two experienced climbers among the expedition party when it was first rostered: George Leigh Mallory and George Ingle Finch.

Even here, however, old boy-ism weighed in. Mallory had spent years working his way up through the ranks of the British mountaineering establishment. He had gone to the right schools, had made the right friends, had become a member of the Alpine Club, and was charming and well mannered as well as technically skilled.

Finch, however, was another matter altogether. Born in Australia and raised in somewhat bohemian fashion after his father moved his family back to Europe at his wife's insistence, Finch had spent a vagabond youth and, by unorthodox means, had become one of the continent's most accomplished climbers. He had definitely not gone to the best schools and had little interest in charming the British establishment. He was respected but not well liked by the old guard. When a pre-expedition physical raised some question about his fitness, Finch was summarily rejected. In fact, there was nothing in his health report that suggested anything seriously wrong with him, but the long knives were out and it seems likely that his enemies in the hidebound British mountaineering establishment leaped at their chance to rid themselves of this outsider.[9]

The old boys then got together and proposed one of their own, forty-eight-year-old William Ling, president of the Scottish Mountaineering Club. This time, though, Mallory put his foot down, complaining to the committee that the expedition team was both too old and too inexperienced at climbing to succeed: "I have all along regarded the party as barely strong enough for a venture of this kind, with the enormous demand it is certain to make on both nerves and physique. . . . You will understand that I must look after myself in this matter. I'm a married man and I can't go into it bald headed."[10]

His fears were brushed aside. As luck would have it, however, Ling declined the invitation and Mallory suggested an old friend and climbing partner, Guy Bullock, as the replacement. The committee accepted. As it later turned out, Mallory's fears proved justified; of the two most experienced Himalaya explorers on the expedition, one dropped out due to illness and retreated to India, and the other dropped dead and was buried en route. Thus, the bulk of the serious exploration and climbing responsibility fell to Mallory and his friend Bullock, just as Mallory had predicted.

The next year, the committee took Mallory's advice to heart and fielded a younger and much more skilled team—one that included George Ingle Finch, who performed superbly. While the expedition failed in its goal of reaching the summit, the team worked together so well that many were called upon again to participate in the 1924 summit bid.

Like the 1922 expedition, the 1924 attempt was to be led by

General Charles Granville Bruce. The Himalaya veteran who had first proposed summiting Everest before the turn of the century, a legendary leader of the Gurkhas who gave the British military khaki shorts, the quintessential British hail-fellow-well-met, Charlie Bruce was a bristle-brush-mustached fireplug of a man (called "Bruiser" by his friends) who was known the length and breadth of India. He was beloved by his colleagues both for his irrepressibly boisterous good spirits and the remarkable organizational and management skills he had demonstrated during the 1922 expedition. As one of his colleagues later wrote, "The very name Bruce is a charm to conjure with all along the Himalayas, but more particularly in and around Nepal. He it was who, by his treatment of the people of the country, great and small, consolidated the permanent way across Tibet which a Mount Everest expedition now follows so comfortably."[11] He was a leader's leader.

He was also unwell. At fifty-eight, age and adventure had caught up with him; he had a weak heart and high blood pressure. The doctors on the expedition's medical review board warned against his going, but were quietly ignored. It was simply inconceivable to everyone that he should not go.

But the selection committee also bought the expedition some leadership insurance: it chose as the Climbing Leader and second-in-command another 1922 expedition member, Lieutenant-Colonel Edward Felix Norton. A skilled mountaineer, the lanky, bearded Norton was well liked and a natural leader: "He sought out advice from his men and took it when it made sense. When he gave orders, he gave credit freely to those whose ideas he was adopting, and when he wished to chart a course that was unpopular, he did so for reasons all could see as being logical. . . .

Respect for his judgment was such that none questioned his authority."[12] It would not be long before these skills would be pressed into service.

The committee also brought back Howard Somervell, the skilled alpinist who had proven himself almost indestructible in 1922 and who, since then, had given up a prestigious medical practice in England to work at the Neyyoor mission hospital at Travancore, in southern India. Surgeon, artist, musician, composer, and mountaineer, Norton said of him, "Somervell has a moral reserve on which he draws to make good any physical disabilities, so that it hardly matters whether he is fit or not—he is always fit to go high."[13]

Captain Geoffrey Bruce, a nephew of General Bruce's whose experience with hill people had brought him to the 1922 expedition as its transport officer, and who had reached a world record altitude in the first climb of his life during that expedition, also returned, as, of course, did explorer Captain John Noel, as photographer and filmmaker. George Finch, who had once again gotten himself sideways with stuffy Everest Committee officials, was blackballed.

These veterans were joined by newcomers Edward Shebbeare from India's Forestry Department, who was to help Geoffrey Bruce; Bentley Beetham, a friend of Somervell's with an enviable climbing record in the Alps; Major Richard Hingston, who signed on as medical officer and had a special interest in the effects of high altitude; John de Vere Hazard, something of a loner who nonetheless reached Camp V; and Noel Odell, the geologist and Alpine Club member who would struggle so heroically to find Mallory and Irvine the day after they disappeared into the clouds.

And finally, there were Andrew Comyn Irvine and George Leigh Mallory themselves, the novice and the veteran, whose names would soon be linked together for all time in one of mountaineering's greatest mysteries. Irvine, in his second year studying engineering at Merton College, Oxford, was something of a protégé of Odell's; they had worked together on a college expedition to Spitzbergen in 1923, and Odell had taken him climbing in Wales. When Finch was denied a place on the expedition, the selection committee, responding finally to Mallory's repeated warnings about the need for strong, young climbers, decided to overlook Irvine's inexperience in favor of his physical strength, unshakable good humor, and, perhaps most important in the end, his extraordinary mechanical skills. Throughout the expedition, working with the most rudimentary of tools, Irvine would be the expedition's Mr. Fix-it. Indeed, he was making improvements on the clumsy and fragile oxygen systems even before the expedition party left England, and kept at it throughout the voyage to India.

As to the matter of George Mallory, however, the committee faced something of a dilemma. As Sir Francis Younghusband put it, "Mallory was a more delicate problem. It was in the highest degree desirable to have him. But was it fair to ask him? If he were invited he could not well refuse. Were the committee justified in virtually compelling him to go? He was a married man. He had already taken part in two expeditions. In the last he had been in two serious accidents, in one of which seven men had lost their lives. He had already played his part—and played it nobly. Could the committee, with any fairness, ask him to do more? On the other hand, might he not be deeply offended if he were not asked—he who had borne all the cold and burden of the day? Might he not be cruelly affronted if he were passed over? It was a difficult point to decide. . . ."[14]

It was a difficult point for Mallory to decide as well. After several unfulfilling years as a schoolmaster and an only marginally successful year as a public speaker, Mallory had at last secured a good job as lecturer and assistant secretary of the Board of Extra-Mural Studies at Cambridge. He, his wife, Ruth, and their three children had just settled into a new home there. Ruth and he were a devoted pair, but he had been apart from her almost as much as they had been together in the previous three years. Mallory knew he would be invited, but he did not volunteer to join the expedition. Indeed he could not decide how he felt about the matter. After a talk with his wife, he wrote to his father, "We have both thought that it would look rather grim to see others, without me, engaged in conquering the summit. . . . [M]y present feeling is that I have to look at it from the point of view of loyalty to the expedition and of carrying through on a task begun."[15]

It was a matter of duty, then. But it was a duty to be performed not without misgivings. Just before he left for India, Mallory confided in his friend Geoffrey Keynes, who later recalled, "He said to me that what he would have to face would be more like war than adventure, and that he did not believe he would return alive."[16]

CHAPTER 3

ABOUT TO WALK OFF THE MAP

*Higher in the sky than imagination had ventured to
dream, the top of Everest itself appeared.*
GEORGE MALLORY

TO THE JONGPENS AND HEADMEN OF PHARIJONG, TING-KE,
KAMBA AND KHARTA.
You are to bear in mind that a party of Sahibs are coming to see
the Cho-mo-lung-ma mountain and they will evince great
friendship towards the Tibetans. On the request of the Great
Minister Bell a passport has been issued requiring you and all
officials and subjects of the Tibetan government to supply
transport, e.g. riding ponies, pack animals and coolies as
required by the Sahibs, the rates for which should be fixed to
mutual satisfaction. Any other assistance that the Sahibs may
require either by day or by night, on the march or during halts,
should be faithfully given, and their requirements about
transport or anything else should be promptly attended to. All
the people of the country, wherever the Sahibs may happen to
come, should render all necessary assistance in the best possible
way, in order to maintain friendly relations between the British
and Tibetan Governments.
Dispatched During the Iron Bird Year
Seal of the Prime Minister[1]

t route through Nepal being closed to outsiders, in 1921,)22, and again in 1924 members of the British expeditions Everest—called Chomolungma, "Goddess Mother of the World," by those who live at her feet—gathered in the tea-growing center of Darjeeling, high in northern India, to prepare for the long, indirect trek to Tibet. "Darjeeling itself," wrote Everest Committee chairman and old Himalaya hand Sir Francis Younghusband, "is 7,000 feet above sea level and is set in a forest of oaks, magnolia, rhododendrons, laurels and sycamores. And through these forests the observer looks down the steep mountain-sides to the Rangeet River only 1,000 feet above sea level, then up and up through tier after tier of forest-clad ranges, each bathed in a haze of deeper and deeper purple, till the line of snow is reached; and then still up to the summit of Kangchenjunga, now so pure and ethereal we can scarcely believe it is part of the solid earth on which we stand; and so high it seems part of the very sky itself."[2]

The 1924 expedition party came from every point on the compass. Norton and General Bruce came early, in mid-February, by mail steamer to Bombay. From there they traveled by rail to Delhi to finalize expedition details, to Calcutta to rendezvous with their expedition supplies, northward across the Indian plains, and, finally, by narrow-gauge railway, up through dense forest to Darjeeling.

They had picked up Geoffrey Bruce en route and met Shebbeare from the Indian Forest Department when they reached Darjeeling. Somervell arrived from Travancore, Odell from the oil fields of Persia, and Hingston from the R.A.F. hospital in Baghdad. Finally, on March 21, Mallory, Irvine, Beetham, and Hazard arrived, having sailed from Liverpool to

Bombay on a new steamship, the *California*, and then traveled north through the by-now steaming jungles to Darjeeling—a voyage of nearly a month.

On March 18, 1999, almost exactly seventy-five years later, Simonson, Hahn, Anker, Politz, Richards, Norton, and Meyers arrived in Kathmandu, Nepal, after a marathon, thirty-hour series of flights from Seattle and other cities through Los Angeles, Osaka, and Bangkok—a far less civilized, if more efficient journey. As Dave Hahn recalls, "by the end of our aviation extravaganza, we were just taking whatever meal got served up without much thought as to how it fit in with the normal sequence of breakfast, lunch, and dinner. We were equally content to let the sun do odd things at odd hours and were perfectly flexible when it came to messing with the calendar at the international dateline."[3]

If the aviation extravaganza had "beat the stuffing out" of Simonson's climbing team, as Hahn reported,[4] it was nothing compared to what Simonson himself had been through. For fully three months he had been working seven days a week, twelve to fourteen hours a day, organizing the expedition and handling what often seemed like "just one damn thing after another."

In the more than three-quarters of a century since the "Iron Bird Year" when the Prime Minister of Tibet issued the 1921 British Reconnaissance Expedition its passport to the Forbidden Kingdom and the Dalai Lama granted access to the region "to the west of the Five Treasuries of Great Snow, within the jurisdiction of the White Glass Fort near the Inner

Monastery of the Valley of Rocks, in the Bird Country of the South,"[5] the matter of gaining entry to Tibet for Everest expeditions has become less lyrical and more bureaucratic.

It has also become more costly. Eric Simonson had applied for and received permission for an expedition to the Tibetan side of Mount Everest long before he had joined forces with Jochen Hemmleb and Larry Johnson to organize the 1999 Mallory & Irvine Research Expedition. There are only a few weeks each year—in late spring, just before the summer monsoons begin—during which climbing Everest is something less than a lunatic proposition, and commercial expedition leaders secure "slots" on the mountain for this period well in advance.

Simonson would have to front some $100,000 in fees for his expedition slot, as well as for film permits, radio permits, satellite phone permits, and countless other details. Much of this he negotiated through the China-Tibet Mountaineering Association, the official agency managing such matters in Tibet and elsewhere in China.

As expedition organizer, Simonson was also responsible for securing "visa-issuing authority" from the Chinese to permit each of the expedition members to be issued visas by the Chinese embassies nearest them: historian Hemmleb in Germany, cameraman Ned Johnston in Malaysia, the climbing team and WGBH/NOVA crew in San Francisco, and the BBC crew in London.

For most of the expedition members, this process went without a hitch. The BBC crew's efforts to acquire visas, however, almost brought the expedition to a halt. Because of its extensive coverage of the Tiananmen Square massacre, the BBC was not regarded with exceptional warmth by the Chinese government. Simonson recommended that the BBC's film crew members identify themselves only as expedition climbers, but instead the BBC's Peter Firstbrook sent an assistant to London with applications specifying that their intention was to make a film in Tibet. The Chinese were not amused. The situation wasn't helped when a reporter for one of the more sensational London tabloids inflated an offhand remark by Larry Johnson about the visa application process into a full-fledged foreign policy conflict. The impasse was eventually resolved through some fancy footwork by Simonson, who arranged for the BBC's entry visas to be issued in Kathmandu, rather than London.

It was the kind of crisis Simonson didn't need. As January slipped into February and the departure date for the expedition loomed, he had better things to do. The telecommunications equipment company sponsorship that he and Larry Johnson had been working on had fallen through, but Simonson used his connections in the outdoor industry to line up five smaller sponsorships with outdoor equipment manufacturers Lowe Alpine, Mountain Hardwear, Outdoor Research, Slumberjack, and Vasque, while Johnson brought in a donation of tents from Eureka. Later, the expedition picked up additional support from the Lincoln Division of the Ford Motor Company, which sponsored the MountainZone.com cybercast; the high-energy snack food company Powerbar; and others, to round out the expedition's $300,000 budget.

The next task was ordering, organizing, and packing some 4,000 pounds of food and gear—15,000 feet of rope, an array of climbing hardware (anchors, snow pickets, ice screws, slings, crampons, oxygen regulators and masks), camp equipment (tables, chairs, stoves), satellite communications equipment and computers, medical equipment and supplies, and some sixty tents of several different types. Simonson also had additional equipment in storage both in Nepal and Tibet that he would pick up along the way, eventually bringing the total to 15,000 pounds.

Simonson broke the food requirements of the trip into two categories: that which would be prepared en route, at Base Camp, and at Advance Base Camp by cooks, most of which could be purchased in Kathmandu; and prepackaged food that would be used by the climbers in the higher camps. In all, the expedition brought about 600 pounds (300 kg) of food supplies from the United States for the high camps—"everything from pressurized cans of Easy Cheese and taco chips to the boil-in-bag pouch meals from army MREs (meals ready to eat) that we bought in surplus stores," Simonson explains. It was a far cry from the shopping list put together for the 1924 expedition which, among other things, specified sixty tins of quail in foie gras and four cases of champagne, vintage 1915 Montebello.[6]

Nothing—especially an Everest expedition—ever goes smoothly. Two years after the 1924 expedition, Everest Committee chairman Sir Francis Younghusband wrote, "Having obtained from the Tibetan government leave for a third Expedition to proceed to Everest, having arranged the finance, and settled the composition of the party, the stores and equipment had to be bought, packed and dispatched. It might be thought that after the experience of two previous Expeditions this would be a simple matter. But finality is never reached in organizing and equipping expeditions any more than in anything else."[7]

Simonson would agree heartily. In the last week before their March 17 departure for Kathmandu, even as he and his climbing team were packing food and gear into dozens of seventy-pound duffel bags, critical items were missing. The Eureka tent company, for example, had shipped tents to Simonson for the expedition, but two days before departure they still had not arrived. Frantic, Eureka sent another shipment of tents by overnight delivery and they arrived just as the team was loading up to head to the airport.

Tents, however, were the least of Simonson's problems at this point. The big problem was money. Simonson explains: "The payment schedule agreement that we had with the BBC was that they would provide the bulk of their funding 'with immediate effect' after we signed the Letter of Agreement at the end of January, and the balance by February 15. MountainZone.com's funding would not be made available until the BBC/NOVA money was in. But the BBC and NOVA had not worked out the details of their own contract with each other, and it was not until nearly February 15, the deadline for the final payment, that the initial payment was made. The money was in the expedition's account for less than an hour before it was sent to the Chinese authorities to cover expedition fees, at this point long overdue. Weeks went by and despite repeated invoices and calls, the BBC failed to make the final payment."

When Simonson arrived in Kathmandu on March 18, the BBC still hadn't met its obligations, the expedition was flat broke, and Simonson was angry. "To cover the expedition's expenses, including some $30,000 for oxygen supplies alone, I had run up huge debts on my credit cards and had to ask all our climbers to pay for their own plane tickets on the promise I'd reimburse them later," Simonson remembers. "It was time for a showdown."

Though they had been asked to arrive in Kathmandu early in order to begin the process of acclimatization and, not incidentally, help with the drudgery of unpacking and repacking all the expedition's gear and food, the BBC film crew arrived at the last minute, the night before the expedition was scheduled to leave Kathmandu for Tibet. Simonson confronted Firstbrook. "I told him flatly that neither he nor any of his crew were getting on to the bus the next day unless the BBC honored its commitment and wired the money that was more than a month in arrears. Then I sent London the same message. That definitely got their attention." Though Simonson relented and let the crew on the bus, the BBC finally transferred their overdue funds to the expedition's account on March 23.

In the early 1920s, the British expeditions had the great advantage of having their food, transport, communications, and logistics largely arranged for them by the Imperial government bureaucracy in India and the military. Simonson's version of this local support was Great Escapes Trekking, a Kathmandu-based organization that provides a wide range of on-site services to expedition organizers, from recruiting qualified Sherpa and cooks to clearing gear through Nepalese customs. When Simonson's climbing team arrived at the airport at Kathmandu, the Sherpa team from Great Escapes was waiting for them.

Jake Norton, who has lived in Nepal, describes the scene: "The interior of the airport is a fairly serene place; the only Nepali citizens permitted inside are those with tickets. While

Eric conferred with a customs official, Dave, Tap, Conrad, Lee, and I lugged something like seventy big duffel bags of food and gear on to baggage carts and we started shuttling them to the door. The moment those remote-control glass doors open, the calm vanishes and you're plunged into a sea of clamoring humanity. Children grab bags and try to haul them off to taxis, from whom they get a commission. There are horns honking everywhere, hotel room hawkers, people yelling and running about. It's an instant culture shock." While the Sherpa cleared a path through the chaos and loaded the duffels into Great Escape's vans and trucks, the climbers guarded the perimeter. Finally, they all piled into the vans and somehow found a route through the mêlée.

"Kathmandu," Norton says, "must be the only airport in the world with a cattle grid across its entrance ramp. Cows being sacred in Nepal, there's no other way to keep the wandering beasts out of the airport."

The vans careened into town along twisting streets, past the huge Pashupatinath Temple complex, with its multiple, still-smoldering cremation pyre platforms along the Bagmati River, through chaotic intersections choked with trucks, taxis, cars, bicycles, motorbikes, rickshaws, and, of course, cows, and finally reached central Kathmandu. At the Manaslu Hotel, everyone grabbed a beer and collapsed in the hotel's backyard garden. Norton, the young Nepal veteran, remembers, "I was more exhausted than on a summit day."

The ancient city of Kathmandu has changed dramatically since Eric Simonson first visited it in 1979. The old city had then been bounded by a ring road beyond which lay lush rice paddies and grain fields. Much of that is gone now. "Like the world over," Simonson says with evident sadness, "the farmland has been gobbled up by sprawl and the air quality has deteriorated dramatically, especially from the two-cycle rickshaw and motorbike engines." This year, the air was even dirtier than usual because the dry winter had spawned forest and brush fires throughout the region. In his diary, climber Andy Politz, another Kathmandu veteran, wrote, "The air quality and dust are getting worse and worse here. With all the lung ailments in this place, the last thing we need is more airborne pathogens carried on the dust."

Still, says Jake Norton, Kathmandu has not completely lost its exotic charm: "If you get up early in the morning and wander around the heart of the city, you can still get a taste of what it was like a hundred years ago—just after sunrise, people come in from small farms on the edge of town carrying baskets of fresh vegetables through the twisting, crowded alleys to the open markets. Vegetable and other food stalls open up and women swat stray cows away from the produce. There are stands and shops selling everything imaginable and you are constantly accosted by merchants who run up to you asking, 'Buy carpet? Tiger Balm? Tea? Change money? Hashish?' It's pretty colorful."

Central Kathmandu is a bazaar for the senses. Bells ring everywhere, competing with horns and whistles. Incense and the pungent smell of marigold petals drift out of innumerable elaborate temples and mix with the fragrance of *daal bhat*, the traditional meal of rice, lentils, and curry being cooked in a thousand tiny invisible kitchens. Huge Buddha eyes painted on buildings seem to follow you everywhere, and the weathered faces of the people themselves crinkle into smiles and whisper *namaste*—"I salute the God which dwells within you"—as they pass, their palms pressed together in blessing.

While the other members of the team spent a day taking in the sights, resting, and trying to stay healthy, Simonson and his Sherpa crew went to work. First they met and worked out the details of the Sherpa's salary and bonuses, then they began pulling Simonson's Kathmandu-based gear out of storage. The next day, he and the cooks purchased several thousand pounds of rice, flour, sugar, dried sheep and yak meat, cheese, canned goods, and fresh vegetables that would keep well (onions, cabbage, cauliflower, potatoes, carrots), as well as a smaller quantity of more perishable vegetables that would be consumed in the early days of the expedition and be replenished by the commercial trekking group Simonson had coming in a few weeks later.

On the 20th, the other team members began to help pack loads as well. Says Hahn, "We all gained a renewed appreciation for Eric's logistical wizardry as we watched him whirl about calling for instantly calculated quantities of propane cooking canisters for this or that camp or replacement tent poles of different sizes and types, and assign tasks to be completed before the whole load could be taken through customs the next day. The rest of us were still in relatively low gear, but Eric had been living and breathing this expedition for months. The challenge for us was to catch up to his level of intensity as soon as possible to take some of the burden of responsibility."

But Simonson was in his element: "For me, this is when the fun finally starts. This is when it all comes together, when we start loading for the trip to Base Camp. And when we finally get there and start unloading again, I know I've had my hands on everything on those trucks and it's all going to work."

By midafternoon, expedition historian Jochen Hemmleb arrived at the hotel. After a short nap, he heard English-speaking voices. Wandering down the hall, he found an open door and, entering, met Eric Simonson for the first time. "My first impression of Eric was, 'My God, this is a big boy!'" he recalls. The two embraced and Simonson led Hemmleb around to the other rooms and introduced him to the rest of the expedition members. That evening the entire group had dinner with Heather Macdonald, a mountain guide for Simonson's company who was spending the season in Kathmandu working for Elizabeth Hawley, the director of the Himalayan Trust established by Edmund Hillary.

The next day, packing continued and more team members arrived: WGBH/NOVA producer Liesl Clark and cameraman Thom Pollard, and independent cameraman Ned Johnston, who was under contract to the BBC.

On the morning of March 22, the Rinpoche, or chief lama, from Thyangboche Monastery, the Buddhist monastery in the heart of the Solu Khumbu region of Nepal from which most of the expedition Sherpa had come, presided over a *puja* (offerings-giving) ceremony designed to provide the expedition with an auspicious send-off. The entire team had bought prayer flags to hang, juniper branches to burn, and rice and other offerings, and received the lama's blessing. The rest of the day was spent in last-minute packing and preparation. That night after dinner, the BBC's Peter Firstbrook and Graham Hoyland finally arrived, complete with forty-five cases of luggage and equipment.

There is a daytime ban on the movement of large trucks in central Kathmandu, so after 8:00 P.M. on the 22nd a large container truck pulled into the Great Escapes compound and the team's Sherpa immediately began loading it for an early departure the next morning. Then at 5:30 A.M. on the 23rd, the truck was moved to customs to be cleared, locked, and bonded. The late arrival of the BBC gear and delays in the clearance of the expedition's oxygen bottles, however, stalled the entire process. Simonson had Dave Hahn and two Sherpa stay behind with the truck while Firstbrook and Hoyland got their gear through customs and the oxygen was loaded.

Meanwhile, the rest of the team climbed aboard a Nepali bus and left for Kodari on the Tibetan border, five hours away. Under Simonson's plan, with stops for acclimatization along the way, the Mallory & Irvine Research Expedition would be at Everest Base Camp in six days.

On March 25, 1924, when the third British Everest expedition left Darjeeling, they faced an overland journey of more than a month. Walking most of the time, riding tough little hill ponies occasionally, they descended from the heights of Darjeeling, through hills terraced with tea plantations, to Tista Bridge, and then trekked northeastward to Kalimpong, Pedong, and the steaming valleys of Sikkim. They would stay in mountain bungalows that could accommodate only half the party at a time, so the group was divided in two, one roughly a day behind the other, and the two snaking lines of ponies, porters (some seventy Sherpa and Bhotias), personal servants, Sirdars (Sherpa leaders), and expedition members themselves slowly made their way toward Tibet, far to the north.

At the beginning, the landscape they traversed was almost

impossibly lush. In his diary, the young Andrew Irvine wrote, "We saw some most beautiful butterflies and got some wonderful wafts of perfume on a very hot breeze."[8] There were tree ferns and wild bananas, scarlet hibiscus and brilliant magenta bougainvillea, the foot-long white trumpet blossoms of datura and orchids of every description. Gradually, as they climbed out of the valley toward the 14,390-foot (4,390-m) Jelep La (*la* means "pass") and the air cooled, they entered rhododendron forests of pink, crimson, yellow, mauve, cream, and white, then rose through stands of evergreens, and finally ascended above the tree line.

Tracing the route used for centuries by mule trains carrying wool south from Tibet, they crossed the Jelep La on April 1, and descended into the Chumbi Valley and Tibet at last. On the lee side of the pass, Chumbi was much cooler and drier than Sikkim and provided a hint of the harshness of the high Tibetan plain, still ahead. As they again began ascending through steadily roughening terrain toward Phari Dzong (*dzong* means "fort"), expedition leader General Bruce described the scene: "In the wooded parts of the Himalaya one often meets with beautiful scenery, magnificent scenery, indeed, combined with real wildness, but the upper parts of the Gautsa Defile . . . impress one with a sense of savage wildness."[9] During the 1921 reconnaissance expedition, Mallory described the approach to Phari Dzong: " . . . after ten miles' dusty walking in the glare of the plain itself . . . Phari seemed to prove that we had come to a new world altogether ruder than the [Chumbi] valley. . . . It is the most incredibly dirty warren that can be imagined."[10]

They arrived at Phari Dzong on April 6 and began an elaborate, days-long negotiation with the Dzong Pen (*pen* means "chief") for fresh ponies and yaks to take them northwest to the next fortress town, Kampa Dzong. General Bruce again: "The Dzong Pen himself, a grasping, avaricious, but feeble, albeit well-mannered individual, was really in the hands of his subordinates, the Gyembus, a truculent, but determined crowd of cheerful rascals, who had clearly not taken on their duties for health's sake alone."[11] Bruce had been through negotiations with these amiable bandits before, but this time he had an ace up his sleeve; he knew that officials in Lhasa had ordered the notorious Dzong Pen to help the expedition and charge fair prices. At an open meeting before all the Phari Dzong leaders, Bruce made a ceremony of writing out a telegram of complaint to the Prime Minister. "This bluff had its desired effect," Bruce notes, "and very shortly an agreement was drawn out and signed, and, after much bowing and ceremonial kow-towing, by general request the telegram was torn up."[12] Two days later, with some 300 fresh pack animals, the expedition resumed its long march.

At the Tang La, 15,200 feet (4,630 m), the expedition party split. General Bruce was, as the London doctors had predicted, feeling unwell and he and Hingston, the expedition doctor, and a local British trade agent traveled farther north into Tibet along an easier route while the main party turned northwest over two more passes toward Kampa Dzong. It was a particularly unpleasant route segment, of which Norton would later write: "This area is the most inhospitable of any we meet on the Tibetan plateau. I have now crossed it four times, both in spring and in summer, and never without encountering a blizzard or constant storms of snow and sleet. . . . Our route lay over a vast gravelly plain, the very abomination of desolation. . . . To the

53

best of my recollection, we had not seen a human being for the last two days."[13] Mallory, however, had found a few kind things to say about the area: " . . . in the evening light this country can be beautiful, snow mountains and all: the harshness becomes subdued; shadows soften the hillsides; there is a blending of lines and folds until the last light, so that one comes to bless the absolute bareness, feeling that here is a pure beauty of form, a kind of ultimate harmony."[14]

After four days of icy nights and relentless daytime head winds, they reached Kampa Dzong, a massive cliff-top fortress gleaming with whitewash and punctuated by both square and rounded turrets. Protected from the incessant wind and described by Norton as "a veritable sun trap," here the expedition would spend the next four days resting, dickering for fresh pack animals, and debating a preliminary plan of assault on Everest.

It was here too that the expedition received the news that General Bruce would not be rejoining them; he had been struck down not by his weak heart, but by malaria, which he had picked up while tiger-hunting in India some weeks earlier, and would return to a hill town outside of Darjeeling to convalesce. Leadership for the expedition now passed into the capable hands of Norton, who was both respected and well liked. But the party would miss Bruce's high spirits: "Bruce is a kind of benevolent volcano in perpetual eruption of good cheer. And of such irrepressible fun that no amount of misfortune can ever quell him," Younghusband later wrote.[15]

Bruce was not the only one suffering. Nearly everyone had digestive disorders, but Beetham had a particularly virulent case of dysentery that would weaken him so thoroughly that (along with a later bout with sciatica) he was effectively taken out of the picture for high-altitude climbing. Mallory had been ill as well, suffering from abdominal pain that was severe enough that Somervell, the surgeon, thought it was appendicitis and had begun considering operating. But the pain eased and Mallory recovered completely.

The expedition left Kampa Dzong on April 15 heading due west on a route that paralleled the Himalaya range, which lay to the south. They had another 100 miles yet to go to their destination. At this point three years earlier, during the reconnaissance expedition, Mallory had written to his friend Geoffrey Winthrop Young, "We are about to walk off the map . . . it's beginning to be exciting."[16] Now, even with the experience of the earlier survey, the landscape before them was largely featureless: a vast dun-colored plain of sand and gravel punctuated here and there by dark patches of quicksand, spiraling dust devils, and distant snowcapped mountains. After another two-day march, they reached Tinki Dzong, conducted the by-now familiar ritual of negotiating for fresh pack animals-donkeys this time-with the Dzong Pen and, after a brief rest, were off again.

From time to time as they marched westward, Everest itself made a distant but hazy appearance. But during the reconnaissance expedition, Mallory had detoured up the Yaru valley, west of Tinki Dzong, and got his first clear view of the mountain that would seize first his imagination and, eventually, his life: "We were able to make out almost exactly where Everest should be; but the clouds were dark in that direction. We gazed at them intently through field glasses as though by some miracle we might pierce the veil. Presently the miracle happened. We caught the gleam of snow behind the grey mists. A whole group of mountains began to appear in gigantic fragments. Mountain shapes are often fantastic seen through a mist; these were like the wildest creation of a dream. A preposterous triangular lump rose out of the depths; its edge came leaping up at an angle of about 70° and ended nowhere. To the left a black serrated crest was hanging in the sky incredibly. Gradually, very gradually, we saw the great mountain sides and glaciers and aretes, now one fragment and now another through the floating rifts, until far higher in the sky than imagination had dared to suggest the white summit of Everest appeared."[17]

The expedition pressed westward, still following a tributary of the River Arun, toward Shekar Dzong. The Arun is one of only a handful of rivers to completely bisect the Himalaya, a feat it is able to perform by the simple trick of being older than the mountains themselves. Over the eons, the river has continued to carve its implacable course southward, cutting through the landscape at the same rate that the Himalaya range rose around it—tangible and timeless proof of the ability of water to move mountains, a sort of Zen meditation on the grandest of scales.

Shekar Dzong, the "White Glass Fort," was the most impressive of the Tibetan fortresses through which the expedition would pass. A massive edifice incorporating a monastery housing some 400 monks, it had been constructed over centuries. Thick-walled, multistoried buildings climbed in tiers hundreds of feet up the steep face of a conical mountain, culminating in a high tower at the very peak. Here, thanks to a cooperative Dzong Pen, the expedition was able to resupply itself quickly and, after only a few days, they turned south across a particularly desolate stretch of plains and eroded hills toward the remote Rongbuk Monastery at the very feet of the Goddess Mother of the World.

During the preceding weeks, the march across the Tibetan plateau had kept the expedition at between 13,000 and 15,000 feet (4,000 and 4,600 m). But at the Pang La, their route rose to nearly 17,000 feet (5,200 m). At the head of the pass, the group climbed a small hill to take in the view to the south. Wrote Norton, "From the Pang La, a striking panorama of the main Himalayan range comes into view, with Mount Everest, its central point, some 35 miles away as the crow flies. . . . From left to right [sic] they run:[18] Gosainthan [now called Shisha Pangma], Cho Uyo, Gyachung Kang, Mount Everest, Makalu, and Kanchenjunga. And that nothing may be lacking from the grandeur of the view, each of the giants is so spaced from its neighbors that none is dwarfed, and each stands dominating the serried ranks of lesser peaks which stretch in a jagged wall from horizon to horizon."[19]

On this day, April 26, 1924, the view also offered Norton one more piece of important good news: "By some freak of the inclination of the rock to the impact of the perpetual northwest wind, the northern face of the whole topmost pyramid of Mount Everest—6,000 feet of it—is at this season almost bare of snow."[20] With rising confidence, the expedition advanced toward its goal.

Dave Hahn is a gentle giant of a guy. Six feet, 2 inches tall, lean but broad-shouldered and possessed of a prominent jaw that breaks readily into a wide, warm smile with a trace of mischievousness around the edges, he gives the outward impression of being one of the more laid-back members of the 1999 Mallory & Irvine Research Expedition team. In truth, says Eric Simonson, his friend and climbing partner of many years, "He's incredibly reliable, conscientious almost to a fault." That's why, when Simonson and the rest of the expedition members left Kathmandu at dawn on March 23, he left Hahn behind to clear the expedition's oxygen bottles and gear through customs and shepherd the BBC crew through the clearance process the rest of the team had gone through days before.

With characteristic modesty, Hahn says, "My role was a small one, really. I was just supposed to stand out like a 6-foot-2 sore thumb and act impatient. The sore thumb part was easy; I don't blend in well in Asia. But the impatient part was tougher; I'm so patient with bureaucratic glitches that I nearly needed CPR when we finally had all the paperwork in hand."[21] For the heavy-duty hassling and palm-greasing, Simonson had also left behind Pemba Tshiri, his cook and champion customs-fixer. Pemba has been with Simonson for years. "The guy's amazing," says Simonson. "He studied in a monastery for years; speaks, reads, and writes Tibetan, Nepali, and English; is brilliant at handling customs; and, most tellingly, figured out a long time ago that if you want to make money and stay alive in expeditions, the thing to do is to be the cook, not a climber."

Despite Pemba's wheedling and Hahn's looming and scowling, the process took much of the day; it wasn't until 3:00 P.M. that the two of them, along with Sherpa Sirdar Danuru "Dawa" Sherpa and the BBC's Hoyland and Firstbrook, finally got the expedition's huge container truck on the road toward China.

The road out of Kathmandu climbs east out of the valley to

Dhulikel, a small resort town on the rim of the basin that only the day before had been the scene of a bloody firefight between the Nepali police and a Maoist extremist group. From Dhulikel, the road winds down through terraced farmlands of almost junglelike lushness, eventually crossing the Sun Kosi (*kosi* means "river"). Shortly thereafter, it turns northward and follows the Bhote Kosi toward the Chinese border. At Lamusangu, the road forks. The right fork turns east, crosses the river, and eventually leads to the approach route for Everest's south side, the route most summit climbs have taken since it was pioneered by Hillary. The left fork continues north toward the Nepali border town of Kodari, along the way passing cliffs full of beehives, some as large as a small car, which are harvested by the famous "honey hunters" of Nepal.

At about the time Hahn left Kathmandu, Simonson was already in Kodari, a ramshackle tumble of buildings wedged into the deep, verdant gorge cut by the powerful Bhote Kosi. After checking the expedition through Nepali immigration, getting their passports stamped, and arranging exit visas, he led them across the "Friendship Bridge" over the river and into China.

There is no "Welcome to the Peoples' Republic of China" tourist information center on the other side, just a handful of unsmiling white-gloved Chinese soldiers at a checkpoint and a bleak no-man's land beyond, threaded by a primitive, incredibly steep one-lane dirt road full of switchbacks and prone to landslides. There are few places on earth where the transition from a warm and boisterous culture to a cold and controlled one happens in the span of only 50 feet; the "Friendship Bridge" is one of them.

"We hired a sort of jitney vehicle, a flatbed with rails built atop a pickup truck body, and piled in," Simonson recalls. "You stand in this thing holding on to the iron railings with your pack at your feet while the vehicle crawls up this terrible road for several miles." The first sign of human civilization, such as it is, and the location of the Chinese customs center, is Zhangmu, a town that zigzags so steeply up a foliage-stripped hillside that each multistory building looks as though it is perched upon the roof of its lower neighbor. As a community, Zhangmu has all the architectural charm of a 1950s-era penitentiary and the rough-and-ready lawlessness of a wild west frontier town. "You can literally get anything you want in Zhangmu," Simonson says with bemused disbelief, "whiskey, women, money-changing, you name it."

What you can't get, apparently, is a decent hotel room. While they waited for Hahn and the container truck to arrive, the expedition members stayed at the Zhangmu Hotel, a classic post-revolutionary Chinese concrete blockhouse, with sterile rooms, worn furnishings, and well-appointed bathrooms in which nothing worked. Like everything else in town, the hotel hung off the hillside. "You enter at the top floor and everything is downhill from there," explains historian Hemmleb with intentional irony. Breakfast at the hotel the next morning consisted of fried peanuts, steamed dough buns, hard-boiled eggs, and a thin rice gruel. "It was fairly grim," says Simonson.

Zhangmu is on Beijing time, two hours and fifteen minutes ahead of Nepal time. As a consequence, Simonson knew Hahn and the container truck would not have made it over the border before it closed at 4:00 P.M., Chinese time, the night before. But by noon on the 24th they still hadn't appeared and Simonson was worried.

The imperturbable Hahn was still in Kodari. It had taken five hours to clear immigration and now he watched calmly as his driver took apart the container truck's rear differential, which had been performing alarmingly on the climb up to the border. In the end they hired another truck, unloaded the roughly 15,000 pounds of gear and supplies from the first one, reloaded it into the second one, and finally made their way over the border and up the switchbacks into Zhangmu. Arriving in midafternoon they, and the rest of the team, unloaded it all once again and shifted the loads into three Chinese trucks Simonson had hired to haul their gear to the foot of Everest. "The Chinese trucks had a capacity of 5,000 pounds of equipment each on 16-foot beds covered by canvas stretched over hoops, like a Conestoga wagon," Simonson explains. "We lashed the loads down, covered them with tarpaulins to keep out the dust, and put two of our Sherpa in each truck to guard them that night."

Simonson had originally planned to leave Zhangmu the same afternoon Hahn arrived with their gear, but the road to Nyalam, the next town, is notoriously treacherous. By late afternoon the sky had turned inky and Simonson was sure a storm was brewing. Instead of leaving, explains Hahn, "We elected to stay in Zhangmu, put away large quantities of Chinese food and beer, and tell each other great and sometimes true stories of the past day's adventures."

That night, as Simonson had suspected, a terrific storm pounded Zhangmu with torrential rain, thunder, and lightning. The next morning, March 25, there was snow on the hills and Simonson was worried about the road ahead. Nonetheless, the team, now augmented by Mr. Liu, their Chinese Mountaineering

Association liaison officer, and Mr. Xu, their interpreter, piled into a convoy composed of the three trucks, a minibus, and a Toyota Land Cruiser. Together they picked their way past a mud slide from the night before and started for Nyalam just as the sun began warming the gorge of the Bhote Kosi.

Zhangmu is situated at about 7,550 feet (2,300 m) above sea level, Nyalam about 12,300 feet (3,750 m). The one-lane gravel road that connects them is ludicrous. It clings tenuously to the east side of the narrow gorge and in many places is cut directly into the cliff face, with huge rock overhangs and drop-offs of more than 1,000 feet to the river below. Climate zones change as the elevation increases, from the humid gorge through evergreen forest and ultimately to the arid flanks of the high Tibetan plateau, a brown, sparsely vegetated landscape composed largely of rock, rock debris, dust, and snow.

After a few hours of slow but steady progress, the convoy crossed to the west side of the gorge, an area famous for avalanches and landslides. There was fresh snow here and the road was deeply rutted in places. "In the past," Simonson recalls, "we've driven on this road in cuts excavated through avalanche debris 20 to 30 feet high, but this year the winter had been so dry that there had been very few avalanches and the road was largely clear." By lunchtime, the team had reached Nyalam safely and booked into the Snow Land Hotel, run by an old friend of Simonson's named Tashi, the unofficial "mayor of Nyalam." Simonson's was the first expedition of the year to arrive, and Tashi was glad to see them.

In Nyalam, the architecture shifts from post-revolutionary Chinese modern to timeless Tibetan stone and mud. The buildings are flat-roofed and squat, their thick stone walls wider at the base than the top and clad in sand-colored mud stucco, a style that would not look at all out of place in a New Mexico pueblo, except that instead of coyotes, yaks nose around in the trash bins. At the four corners of every roof, a short chimneylike construction serves to hold in place firewood, which edges the rooftop to a depth of perhaps 3 feet. It is hard to tell whether the Tibetans adopted this practice to dry the wood quickly or keep it safe from thieves; firewood is a valuable commodity in these stark hills. Through the streets of Nyalam roamed a swarthy mix of Chinese truck drivers and Tibetan yak drivers, most of whom clustered at a stunningly out-of-place establishment that was part karaoke bar, part brothel.

The team spent the afternoon lazing in the sunshine and taking short hikes designed to speed the arduous process of acclimatizing to the thin, cold air. That night, Tashi put on a big spread: "We had a fine dinner of tea, rice, potatoes, green beans, fried onions, a few awesome mystery meat plates, and some cauliflower, not forgetting the egg-drop soup and the scrambled egg/tomato dish," Hahn later reported.[22]

The next day, March 26, Simonson sent the trucks ahead to Tingri but kept the climbers in Nyalam to clamber about the hills above the town and push the acclimatization process further. In twos and threes they went, hiking up the snow-clad slopes and rocks. Hemmleb and Anker headed up one ridge; Simonson, Richards, Norton, and Politz, another; and Hahn, Pollard, and producer Liesl Clark, yet a third. It was cold and windy and it snowed off and on, a foretaste of what was to come. Hoyland and Firstbrook, who were effectively a day behind the rest of the group in acclimatization, had altitude headaches and took only short walks.

It was also at this point, in Nyalam, that the BBC's Firstbrook presented Simonson a final contract different in many respects from what had been agreed to in January. "Assuming for a moment that this wasn't a case of galloping incompetence, it was a brilliant move," Simonson says. "Their lawyers had spent six weeks rewriting this thing, and Firstbrook knew I had no access to legal counsel here in the middle of Tibet and only limited ability to negotiate, since we were already halfway to Everest. It was an event that made it hard for me to trust the BBC folks from that point on. In any event, I refused to sign the contract."

Early on the morning of March 27, the expedition team was back on the bus ascending northward again to the lip of the Tibetan plateau at the Tsong La, almost 17,000 feet (5,200 m) above sea level. "We stopped at the top of the pass, where the view is spectacular," Simonson explains. "You get a terrifically clear view of Shisha Pangma and Gaurisankar and a good section of the Himalaya range. There are big stone cairn monuments and the air crackles with all the colorful prayer flags snapping in the wind."

Beyond the Tsong La, the road descends steeply to the Tibetan plateau. "It was not a boring drive," deadpans Hahn. "Our driver, Tsering, is like many drivers in these parts in that he likes to let a vehicle drift on a descent. But he is good at it, and so when our bus would get a few wheels in the air upon hitting some obstacle, we weren't alarmed."[23]

At the bottom of the descent, the road—the "Friendship Highway"—runs out along a broad, dry valley and turns east. Quite suddenly, far away to the southeast, Everest itself appears, flanked on the right by Gyachung Kang and Cho Oyu. "It is a magnificent view," Simonson recalls. "We stopped the bus and

1924 British Everest Expedition: (back row, from left) Andrew Irvine,
George Mallory, Edward Norton, Noel Odell, John MacDonald; (front
row, from left) Edward Shebbeare, Geoffrey Bruce, Howard Somervell,
Bentley Beetham (Members not shown: General Charles Bruce,
John Noel, John de Vere Hazard, Richard Hingston.)

John Noel with his cine camera on the North Col, 1922

The first summit team in 1922: (from left) Henry Morshead, George Mallory, Theodore Somervell, and Edward Norton

Last photo of Mallory and Irvine departing from the North Col,
June 6, 1924

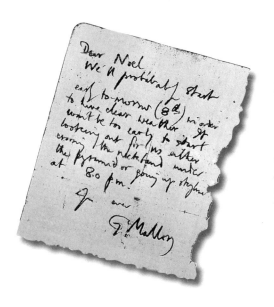

Mallory's note to Odell   Mallory's note to John Noel

Above left: Noel Ewart Odell
Above right: Edward Felix Norton

Below: Pony train on the approach to Everest, 1924

Camp II on the East Rongbuk Glacier, 1924

Sandy Irvine outside his workshop tent at Everest Base Camp, 1924

Geoffrey Bruce

Theodore Howard Somervell

Left: Norton at
28,000 feet (8,530 m),
climbing toward the
Great Couloir.
Second Step at upper
left, summit in the
background

Below: Irvine with
his modified oxygen
apparatus. Note
characteristic shape
of oxygen bottles

The ice chimney on the North Col in 1924 with the
rope ladder constructed by Sandy Irvine

all piled out into the silence of the plateau. The sky was the kind of brilliant blue you only get in Tibet, and there was a huge plume blowing east off the mountain's summit. Some of us had been here before, but it is always a thrill. Jochen, for whom this was a first, was beside himself with excitement."

In his journal, Hemmleb would write, "I distanced myself from the rest of the group to experience this moment in solitude. After having studied this mountain in countless photographs, I thought I'd be prepared for this first sighting. But I wasn't. After a few minutes, a feeling of warmth and contentment came over me and I marveled at how something as nonorganic as a mountain can move one so deeply."

The route carries on across vast stretches of dusty plain, interrupted from time to time by small villages and the ruins of nineteenth-century fortresses destroyed when the Nepalese invaded Tibet. On the bus, watching the ancient hamlets and new public works projects roll by, Andy Politz wrote in his diary: "The Chinese are trying to kill the Tibetan culture with kindness by building infrastructure—hydroelectricity, housing, road improvements, communications. Every other nation will look upon this as improving the standard of living for the Tibetans, but I can't help but think that the effect on this intensely spiritual culture is insidious. When they can turn the handle on a faucet and water flows out, people have been robbed of the experience of walking to a pure, flowing brook and drinking from the spirit of the earth."

The expedition had reached the plains of Tingri, a vast region that has been inhabited by nomadic tribes for centuries. Here, in places, the soil is fertile enough for farmers to irrigate the dry land to raise barley and potatoes during the short growing season. But for the most part, the plains in late March are a dull gray-brown tableland, cut occasionally by meandering streams that eventually wander off and lose themselves in parched alkali flats. Here and there, darker brown hills, worn down to nubs by the ages, break the otherwise flat expanse. Vegetation is sparse and, at this time of year, wind-burnt and lifeless.

Finally, the convoy topped a rise and Tingri itself rose out of the shimmering haze of the plateau, a random cluster of low-slung Tibetan buildings scattered around the base of an isolated hill. The bus rolled up to a hotel rather grandly named the Everest View (spelled "Veo" on the sign outside). "It's a typical Tibetan inn: stone and mud walls, dirt floors, primitive beds, and a communal toilet up on the roof," says Simonson, as if trying to persuade the group they will be having a genuine cultural experience. "But the food is great; the cooks come from Sechuan." Later the team discovers it's true. At supper, they sat down at a big table in the middle of which was a huge lazy Susan heaped with plates of food that, Hemmleb later admitted with amazement, "was fabulous."

Tingri (14,400 feet; 4,390 m), a town of perhaps 500 souls, is the northern terminus of the ancient yak route across the Himalaya. From Tingri the route climbs to the Nangpa La, skirts the western slopes of Cho Oyu, and finally descends to Namche Bazaar, in the heart of the Khumbu region of Nepal, ancestral home of the Sherpa. For centuries, yak trains carried salt from evaporated basins on the Tibetan plains and dried sheep meat to Nepal by this route, returning weeks later with buffalo hides for shoes and other trade goods.

As in Kathmandu, Simonson kept gear stored in Tingri. The

Sherpa crew he sent ahead from Nyalam had already loaded this gear, along with four fifty-five-gallon drums of kerosene and one fifty-five-gallon drum of gasoline (eventually to be transferred to jerry cans), into a fourth truck. On March 28, the Sherpa drove three of the four trucks south toward the bleak Rongbuk Valley and Base Camp.

That night, Hemmleb found a kindred soul in BBC producer Graham Hoyland, who had been equally moved by the expedition's first sighting of Everest from the plains of Tingri. The forty-two-year-old Hoyland, who summited Everest from the south side in 1993, comes from a long line of climbers. His father had started him climbing at the age of five on the island of Arran, in Scotland. Before he was killed on Mont Blanc in the thirties, Graham's uncle, John Hoyland, had been called "potentially the best mountaineer of his generation" and compared to Mallory as one of "whom it seemed safe to expect so much."[24] And, of course, there was "Uncle Hunch," the legendary Howard Somervell himself, who had climbed with Mallory in both 1922 and 1924. In 1990, on another BBC film expedition, Graham Hoyland had climbed most of the route his granduncle Somervell had taken on the North Face.

Hemmleb felt a great deal of respect for how hard Hoyland had worked to get the BBC interested in a search expedition, and felt sad that the politics of dealing with the BBC made developing a closer, more personal relationship difficult. Now, with the joint expedition underway, Hoyland had one clear ambition: to find the camera Howard Somervell had lent Mallory on the final, fateful summit day in 1924. When the expedition reached the point on the plains of Tingri at which Everest finally heaved into view, Hoyland, like Hemmleb, could feel a deep sense of satisfaction perhaps unreachable by the other team members. That night, however, Hoyland also told Hemmleb he had a premonition that something would happen to him on the expedition, as indeed something did.

The next day, the expedition team stayed in Tingri to acclimatize again. Team members hiked out into the surrounding hills, working on themselves as much psychologically as physiologically. In his diary, Politz wrote: "There's a major altitude headache knocking at the door. To keep it away, I drink water and tea all day long. Already the lactic acid is building up in my legs and they're tired. I'm going to take it slowly; easy on the legs and torso for the first two weeks; there's too much at stake for me to ruin my chances by racing up or down the mountain . . . it's going to take sheer backbone to get this done."

That night, after a suitably spicy Sechuan dinner, the team finished loading the fourth truck and turned in. The next morning, March 29, the expedition members stumbled out into the chill predawn darkness, climbed into four Toyota Land Cruisers, and, followed by the fourth truck, rolled out of town, heading first east toward the rising sun, then south for Everest, at last. Hemmleb, however, stayed behind, struggling with a chest infection. Simonson felt Hemmleb would recover more quickly in Tingri than at the higher altitude of Base Camp and, though the illness caused Hemmleb to question privately his ability to perform on the mountain, Simonson turned out to be right; two days later he rejoined them, fully recovered.

Mallory, Irvine, and the rest of the 1924 Everest expedition would have no difficulty recognizing the 16,800-foot (5,120-m) Pang La today; it is virtually unchanged. There are a few more cairns topped with wind-ravaged prayer flags, perhaps, and the rough yak track is now a rough four-wheel-drive vehicle track, unpaved and rutted. But the pass itself is still searingly bleak. The wind is still fierce and rips tears from the eyes. The air is still cold and biting. The view is still breathtaking, stretching some 100 miles along the entire central Himalaya. On this day, March 29, 1999, the range was almost unnaturally clear. Some three dozen miles away, the stupendous mass of Everest rose into the brilliant azure sky as if it were still growing, which indeed it is, at roughly 1 centimeter a year. As in 1924, very little snow marked its North Face. No plume streamed from its summit. It would have been a perfect summit day.

After staring gape-mouthed at the scene before them, the team returned quietly to their cars and descended through a series of steep switchbacks until the road reached the broad, desolate valley of the Dzakar Chu (*chu* means "river"). Later, after passing through the settlement of Chosang, the convoy turned south into the long Rongbuk Valley, gateway to Tibetan Everest.

In 1924, acting expedition chief Norton described the landscape through which the 1999 expedition team now traveled: "The stage from Chödzong to Rongbuk bears to the wide plains behind and the big glaciers ahead somewhat the same relation as, in an approach march of the Great War, the ruined areas bore to the fertile fields of France behind and the stricken battlefield ahead. For it is a cheerless, desolate valley suggestive at every turn of the greater desolation to which it leads. . . . The hills on both sides are ugly brown humps of limestone devoid of any beauty of colour or form. . . . The marked drop in temperature and the bite to the wind that blows straight off the big snow-fields above further serve to emphasize the fact that the land of ice and snow is getting very near."[25]

If he notices the bleakness, Jochen Hemmleb doesn't mention it in his journal. From his entry for March 31, 1999: "Then, after another bend, Everest itself appeared in all its splendid grandeur. The huge North Face with all its familiar features, the towering Northeast Ridge, the icy West Shoulder with Nuptse behind. I'd never have thought that the mountain, still 12 miles away, could be so incredibly big. Past the Rongbuk Monastery, highest in the world. Past the site of the 1924 expedition's Base Camp. Finally, a sort of bay in the vast terminal moraine of the Rongbuk Glacier and a cluster of yellow tents: our 1999 Mallory & Irvine Research Expedition Base Camp.

"I am here at last."

CHAPTER 4

THE WHOLE BANDOBAST[1]

It is a very complicated business to arrange the
carrying to the high camps . . .
GEORGE MALLORY

Everest climbers call Rongbuk Base Camp "the gravel pit" with only the faintest hint of affection. It is an unrelievedly barren spot, a vast gray glacial outwash plain roughly 500 yards wide and hemmed in by equally gray foothills that look beaten to exhaustion by nearly continuous wind, freezing temperatures, sudden blizzards, ice, and the inexorable force of time. Were it not for the astonishing and immediately recognizable mass of Everest just to the south and the brilliant blue sky above, it might as well be the surface of the moon. Expeditions make this garden spot home for months at a time—tangible proof of the mountaineering theory of relativity: relative to the predictably nasty conditions at the higher camps—cold, wind, snow, lack of oxygen—Rongbuk Base Camp, elevation 17,060 feet (5,200 m) is downright cozy. In the spring of 1999, the Mallory & Irvine Research Expedition was the first to reach the valley, and the landscape they came upon was as pristine as it had been when the British first arrived in 1921. In his diary, Andy Politz would note, "The Buddhists believe there are five major elements:

earth, water, fire, air, and space. Looking around, it isn't hard to understand; it is a landscape of austerity, simplicity."

A day ahead of the climbing team, Eric Simonson's Sherpa had made as comfortable a camp as could be expected in such an environment. On the east side of the valley, bright yellow Eureka sleeping tents had sprung up from the unpromising gravel like giant early crocuses. Big Chinese army tents, regulation drab but looking positively verdant in their monochrome surroundings, had been erected to house the expedition's kitchen and to provide storage space. Two 20-foot-wide Mountain Hardwear "space dome" tents, which looked like psychedelic fabric versions of Buckminster Fuller's geodesic domes, also stood on the rocky plain: an orange one for communications and another, violet and pale blue, for dining. A series of plastic pipe sections delivered a constant trickle of fresh water from a stream flowing from a side valley.

For power generation, ten solar panels had been assembled and a low stone wall built around them to ward off stray yaks. The panels were hooked up to a charge controller that kept the camp's two deep-cycle 12-volt batteries from being overcharged by the intensity of the Tibetan sun. The batteries, in turn, were connected to a voltage inverter that produced 110-volt AC power. With that, the communications systems were soon up and running—walkie-talkies, computers, satellite phone. The expedition also had a backup gasoline-powered generator, but so long as the weather remained reasonably bright, it would not be needed.

On March 30, 1999, when everyone but Jochen Hemmleb had arrived, Rongbuk was a good deal more than "reasonably bright." Tap Richards recalls, "It was just unbelievably warm.

The sun was strong, there was absolutely no wind, and some of us were wandering around in T-shirts." More significantly, the mountain itself was black, not white. The winter had been exceptionally dry—very like 1924—and conditions for mounting a search were ideal. But Andy Politz, who had been here before and knew Everest well, quietly wrote in his diary, "As good as conditions are, I can bet this mountain will have something to shake us up. We'll need to cover all our bases and leave no strings untied."

As the team finished establishing the camp and sorting out the loads, Simonson tended to spiritual matters. He sent a delegation back down the valley to the Rongbuk Monastery to recruit the head lama for the expedition's second and most important *puja*. "The *puja* is just incredibly important to the Sherpa," Simonson explains. "If something goes wrong on an expedition, it's because something was wrong with the *puja*, and if things go right, then it was because the *puja* was correct. You don't have to be a Buddhist to want the *puja* to be perfect."

The Sherpa had spent hours building a large stone altar, which was now strewn with offerings—rice, whiskey, beer, money. Earlier the Sherpa had collected branches of juniper to burn as incense. Finally everything was suitably arranged, the lama arrived with an acolyte, and the ceremony began. The lamas chanted prayers, rang simple bells, and thumped hand drums for nearly an hour until finally the Sherpa climbed atop the altar and erected a mast strung with multicolored prayer flags. Then, amid much drinking of whiskey and beer, Sherpa and western climbers alike threw rice and *tsampa* (barley flour) into the air for good luck. Says Dave Hahn, "I took the opportunity amid the happy confusion to slip a little sweet-smelling sagebrush from Taos, New Mexico, on to the fire. Some of the guys smuggled their ice axes or crampons on to the blessing pile. I noticed Phinjo Sherpa, our oldest, most experienced, and most humble climber, working a few extra prayers in, throwing extra offerings on the sly. . . . We may not all be good Buddhists, but we welcomed the opportunity to come together as a team and be reminded that life is precious and fragile."[2]

Then it was time to begin the elaborate ritual of negotiating with the yak drivers. The great advantage of the Rongbuk approach to Everest is that yaks can be used to carry loads all the way to Camp III, high on the East Rongbuk Glacier. The Chinese Mountaineering Association liaison officer, Mr. Liu, had arranged with the local district "headman" for the provision of forty-two yaks and fourteen yak drivers from the surrounding area. The yaks and drivers arrived on April 2 and the game began. "The yak drivers get paid by the trip," explains Simonson, "so it's in their interest to take as little as possible in order to have to make multiple trips." There was another issue as well. After the hard Tibetan winter, the yaks themselves are weak and can carry loads of only about fifty pounds (twenty-five kg) on each side. The yak drivers bring their own Tibetan weighing scales, and hours are spent haggling—heatedly but with good humor—over what constitutes an acceptable load.

Hahn describes the delicate negotiations: "The yak drivers heft the bundles, point at their yaks, and say, 'You must be joking.' Actually, we have no idea what they're saying. Then we heft the same bundles and say, 'My yak at home can lift this, no sweat.' The yak drivers lift again and say, a little louder this time, 'Surely you jest.' Then we lift the bags once more and say,

'Check out these nifty colored duffel bags; these yaks will love carrying them.' And so it goes, on and on."[3] The first yak train left on April 3, following in the wake of Conrad Anker, Jake Norton, Tap Richards, and Thom Pollard, who had started up the valley the day before.

The approach to Everest from the north is done in stages. From Base Camp, the route runs south along the Rongbuk Valley, and gradually funnels into a narrow trough between the left lateral moraine of the main Rongbuk Glacier and the mud and rock hillside of the eastern wall of the valley. This wall is composed of hundreds of unstable mud and rock pinnacles, some as high as 100 feet (30 m), from which rocks rain down regularly on the path below. The trough itself alternates between rugged boulder fields and sandy segments flat as a beach. After perhaps 2.5 miles (4 km), the route traverses up across a steep slope of loose scree and turns left into a side valley.

The 1921 reconnaissance expedition's preliminary survey of this area missed the significance of this valley entirely. The unimpressive stream that tumbles out of it gives little hint of what lies out of sight around a bend to the south—the 8-mile-long (13-km) East Rongbuk Glacier—the main highway to the North Col and the best approach to Everest's North Face.

The long trek up the East Rongbuk Valley is spectacular, if wearisome. After the ascent from the main Rongbuk Glacier, the route passes the site of the 1922 and 1924 British expeditions' Camp I along the left bank of the East Rongbuk River. Beyond the camp, the route follows the river and then crosses a short moraine ridge to a hummocky gravel landscape pocked with small lakes that is, in fact, the snout of the East Rongbuk Glacier in disguise. Here the path crosses to the right lateral moraine and then passes through a series of connected, uneven boulder fields that undulate, exhaustingly, for another 2 miles (3 km) to a flat spot on the moraine ridge that served as the 1999 expedition's first, or "intermediate," camp, at 19,325 feet (5,890 m).

From here, the path descends steeply, crosses the meandering threads of the river, and ascends some 250 feet (80 m) to the crest of the glacier's medial moraine, reaching perhaps the most extraordinary feature of the entire route. Ahead, on both sides of the moraine, are row upon row of huge shark-tooth ice pinnacles. This is the start of what, in the past, has been called "the trough" of the East Rongbuk Glacier. But the glacier itself has lost more than 100 vertical feet within the past decade alone, and the trough today seems more like a highway than a chasm. The fantastic pinnacles, like frozen sentinels guarding the upper valley, create a fairy-tale landscape, an impression accentuated when they are magically backlit by the lowering afternoon sun. The path between the pinnacles rises gently but steadily for roughly another 2 miles (3 km), almost to the base of Changtse, Everest's northern neighbor. At the point where the Changtse Glacier joins the East Rongbuk Glacier from the right, the route drops down off the medial moraine, meanders along the base of the pinnacles, and finally reaches a relatively flat plain that is the 1999 Mallory & Irvine Research Expedition's Camp II, 20,000 feet (6,100 m) above sea level.

Roughly 1.5 miles (2.5 km) up the valley from Camp II, the path rises above the surface of the glacier at last, revealing a vast bowl of smooth, polished ice, a glittering world of blue and white nearly a mile wide and rimmed by a continuous band of steeply rising ridges.

As stunning as this vision is, it shrinks to insignificance when the moraine bends gradually around to the right to reveal, vaulting far above the surrounding peaks and ridges, the towering Northeast Ridge of Everest, razor-thin and tipped by the menacing black teeth of a formation called "the Pinnacles." Nothing can prepare you for this prospect. In the deep silence of the upper East Rongbuk basin, Everest is massive, humbling, impossibly high.

A mere speck upon the shimmering whiteness of the basin, Camp III—Advance Base Camp (ABC)—huddles on the moraine in the shadow of the eastern flank of Changtse, at 21,200 feet (6,460 m). Simonson's plan of attack from Camp III was straightforward: "I was exclusively focused on establishing ourselves quickly on the upper mountain: building and stocking the camps, getting the climbers up high, and getting ourselves into position to climb and search. Our goal was to be ready to go high in early May, the point at which weather on Everest tends to be at its best. That meant having Camp V on the North Ridge established and stocked by the end of April."

To reach that goal, the strategy was to get climbers and Sherpa up to Advance Base Camp as soon as possible and then, even as the camp was being set up, push a route up to Camp IV, 23,200 feet (7,070 m), atop the North Col. (A col is a dipping ridge between two peaks, in this case Everest and its lesser neighbor Changtse.)

"Getting the gear for all the higher camps up to ABC took two and a half yak trains, each with a four-day round trip and a rest day in between," Simonson explains, "which meant it was well past the middle of the month by the time we got all our gear up there." In the meantime, groups of climbers were ascending and descending as well, carrying gear up to ABC, stopping overnight at Camps I and II on their way up and back (later using only Camp II or going all the way in one long push). They were practicing a rule that had taken many years and not a few lives to learn: "Climb high, sleep low." This is how the body and the brain learns to cope with inadequate oxygen. By pushing the limits, then retreating to safety, repeatedly, human beings can gradually acclimatize to the thin air of the high Himalaya. The Sherpa, of course, have less difficulty than sea-level dwellers; they live high, as it were, all the time.

It would take several days of hard work to turn the more than 100 yak loads of gear and supplies dumped at Camp III into a miniature version of Base Camp. "My dad was a contractor and I've worked part-time at construction sites for years," explains Tap Richards, "and my dad had told me there's always something to be done on the job site. If you find yourself standing around with your hands in your pockets, then the house must be done. The same goes with expeditions; there's always something that can be done. Jake is a builder too and understands this; I think that's one reason we climb well together."

On April 5, as that work was underway, Conrad Anker, Dave Hahn, and two Sherpa, Pa Nuru and Ang Pasang, began putting in the route to the top of the North Col. From ABC they followed the stony lateral moraine at the edge of the ice bowl as it curved around to the west beneath the eroding face of Changtse to the dead end created by the col. They stopped to consider their options.

The col itself is a 1,300-foot-high (400-m) frozen cascade of ice waves stacked one atop another and crisscrossed at various elevations by yawning crevasses. The side of the col facing the East Rongbuk basin is in the lee of the prevailing west wind and thus accumulates snow in its upper reaches. But much of the lower half is solid ice. "This year, it was pure water ice, polished, transparent, and varying in color from clear to sapphire blue to nearly black," Simonson reports. Scaling the col involves a series of short, nearly vertical steps interspersed with steep snow slopes and twisting crevasse detours. Taken together, it is one of the more difficult segments of the route to the summit from this direction.

Off to the right, there is an attractive snow slope that is the obvious choice for a route to the top. It is also often a lethal choice. Accidents and avalanches are common here; it was in this spot that an avalanche killed seven Sherpa in 1922 and almost took Mallory and Somervell as well. Anker decided to go straight up the ice wall instead.

Conrad Anker, a superb climber used to scaling big rock walls in Yosemite and Antarctica, was the expedition's most experienced technical climber, the one the others turned to instinctively to lead difficult pitches. Describing his respect for Anker's skill, Politz says, "Tibetans believe that you can explain the entire universe in a grain of sand; Conrad has found his explanation of the universe hanging on ropes, taking huge risks, and having a head that's so rock solid that, with danger and panic knocking at the door, he still stays focused. It's uncanny." Despite this ability, Simonson explains that Anker has another side as well: "He also has an exuberant, almost childlike enthusiasm. He gives the impression of being a barely controlled bundle of energy. You can see it when he walks: he bounces, as if he has too much energy to keep him rooted to the ground."

While the two Sherpa paid out rope and Hahn watched, Anker climbed quickly, installing ice screws to anchor the rope. In stages, he and the Sherpa ascended roughly a third of the way up the col, in the process finding a safe route through the particularly steep and deeply crevassed central section of the route, before descending for the day. The rest of the climbing team—Jake Norton, Dave Hahn, Tap Richards, and other Sherpa—spent the next two days pushing the route higher until finally, on April 8, Anker, Norton, and Thom Pollard pitched the first tent of Camp IV on a protected ice terrace just below the lip of the col—a major event.

The next day, the expedition's first crisis: Graham Hoyland, forty-two, the BBC producer and grandnephew of 1920s expedition member Howard Somervell, the man who had spent the better part of two years nursing the idea of an expedition through the balky bureaucracy of "the Beeb," had suddenly been struck by numbness along his left side. Quickly diagnosing TIA, Transient Ischemic Attack, a disruption of blood flow, and thus oxygen, to the right side of the brain, Simonson put him on a high flow of oxygen and immediately sent him down from ABC to Base Camp, accompanied by expedition doctor Lee Meyers and four others. In fact, their help wasn't needed and by the 11th he was fine again, if a bit unsettled. After all, he was an experienced Everest climber, not a beginner. Though the crisis had clearly passed and he could certainly be of value even at Base Camp, Hoyland's boss, BBC series director Peter Firstbrook, hustled him off the expedition to

Kathmandu, an ignoble and, to the rest of the expedition members, unfair fate for someone who had been so central to the idea of the expedition in the first place. "It was an emotional trip," says Meyers, who accompanied him. "Graham was sure this would be his last trip to the Himalaya."

While most of the expedition members rested for nearly a week at Base Camp, Andy Politz was still up at ABC, living with the Sherpa. "The Sherpa immediately welcomed me into their company," he says. "We drank tea and cooked together, and they taught me how to make *corsani*, a fiery paste made by grinding hot chilies, garlic, and salt between two stones. We slathered the *corsani* on boiled potatoes, and I could feel the germs in my throat and nasal passages jumping overboard."

In all, there were twelve Sherpa on the expedition, most from the Nepali towns of Pangboche and Phortse. The cook, Pemba, had a helper, and the rest were climbers, under the leadership of their Sirdar, Danuru "Dawa" Sherpa. "I've known many of our Sherpa for years," says Simonson. "They're incredibly strong and hard workers, and we try to take very good care of them. Between base salary, carry bonuses, equipment allowances, and tips, the Sherpa walk away with close to $3,000—roughly twenty times the average Nepalese annual income—for a few weeks of hard work."

Having Politz stay with the Sherpa was an easy choice for Simonson: "I knew Andy would fit right in. He's deep, thoughtful, almost Zen-like sometimes, and strong as an ox physically." Shorter than the rest of the climbers, Politz is a heavily muscled, barrel-chested rock of a man, the kind who looks like he lifts weights all day but actually never touches them. "It's all genetic; incredibly unfair," Simonson says with feigned disgust. Despite his bulk, there is something deeply gentle and settled about Andy Politz. The only member of the climbing team who is married and has children, he also seemed to be the one member of the climbing team for whom climbing is just a small, though related, part of a more complex world view. "Back home," Politz explains, "I spend part of my time teaching kids at an alternative school to understand that their dreams are their rite of passage, that who they can become can be determined by what they can dream, and that those dreams are accessible." Politz's own dreams were changing; this would probably be his last trip to Everest.

During the course of the week, Politz and the Sherpa made several trips up the North Col to Camp IV, carrying supplies for the higher camps. Without the benefit of descending to the denser air of Base Camp to speed his acclimatization, Politz found the going hard and turned to philosophy for support. About his first ascent to the col, he wrote, "The entire lower half of the col was an exercise in surviving torture; I'm simply not acclimatized and fit enough yet. The col is so far, it is so hard to move uphill, so easy to descend. I can't attain the pace I want to make and am miserable. Then I remember that the Buddhists believe that desire is the root of all pain. It is my desire—to climb at a certain pace, to reach certain goals—and my inability to satisfy that desire at this stage of the game that is creating the torture. I slow down and find a pace in which climbing, breathing, and balancing become a kind of meditation. I leave desire behind and life becomes fun rather than a burden. Before I know it, I'm on top of the col and transfixed by the crystal-clear, cloudless view of the Northeast Ridge and North Face of Everest."

Descending from his first climb up the col, exhausted, Politz noticed a flock of goraks (Himalayan ravens) take flight from what appeared to be a tan-colored pile atop the polished blue ice of the upper glacier. Unable to resist his own curiosity, he willed his weary body off the trail back to Camp III to investigate. That night he wrote in his journal, "I am in shock. It looks like I found a camp today from the 1922 British expedition. There were bronze tent pegs[4] made in England, ancient unused ice pitons, some four-strand cotton rope in several sizes, tin cans of an old-fashioned lapped and soldered construction, and a tent of what looked like ¾-ounce Egyptian cotton. The stitching was by machine, but with two passes of a single needle. The tent was, of course, frozen into the ice and I was dying to know what the goraks wanted that was in there, but we were on an archeological expedition and I knew we'd have to examine the site carefully. It is this extraordinarily dry winter and warm, early spring that has revealed the old camp. I'll bet it hasn't melted out of the ice in the entire seventy-seven years since it was abandoned."

When Hemmleb, the expedition's historian, reached the site a few days later, his initial thought was that it encompassed relics from three different camps—a 1933, not 1922, British expedition; a 1958 Chinese-Russian reconnaissance expedition; and either a 1975 Chinese or 1981 French expedition—all possibly merged over time by the movement of the glacier. In fact, it was none of these. On his return from Tibet, Hemmleb unearthed conclusive evidence that the artifacts found at the site were all from the controversial 1960 Chinese expedition.[5] The Chinese had used British-style tents well into the 1970s, and pictures from the 1960 expedition clearly showed pitons and tent pegs identical to those found at the site, equipment that the Chinese were known to have purchased in the West. The clincher, however, was a simple wooden-handled piton hammer found inside the collapsed cotton tent. In a Chinese movie of the 1960 expedition, an identical hammer appears dangling from a string hanging from the shoulder of one of the Chinese climbers. Indeed, Jake Norton would find another such hammer a few weeks later high on the mountain, with a similar string still attached.[6]

Meanwhile, down at Base Camp, a group of trekkers organized by Simonson's company had arrived from Kathmandu by way of Lhasa. Among them was Larry Johnson, the man who had given Jochen Hemmleb the confidence to pursue his dream of a research expedition, and who had made the crucial connection with expedition leader Eric Simonson. It was his first visit to Everest. After a day of acclimatization in Tingri and only a tantalizing glimpse of a distant Mount Everest through late-afternoon haze, his group had reached the Pang La to find the entire Himalaya range shrouded in mist. As the expedition had before them, they wound down from the pass and across the desolate valley bottom, and turned south toward Rongbuk. "As we passed the last of the small Tibetan villages, the sky began to clear. We picked our way along a road that wasn't much more than two ruts in a boulder field until, finally, a great snow ridge came into view and it hit me that this was the great West Ridge of Everest. Then the entire North Face came into view, its fresh snow glistening in the afternoon sun. Before long I was standing beside the Rongbuk Monastery, with its great stupa silhouetted against the mass of Everest just behind. For thirty-five years, I had dreamed of being in this spot. I never believed it would happen."

Larry Johnson, fifty-two years old, is a quiet man with gentle, downsloping eyes that sometimes seem to have seen too much over too many years. He is instinctively deferential; he avoids the limelight. He does not wear his heart on his sleeve, so much as his heart seems to precede him into a room; it is big and generous. "As I was standing there at the monastery, two of my trek companions came up and stood on either side of me. 'How do you feel about all this?' one asked. The next day, I would meet for the first time the young man I had promised to help get to Everest to pursue his dream. I had kept my promise to Jochen Hemmleb, and he was here. Now I was too. Tears made muddy tracks through the road dust on my face."

Up on the mountain, the climbers were struggling to establish Camp V. The mountain wasn't making it easy. The route from Camp IV slopes first downward to the actual saddle of the North Col, then climbs up a long, rounded, steeply ramped snowfield that falls off sharply into voids on both the left and right. Above the upper tip of the snowfield, the going gets really rough, a steady slog up a 30- to 35- degree slope of down-tilting rock slabs and snow patches. This is the North Ridge, a massive buttress that climbs from the col to the high northeast shoulder of Everest, which, in turn, is joined by the long, serrated, steeply rising Northeast Ridge to the summit itself. But the terrain is only one of its challenges; the greatest danger is the unremitting wind, which, on this trip, reached as high as 100 miles per hour. It freezes exposed skin instantly, makes staying upright with a pack difficult, and saps strength with extraordinary speed. The wind had driven back an attempt by several of the Sherpa to establish Camp V on April 15. Jake Norton was driven back two days later. Finally, on April 19,

Conrad Anker and eight Sherpa succeeded in fixing rope up to 25,600 feet (7,800 m), and Camp V was in place. Meanwhile, other climbers were hauling supplies for Camps V and the yet-to-be-established Camp VI up the col to Camp IV.

One of those climbers was historian Hemmleb, who, on reaching the North Col, had achieved his own climbing goal for the expedition. "I had long ago decided that the North Col was probably the limit of my capabilities as a climber at this point, even though Simonson thought I could go higher. But I had attained both my goal and my dreams now; how much higher can you go than that?"

In the days that followed, climbers and Sherpa shuttled additional supplies to Camps IV and V and finally headed down to Base Camp once again for a rest. Incredibly, almost everyone was still healthy, a happy condition that owed as much to Simonson's expedition management skills and passion for hygiene as it did to the climbers' hardiness and the relatively good weather. Expedition doctor Lee Meyers kept busy, none-theless, treating every manner of ailment including, at one point, extracting an impacted tooth for one of the Sherpa in the mess tent.

The team was also working together smoothly and was in high spirits. There were occasional conflicts between the climb-ing crew and the film crews and, for that matter, between the two film crews themselves. At least in the former case, some level of conflict was probably inevitable; Simonson's priority was the search and the welfare of his climbers, both American and Sherpa. The film crews' priority was making a movie, though they seemed to disagree about how best to do that. But for the most part, Simonson seemed to have picked a remarkably congenial group, one whose members enjoyed not only each other's company but each other's respect as well.

Simonson himself, normally a no-nonsense leader, had adopted a consciously deferential leadership style on this trip, out of respect for the experience and skills of the team members. "I'm fairly obsessive/compulsive on an expedition," he explains, "but I was dealing with topflight climbers here, and I tried to focus my tendency to get intense only where it would make a real difference. If something didn't really matter, I could just lean back and mellow out. I tried not to overanalyze things, to go with my instincts and stay open to changing my mind. Things change on a mountain like this; weather changes, routes change, people's strength varies, and you have to stay flexible, take in new information, then cut a decision and move on."

Says Politz, who had effectively become Simonson's right-hand man on this expedition, keeping track of gear and supply carries and the status of the higher camps: "I've known Eric for twenty years, ever since I apprenticed under him at RMI, and I'm continually impressed by his ability to quietly assess situations and make good decisions. He has so much experience and an unerring ability to pick good people. I've always been confident that anything he's in charge of is going to work out pretty well. And if it doesn't, he's got a fascinating ability to cobble something together with whatever is at hand to make it right. He can be hard and he doesn't suffer fools or anyone who doesn't put the needs of the group as a whole to the forefront, but the overall package is pretty impressive."

Gradually, the climbers had sorted themselves out into distinct roles. Hahn, when he wasn't hauling gear uphill or in the communications tent writing exceptionally literate dispatches, played the camp clown, a relaxed and irresistibly funny giant. But the clowning is a ruse: "In fact," Simonson says, "Dave's very astute. He's quick to pick up subtle undercurrents in any situation. He's also remarkably self-sufficient, capable of holing up in a storm without going crazy. He has a quiet core."

Conrad Anker's exuberance kept the atmosphere of the camps upbeat and energetic, as did Richards and Norton, the "young Turks," who were eager, hard-working, earning their spurs. "I got used to calling them Tap'n Jake, as if they were one unit, which is unfair because they're distinct individuals," comments Simonson. Politz adds: "Tap tends to be the quiet one; he has a slow, gravelly voice that he only uses when he has something worthwhile to contribute, while Jake, who is incredibly well educated, has opinions on everything. They're both excellent climbers, with a good sense of the properties of snow and strong technical skills. But they don't yet have the understanding that time can be a tool, that you can apply time and patience to a situation and get an entirely different result. That's a skill Eric has and that they'll develop too. What they do have is the willingness to jump in and burn a hell of a lot of calories to get the job done, which is a help to us older guys."

Both of the WGBH/NOVA crew members, producer Liesl Clark and high-altitude cameraman Thom Pollard, as well as BBC contract cameraman Ned Johnston, impressed the climbing team with their strength and commitment. Clark, highly professional and doggedly hardworking, made several trips to ABC. Johnston, quiet, mature, and relaxed amid the high-pressure film producers, had little climbing experience but nonetheless made it as high as Camp IV. Pollard, gregarious and eager, pitched in with route-pushing and gear-hauling, made no fewer than ten carries to Camp IV, spent several nights at Camp V, and climbed as high as Camp VI, 26,900 feet (8,200 m).

Hemmleb, perhaps inevitably, was initially considered the egghead. But his determination, his depth of knowledge, his willingness to do the grunt-work of hauling loads, and his climbing skill quickly earned him the admiration of the older hands. And very soon, now, they would require his special knowledge to reach their goal.

At this point in the expedition, Simonson's principal personnel worry was the BBC's Peter Firstbrook, who was not well. A diabetic and, partly as a result, less fit than the rest of the team, Firstbrook had only once gone above Base Camp, to Camp I, from which he had to be evacuated because of the onset of rales, a lung ailment that signals High Altitude Pulmonary Edema (potentially life-threatening fluid in the lungs). Now he was suffering from almost continuous headaches. Simonson recalls, "He had deteriorated throughout the course of the expedition, and got so sick that our expedition doctor, Lee Meyers, and I were constantly afraid he was going to die."

Meyers, a big, grimacing bear of a man whose strength, to everyone else's astonishment, surpassed his girth, is a specialist in emergency medicine with extensive knowledge of high-altitude ailments. He had been treating people in other expeditions as well, but Firstbrook was his main worry. "During the next several days, his face got puffy and the headaches worsened—a possible sign of cerebral edema, the kind of thing that could kill him in a couple of hours," Meyers remembers. Fearful about and frustrated with Firstbrook's refusal to heed his warnings, he sent an only half-kidding note from Base Camp up to Simonson at ABC that said simply, "I quit."

"I thought it interesting," comments Simonson, "that when Graham Hoyland got sick, Firstbrook insisted that he leave the expedition immediately, citing BBC rules. But when Firstbrook himself became ill—much more seriously ill than Hoyland—he simply refused to leave, despite our doctor's orders." To the rest of the expedition members, the general conclusion was that, for whatever reason, Firstbrook simply wanted to get rid of Hoyland.

While Simonson and Meyers worried about Firstbrook, the climbing team left Base Camp and began the process of ascending to the higher camps. It was time to begin the formal search for Mallory and Irvine. Everything was in place. The weather was perfect. Anticipation and excitement ran through the team like an electrical current.

A couple of weeks earlier, some of the trekkers had asked their colleague, expedition coordinator Larry Johnson, what he thought the chances were that the expedition might find anything. Johnson, who along with most of the trekkers had by now returned to Kathmandu, recalls, "I thought about the question for a while, part of me worrying that any answer might jinx the whole enterprise. But everything seemed perfect for the job. We had a great high-altitude team to do the search. We had a highly competent expedition leader who was committed to the task. We had Jochen, our researcher, to steer the climbers to the spot most likely to reveal traces of Mallory and Irvine. And we had the weather: clear and dry, with almost no snow on the North Face. I believed we'd succeed. I was sure of it."

CHAPTER 5

AN INFERNAL MOUNTAIN

I can't tell you how full of hope I am this year . . .
GEORGE MALLORY

Arriving in the upper Rongbuk Valley on April 28, 1924, the British Everest expedition's ascent started badly and got progressively worse. The weather was appalling. As expedition members struggled to set up their Base Camp, Norton wrote in his diary: " . . . this was one of the coldest days I had ever known . . . and we all worked muffled to the eyes in our full outfit of woolen and wind-proof clothes, ear-flapped caps and mitts . . . and then came down the snow."[1] In his diary, Andrew Irvine was more succinct: "Bloody morning, light driving snow, very cold and felt rather rotten."[2]

The 1924 expedition carried simple two-man canvas tents and larger canvas wall tents, both held up by tent poles at each end and guylines. Irvine describes his first day at Base Camp: "We got all the tents up and I started my job of getting six new pattern and four old pattern oxygen apparatus ready. A primus [stove] for soldering was very welcome in the mess tent, as the wind was well below freezing. Spent all evening trying to mend Beetham's rather old fashioned reflex camera."[3]

In fact, this could have been Irvine's entry for almost any day during the previous monthlong trek to the mountain, for he had spent virtually every moment when they were not traveling slaving over the expedition's fragile and poorly engineered oxygen sets. There seemed nothing he could not fix or improve, a skill he had developed while still a child. He had graduated early from making scale-model sailboats and was soon fixing, and ultimately rebuilding, the family car. Odell later wrote of his protégé, "Though lacking in mountaineering experience it was felt that the natural aptitude he had already shown, together with his undoubted gifts of mechanical and general practicable ability, not to speak of temperamental suitability, fitted him for inclusion in the party, before older men of greater experience in mountain craft."[4] Irvine would validate Odell's confidence again and again.

Even before the expedition had left England, Irvine had sent design modifications to the oxygen apparatus manufacturer that would have both lightened and strengthened the 1922 prototypes. His advice was ignored. A few days into the trek from Darjeeling, he wrote in frustration to a friend, "The OX. AP. has already been boggled. They haven't taken my design, but what they have sent is hopeless, breaks if you touch it, leaks, is ridiculously clumsy and heavy. Out of ninety cylinders, fifteen were empty and twenty-four had leaked badly by the time they got to Calcutta. Ye Gods!"[5] A few days later, he discovered that all but one of the backpack frames that were to carry the cylinders had been damaged en route, and he immediately began repairing them with whatever materials were at hand. During the next three weeks, using only the most basic tools, he worked almost every evening, often late into the night, repairing, strengthening, and lightening the entire apparatus and, in between, repairing lanterns, torches, tents, cameras, tripods, broken ice axes, and crampons. The battle with the oxygen cylinders and regulators was never-ending. By mid-April, Irvine wrote, " . . . we had a demonstration of oxygen apparatus—'How to test for leaks.' We found leaks all right, but couldn't cure them."[6] Despite having been refilled in Calcutta, by the time they reached Shekar Dzong, 30 percent of the cylinders were empty again.

The irony of all this was that few, if any, of the expedition members really wanted to use supplemental oxygen anyway. Despite proof from the 1922 expedition that oxygen could make a dramatic difference at high altitude, there still existed a typically British prejudice that using it was somehow "unsporting." When Irvine got the word that Norton had decided that he (Irvine) and Mallory would be doing the expedition's first summit attempt together, with oxygen, he was both delighted and disappointed: "I'm awfully glad that I'm with Mallory in the first lot, but I wish ever so much that it was a non-oxygen attempt."[7]

If these frustrations got to him, no one ever saw it; he did not complain. For all his youth and inexperience, by the time the expedition reached Base Camp, Irvine had earned both respect and admiration from his fellows, not just for his remarkable skill as an engineer and all-around handyman, but also for his unshakably even temper.

With General Bruce effectively out of the expedition, Edward Norton had moved to fill his shoes with remarkable ease, passing his role as leader of the climbers to Mallory. Though he had great affection for the sidelined Bruce, Mallory couldn't have been happier. In a letter to his wife he wrote, "I'm bound to say I feel some little satisfaction in the position. . . . With Norton, of course, I shall work in complete harmony; he is really one of the best." In an April 19 letter to a member of the Everest Committee, he wrote, "I must tell you, what Norton can't say in a dispatch, that we have a splendid leader in him. He knows the whole bandobast [plan of attack] from A to Z, and his eyes are everywhere, is personally acceptable to everyone and makes us all feel happy, is always full of interest, easy and yet dignified, or rather never losing dignity, and is a tremendous adventurer."[8]

This latter note was as revealing about Mallory himself as it was about Norton. Only Mallory, after all, had been on all three British expeditions. He might well have been expected to be named leader of the climbers for the 1924 expedition at the outset, but Norton was named to that post instead, and for good reason. As brilliant as he was as a climber, Mallory was a walking organizational disaster. So focused did he become on whatever the climbing task was before him, that he tended regularly to forget items of some significance—like his boots or, in one of his last acts of forgetfulness, his compass and night lantern. If Mallory was generous with his praise for Norton, it was not faint praise; he recognized in Norton the better manager.

The two men, Mallory and Norton, had spent weeks developing a plan of attack for the summit effort, proposing, debating, and modifying different options (indeed, Norton had sent his initial plan around to all the climbers the previous Christmas). By the time the expedition reached the foot of the Rongbuk Glacier, the plan was firm. In Norton's words:

Camps I, II, and III had to be established and stocked; the route from Camp III to the North Col had to be reconnoitered by a party of climbers, for the route follows a steep glacier, and it was certain to have changed since 1922. Camp IV must be established and stocked with stores and oxygen both for itself and the higher camps. Next [Geoffrey] Bruce and [Noel] Odell were to escort a party of fifteen porters to a site for Camp V at about 25,500 feet, there to prepare the camp and dump tents and stores for it and for higher camps. Somervell and I were then to start from Camp IV, sleep one night at Camp V and another at Camp VII (at about 27,500 feet), and while we were climbing to the latter, Mallory and Irvine were to go from Camp IV to Camp VI at about 26,500 feet, there to sleep. With this programme to precede our combined attempt on the summit on May 17, it will be understood that time pressed.[9]

It was a brilliant plan, worthy of the work that Norton and Mallory had put into it. Its only weakness was that it did not account for either the difficulties to be encountered on the as yet unexplored Northeast Ridge or the vicissitudes of the weather. In short, it was doomed from the start. It didn't help any that the head lama at the Rongbuk Monastery had taken to a hermit cell to meditate and was unavailable to bless the enterprise. In his stead, the other lamas sent the expedition off with this cheerless message: "Chomolungma, the awful and mighty Goddess Mother, will never allow any white man to climb her sacred heights. The demons of the snows will defeat you utterly."[10]

This warning notwithstanding, they wasted no time getting started, following the route used by the unsuccessful 1922 expedition and all the North Col route expeditions ever since, including the 1999 expedition.

To save the strength of the climbers, the expedition had arranged through the Dzong Pen at Shekar Dzong for some 150 local porters to carry loads to establish Camp I just above the point where the East Rongbuk valley joined the main Rongbuk Glacier, and to carry supplies as far as Camp II, farther up the East Rongbuk at about 19,800 feet (6,030 m). The local porters were put in the charge of three non-commissioned officers (NCOs) of Geoffrey Bruce's Gurkha regiment, two of whom had been on the 1922 expedition. Within a couple of days, this work was completed virtually without a hitch.

The next step was for the expedition's own Nepali porters (mostly Sherpa) to move these supplies from Camp II to a new Camp III high up on the East Rongbuk Glacier at 21,000 feet (6,400 m), just above the trough of the glacier—a straight-forward task that would prove dangerously difficult. Two groups of twenty porters each would be involved. The first would carry supplies to Camp III. This group was led by Mallory and Irvine, who would stay at Camp III to become acclimatized and test the oxygen equipment. Odell and Hazard accompanied them in order to try to establish a route to Camp IV. Captain John Noel, the photographer, was also in this first group. The second group, led by one of the Gurkha NCOs, was to climb to Camp II and then shuttle supplies to III. A reserve group of twelve porters was kept at Base Camp "to replace casualties." There was trouble almost immediately.

The first group left on May 3 and arrived at Camp III on May 5. The second left Base Camp May 4 but got caught in a blizzard above Camp II. Mallory came down from Camp III to guide them up, but the porters could go no farther; they dumped their loads a mile below Camp III and retreated to Camp II. This left the porters at Camp III stranded without adequate food or blankets through two nights during which temperatures dropped as low as 22 degrees Fahrenheit below zero. Gradually, these porters too straggled down to Camp II, frozen and exhausted. Unaware of this developing crisis, Norton, Somervell, and Beetham headed up from Base Camp on the 6th, arriving at Camp II on the 7th to find it fully occupied with dispirited porters.

"There had been a severe breakdown," Geoffrey Bruce reported of the scene when he arrived the next day with the reserve porters, "which would undoubtedly have developed into a complete collapse of the porters had Norton not been present at the critical moment to keep them on their feet and restore their ebbing courage and spirits." To sustain the weakened porters, Norton had no choice but to break open the food, tents, and other supplies that had been intended for the higher camps. "Fortunately for us all," Bruce added, "he was one of those really great leaders of men, who by their own resolution and courage inspire their comrades and followers with some measure of their own qualities."[11] Norton let the weakened group rest and rallied the stronger porters to ferry the dumped supplies the last mile to Camp III.

But on their way to Camp III another blizzard blew in, far worse than the first, and pinned the entire party at Camp III for two viciously cold days. Amazingly, through all of this chaos Irvine continued to work on the team's oxygen apparatus: "Irvine's capacity for work was immense," wrote Bruce. "After the most grueling day on the glacier, he would settle down with his tools inside a tent, improving the oxygen apparatus, or mending stoves, regardless of time or temperature, long after the rest of us were in our sleeping bags."[12]

At dawn on the third morning of this second storm, Mallory descended to Camp II to report to Norton. "He had a terrible story to tell of [Camp III]. Everything there was at a standstill. The men were done—incapable of any work. The mountain above, whenever parting clouds revealed her, was smoking angrily with driven mist and snow. The gale was tearing over her ridges a hundred miles an hour, madly flinging the snow a thousand feet into the air. Odell and Hazard had tried the Ice Cliff, but had not been able to go far and had dumped the ropes and pickets on the cliff and returned."[13]

Norton called a general retreat back to Base Camp. He had no choice; two porters and one of the Gurkha soldiers were injured or ill (two later died), and the system for establishing and supplying the higher camps he and Mallory had devised was in a shambles. And even if it hadn't been, neither the porters nor the expedition members themselves were equipped to survive such appalling weather. The porters had little more than the clothes on their back and blankets provided by the expedition. The expedition members, who had been given only £50 for their personal "kit," were not a great deal better off. They had ventured into one of the harshest environments on earth in clothing that can only be described as pathetically inadequate.

"Personally," Norton wrote, "I wore a thick woolen vest [undershirt] and drawers, a thick flannel shirt and two sweaters under a lightish knickbocker suit of windproof gaberdine the knickers of which were lined with light flannel, a pair of soft elastic Kashmir putties [leggings wrapped like a bandage from ankle to knee] and a pair of boots of felt bound and soled with leather and lightly nailed with the usual Alpine nails. Over all I wore a very light pyjama suit of Messrs Burberry's 'Shackleton' windproof gaberdine. On my hands I wore a pair of long fingerless woollen mitts inside a similar pair of gaberdine. . . . On my head I wore a fur-lined leather motor-cycling helmet, and my eyes and nose were protected by a pair of goggles of Crooke's glass, which were sewn into a leather mask that came well over the nose and covered any part of my face which was not naturally protected by my beard. A huge woollen muffler completed my costume."[14] Around the camps, the climbers wore a ragtag assortment of old tweed trousers and Norfolk jackets, shirts, sweaters, even shorts, and thick, knee-high woollen socks; on their heads, rather stylish fedora hats. Says historian Audrey Salkeld, "When George Bernard Shaw saw pictures of one of the early Everest parties, he was amazed: it looked, he said, like a picnic in Connemara surprised by a snowstorm."[15]

The retreat to Base Camp was no picnic, and the wait there for better weather was sheer agony for Mallory. Noel recalled, "He seemed to be ill at ease; always scheming and planning. It was obvious to me he felt this set-back more acutely than any of us. He was a highly strung man."[16] He was also, characteristically, swinging back and forth from high confidence to low doubts. In a letter to a friend during the 1922 expedition that was at once disconsolate and hopeful, he wrote, " . . . it is an infernal mountain, cold and treacherous. Frankly, the game is not good enough: the risks of getting caught are too great; the margin of strength when men are at great heights is too small. . . . And then, given the right weather, there's quite a good chance of reaching the top. . . ."[17] Now, in a letter to his wife, Ruth, he expressed the same extremes of emotion: "Dear Girl, this has been a bad time altogether. I look back on tremendous efforts and exhaustion and dismal looking out of a tent door into a world of snow and vanishing hopes. And yet, and yet, and yet. . . ." [18] Time was running out, but his hopes clearly had not yet vanished.

Norton was worried about time too. He was obsessed with the threat of the onset of the monsoon. During the 1922 expedition, it had begun on June 1, burying the mountain in snow and creating the avalanche conditions that killed seven porters and very nearly swept Mallory and Somervell away as well. To Norton, the new strategy was simple: "We must at all costs establish the North Col Camp; then a fine interval before the arrival of the monsoon proper might just give us the time to put in one serious attempt at the summit."[19]

By May 17, after the expedition at last received the blessings of the Holy Lama of Rongbuk himself, the weather cleared and the expedition members and porters were ready to begin another assault. The date for the summit attempt was now the 29th—fittingly, Ascension Day. They reached Camp III on the 19th, ready to push up to the North Col at last.

On May 20, avoiding the easier slope that had avalanched in 1922, Mallory led Norton, Odell, and one of the Sherpa on a direct line up the ice wall of the col, finding a narrow ice "chimney" by which to gain significant altitude. Norton later described Mallory's performance: "Confronted with a formidable climbing obstacle Mallory's behavior was always characteristic: you could positively see his nerves tighten up like fiddle strings. . . . Up the wall and chimney he led here, climbing carefully, neatly, and in that beautiful style that was all his own."[20]

Kicking steps in snow, chopping steps in ice, and skirting crevasses, they struggled to find a route that would be safe for the porters to follow later, laden with supplies. Near the top they reached a steeply sloped, avalanche-prone pitch and paused to consider a traverse. Mallory decided to take the slope vertically as high as feasible and only then traverse to the other side, which he did safely, with Norton and Odell belaying him. At 2:30 P.M., they reached a shelf just below the top of the col that would serve as the site for Camp IV, as it had in 1922. Mallory and Odell pressed upward again to find a route to the top of the col, and Norton fixed rope along part of the route they had just ascended.

The entire party returned to Camp III by 6:30 P.M., though not without incident. On the way down, unnoticed by the others, Mallory, descending unroped, had a nearly fatal fall into a crevasse: "The snow gave way and in I went with the snow tumbling all around me, down, luckily only about 10 feet before I fetched up half blind and breathless to find myself most precariously supported only by my ice axe somehow caught across the crevasse and still held in my right hand—and below that a very unpleasant black hole." When no one responded to his cries for help, he wedged his body in the crevasse and then dug a passage back up to the surface along the sloping face of the crevasse. "So much for that day," he later wrote matter-of-factly.[21]

The next day Somervell, Irvine, Hazard, and twelve porters ascended the face of the col carrying tents and supplies for Camp IV. Snow began falling almost the moment they reached the bottom of the col, but they pressed ahead anyway. Irvine, the youngest and strongest of the team, hauled the loads one by one up the chimney pitch. Leaving Hazard and the porters to complete the climb to the terrace camp, Irvine and Somervell then descended through the worsening storm. Snow fell throughout the night and until 3:00 P.M. the next day. Unable to move, Hazard and the porters stayed a second night, during which the temperature fell to a record 24 degrees Fahrenheit below zero.

On the morning of the 23rd, the weather cleared and Odell and Bruce set off to join Hazard and push the route above Camp IV, but the snow was too deep to attempt the climb up the col. Later, to their astonishment, Hazard arrived at Camp III, but with only eight of his twelve porters. They had been forced to abandon Camp IV, but at the top of the col four of the porters had been too frightened to descend.

Quietly disgusted by Hazard's lack of leadership, Norton now had a rescue operation on his hands instead of a summit assault: "It was quite evident that they must be rescued. . . . It was equally obvious that it was at present out of the question to continue our attempts on the mountain. . . . We were about to send three of the four climbers detailed for the first [summit] attempt on what must be a severe test of endurance, and this would still further diminish our chances of success. . . . But at the time these seemed but minor considerations; the only thing that mattered was to get the men down alive."[22]

And this they did, though it would take a heroic effort on Somervell's part to retrieve the last two after they slid down a steep snow slope to the very edge of oblivion. They all descended safely and "the next morning we thankfully turned our backs on Camp III and, escorting a miserable little convoy of the halt, the lame and the blind, reached Camp II in due course in the teeth of a north-east wind and with snow falling again."[23]

Another retreat, another plan. After a prolonged debate at Camp I, the team agreed to mount two quick, stripped-down summit attempts as soon as the weather improved. They would involve two climbers each—first Mallory and Bruce, then Norton and Somervell. And because their numbers had been cut sharply by the previous epics, there were not enough porters to carry oxygen cylinders, so they agreed to forego oxygen sets. If this decision dismayed Irvine who, after all, had slaved over the apparatus for weeks, he never let on. Mallory, however, was disappointed. A late convert to supplemental oxygen, he now knew at some instinctive level that if he was going to make it this time—and this would no doubt be his last time—it would be on oxygen. Still, he signed on to the overall plan.

The weather did improve and, after several days' rest, the climbing teams, the fifteen toughest porters (now dubbed "the Tigers"), and Odell and Irvine serving in a support role arrived at Camp III once again. Irvine, during his "rest," had fashioned a rope ladder with wooden tent pegs as treads to speed the porters up the North Col chimney.

At 9:00 A.M. on May 31, in perfect weather at last, Mallory and Bruce started up from Camp III with nine porters.[24] Odell and Irvine joined them later at Camp IV; Norton and Somervell would arrive the next day. And on June 1, finally, Mallory and Bruce, with eight porters, ascended the long North Ridge toward the Northeast Shoulder of Everest—the route to the summit.

The weather was clear, but the moment they cleared the

protective seracs above the camp, gained the top of the col, and started up, the little party was slammed by the ferocious and nearly constant wind that screams over the North Ridge from the west. "Progress up the north ridge of Everest does not lend itself to description," Norton later wrote. "It is a fight against the wind and the altitude, generally on rock, sometimes on snow, at an average angle of 45° [sic]."[25] Up they staggered nonetheless until, at about 25,000 feet (7,600 m), half of the porters gave out, dumping their loads. Mallory, Bruce, and four of the Tigers made it to their proposed Camp V at 25,300 feet (7,710 m), and Bruce and one of the porters spent the rest of the late afternoon shuttling up the dumped loads while Mallory established tent platforms. They were in position.

The next morning, however, even as Norton and Somervell and their porters began climbing up to Camp V, they met a descending porter with a disgusted note from Mallory: "Show's crashed—wind took the heart out of our porters yesterday and none will face going higher today."[26] Not only were two of the porters ill, but Bruce had strained his heart shuttling loads the night before. There was nothing to do but descend.

In the fierce wind, the two parties said little as they passed each other a while later. Somervell remembers, "It was a grievous disappointment, and must have been worse for them than for us. The number of attempts on Everest was cut down by one, and it was just possible that Norton and I would have the only chance given to the whole Expedition of climbing to the summit."[27]

Two days later, they very nearly did it. After a "fair night" at Camp V, Norton and Somervell and three of their porters headed higher up the North Ridge and traversed away from the ridge's eastern edge toward the "Yellow Band," the 700-foot-

(200-m-) thick horizontal bed of striated golden limestone beneath the Northeast Ridge. But once again, by early afternoon the porters (one of whom was injured) could go no farther, and Camp VI was established at 27,000 feet (8,230 m), shy of the goal but still the highest in history.[28]

That night, Somervell had an odd vision: "I remember a curious sensation . . . as if we were getting near the edge of a field with a wall all round it—a high, insuperable wall. The field was human capacity, the wall human limitations. The field, I remember, was a bright and uniform green, and we were walking towards the edge—very near the edge now, where the whitish-grey wall said: 'Thus far, and no farther.'" The vision would prove prophetic.

On summit day, Norton and Somervell climbed up to the Yellow Band and began a long, slantwise traverse to the right along its face, according to Norton roughly 500 to 600 feet (150 to 180 m) below the crest of the Northeast Ridge.[29] "This was a line Somervell and I had always favoured," Norton wrote, "in preference to the actual crest, which Mallory advocated."[30] However preferable, it was not easy. Here, the North Face of Everest is an endless series of uneven slabs that slope sharply downward at an angle of roughly 45 degrees. There is relatively little snow, since most of it is simply blown away by the persistent wind, but the slabs are typically littered with gravel, making footing treacherous. In addition, of course, there is precious little air to breathe. "The imaginative reader," Somervell would write, "must not picture to himself a couple of stalwarts breasting the tape, but a couple of crocks slowly and breathlessly struggling up, with frequent rests and a lot of puffing and blowing and coughing."[31]

Somervell, in particular, was struggling. The cold, dry air of Everest had virtually destroyed the lining of his throat and he had been coughing almost continuously. Now, his breathing had become more labored than he could explain. At about 28,000 feet (8,530 m), Somervell could go no farther.

Norton explained what happened next:

I left him sitting under a rock just below the topmost edge of the sandstone band and went on. I followed the actual top edge of the band, which led at a very slightly uphill angle into and across the big couloir [the Great Couloir, a huge vertical gash on the North Face]; but to reach the latter I had to turn the ends of two pronounced buttresses which ran down the face of the mountain. . . . From about the place where I met with these buttresses the going became a great deal worse; the slope was very steep below me, the foothold ledges narrowed to a few inches in width, and as I approached the shelter of the big couloir there was a lot of powdery snow which concealed the precarious footholds. The whole face of the mountain was composed of slabs like the tiles on a roof, and all sloped at much the same angle as tiles. I had twice to retrace my steps and follow a different band of strata; the couloir itself was filled with powdery snow into which I sank to the knee or even to the waist, and which was yet not of a consistency to support me in the event of a slip. Beyond the couloir the going got steadily worse; I found myself stepping from tile to tile, as it were, each tile sloping smoothly and steeply downwards; I began to feel I was much too dependent on the mere friction of a boot nail on the slabs. It was not exactly difficult going, but it was a dangerous place for a single unroped climber, as one slip would have sent me in all probability to the bottom of the mountain.

The strain of climbing so carefully was beginning to tell and I was getting exhausted. In addition, my eye trouble was getting worse and was by now a severe handicap. . . . It was by now 1 P.M., and a brief calculation showed that I had no chance of climbing the remaining 800 or 900 feet if I was to return in safety. . . . In an hour I had gained but little—probably under 100 feet in height, and in distance perhaps 300 yards.[32]

Even without the blurring vision, at a climbing rate of only 100 feet per hour, it would be dark before he made the summit and he was prepared for neither a nighttime descent nor an overnight bivouac. As Somervell put it, "We had been willing always to risk our lives, but we did not believe in throwing them away. So we decided that we must go down the mountain and own ourselves beaten in a fair fight. . . . We were somehow quite content to leave it at that, and to turn down with almost a feeling of relief that our worst trials were over."[33] And so the two groped their way back from whence they had come. At one point, Somervell's ice ax slipped from his numbed fingers and skittered all the way down the North Face and out of sight—proof of how steep the slope they were on really was. The two stopped briefly at Camp VI to borrow a section of tent pole for Somervell to use in its place.

It was at this point on their descent to the North Col, with Norton ahead of him, that Somervell nearly perished. Another coughing fit wracked him and suddenly there was an obstruction in his throat. He could not breathe. He could not call out. He sat down to die. Then, desperate, "I pressed my chest with both hands, gave one last almighty push—and the obstruction came up . . . though the pain was intense, yet I was a new man."[34] He had coughed up the desiccated mucous membrane of his throat.

Both summit attempts had failed. As far as Norton was concerned, the 1924 Everest expedition was over. Down at the North Col, however, Mallory had other ideas. While Norton and Somervell had been battling the mountain, Mallory had recruited Bruce and Irvine and a few of the porters at Camp IV to descend to Camp III, retrieve the oxygen apparatus and cylinders, and carry them back up to the North Col again. The night Norton and Somervell returned, he presented his plan: he and Irvine would climb to Camp V and Odell would follow a day later, in support. They would spend the next night at Camp VI, using very little oxygen to get there. Then they would make their summit bid, with oxygen.

"I entirely agreed with his decision," Norton reports, "and was full of admiration for the indomitable spirit of the man, determined, in spite of his already excessive exertions, not to admit defeat while any chance remained, and I must admit— such was his will power and nervous energy—he still seemed entirely adequate to the task."[35]

He did not, however, think Mallory's decision to take Irvine wise. Odell was fit, at the peak of his acclimatization, an experienced mountaineer, and the expedition member actually in charge of the oxygen systems; Norton thought him a better partner for Mallory. Irvine was struggling with the team's pervasive throat malaise, his fair skin was so badly sunburned by now that his face was ravaged, and he was, of course, far less experienced than Odell. Mallory's expressed reason for choosing Irvine was that it was he, not Odell, who had the mechanical genius to modify the apparatus and keep it working. But it was also clear that Mallory had developed a close bond of affection with Irvine, as perhaps mentor and student might, and he wanted Irvine as his climbing partner on this last attempt. There was no dissuading him, and Norton did not try. Indeed, a few hours later Norton had other troubles: he was struck completely blind. And while he knew the snow blindness would pass, the pain was excruciating.

The next day, as the expedition team tried to make Norton comfortable, blocking out the light in his tent, Odell noted that Mallory, readying himself for the expedition's final try for the summit the next day, was vibrating with nervous energy: "Who with the fighting spirit of Mallory, or with the long-tried obsession of attainment of the greatest goal of his ideals, could be otherwise than impatient to be off on the culminating challenge of a lifetime, nay, even of a whole generation of mountaineers!"[36]

On June 6, at 7:30 in the morning, taking little more than their oxygen sets, they were gone.

"This was the historic climax of our adventure," wrote the expedition's official observer, the photographer and adventurer John Noel. "For Mallory and Irvine had gone for ever from our sight. Up and up into the blue they had gone, higher and higher—higher than men have ever reached before. Odell got a single fleeting glimpse of them within 600 feet of the summit [sic] and still going up. Then he saw nothing more. What happened no one knows. They never came back."[37] (See "Two Tiny Dots—What Does Captain Noel's Film Really Show?" in Appendix 1, Everest North Side: Resolved and Unresolved Mysteries.)

CHAPTER 6

THE "ENGLISH DEAD"

Again and for the last time we advance up the
Rongbuk Glacier for victory or final defeat.
GEORGE MALLORY

At 11:45 A.M. on May 1, 1999, the radio in Dave Hahn's jacket pocket crackled: "The last time I tried a boulder in hobnail boots, I fell off," someone mumbled through the static. All morning as he climbed in the vicinity of 27,000 feet (8,200 m), he'd been picking up nonsensical cell phone messages bouncing off the ionosphere from God only knew where. The damn radio never shut up, so he shut it out of his mind and kept going; it was taking all his concentration just to keep his footing. A moment or two later, another bizarre, fractured message: "Why don't . . . come down . . . tea and Snickers?" He stopped this time; was that Conrad's voice? He looked around the tilted wasteland across which he'd been picking his way, and saw Tap Richards waving at him and pointing at Conrad Anker far down the rock and snow slope of Everest's North Face. Just then, another message came through, this one unambiguous: "Mandatory group meeting!"

Two miles below and 12 miles away at Base Camp, Jochen Hemmleb had been monitoring the same peculiar messages, but with much greater interest. Peering through a high-powered telescope, he could see five climbers converging from several points on a wide, dish-scooped section of the North Face known as the "snow terrace" until they reached its lower edge. Then the radio went silent. It was May 1, May Day, a workers' holiday in many nations. For the workers on Everest, however, it was another work day, but one that would end in celebration nonetheless.

The problem all along was the ice ax. For almost a decade after Noel Odell last saw Mallory and Irvine climbing into the mists high on Everest, never to return, no one had a clue what had happened to them. Then, on May 30, 1933, during the next British Everest expedition, climber Percy Wyn-Harris found an ice ax high on the Northeast Ridge at 27,760 feet (8,460 m). It lay some 750 feet (230 m) east of the prominent rock formation called the First Step and 60 feet (20 m) below the ridge crest.

Somervell, of course, had dropped his ice ax while descending the Yellow Band in 1924, but the Yellow Band is beneath the site where the ax was found, not above it. Clearly, it was not his, and no other expeditions had been on the mountain between 1924 and 1933. The ax could only have belonged to either Mallory or Irvine. Immediately the world assumed that one or both of them had fallen to their deaths, losing the ax in the process.

The ax was found to have two marks on its handle, a small cross made by Wyn-Harris's servant, Kusang Pugla (to distinguish it from other ice axes in the 1933 expedition), and three parallel inked nicks, which Odell noticed when he examined it in 1934. It was not until 1962 that one of Andrew Irvine's brothers found an old swagger stick belonging to Irvine that had identical identification marks. The ice ax, therefore, had been Irvine's. If you want to find Irvine's remains, the common wisdom went, look on the broad snow terrace several hundred feet below the site where the ice ax was found.[1]

But Jochen Hemmleb was not convinced. The assumption that Irvine, and possibly Mallory, had fallen from the site where the ax was found seemed to him unlikely: "Russell Brice described the ridge to me as quite broad at this location; it's simply not the kind of place from which one falls. What is more, there are a couple of ledges below the ridge crest there that would easily stop a fall in the unlikely event one happened." Something else bothered him as well: the ax was found simply lying flat on a slightly inclined slab of rock, not caught or wedged in any way, and it was undamaged. "It is far more likely that it was put down deliberately than that it somehow slid to this position in an accident," Hemmleb points out. Noel Odell had said virtually the same thing sixty-five years earlier: "It seems to me very possible that one of them—and more plausibly Irvine, who was less used to carrying an axe on a rock climb than Mallory—may have decided to leave his axe on the ridge during the ascent, to be picked up on the descent, in view of the climbing being almost entirely on rock under the conditions prevailing at that time."[2]

Says Hemmleb: "There is little reason to assume a connection between the location at which Irvine's ice ax was found and the answer to the mystery of what had happened to either him or Mallory. Was there a possibility? Perhaps, but it was neither the only nor the most likely possibility."

As Hemmleb had reexamined the history of North Face

expeditions, it had become clear to him that the only hard bit of data about Mallory and Irvine themselves (as distinct from artifacts like the ice ax) was that the Chinese climber Wang Hongbao had found a body he had adamantly described as "English, English!" during what he said was a short stroll from the 1975 Chinese expedition's Camp VI.

Wang had been a member of a search party looking for Wu Zongyueh, who had disappeared between Camps VI and VII on May 4, 1975. Wang was at Camp VI with another climber, Zhang Junyan, the day after Wu disappeared and had decided, while waiting for another climber to arrive, to go for a short walk. Returning twenty minutes later, he told Zhang (and, later, others) that he had come across the body of a foreign mountaineer.[3] It wasn't until 1979, while participating in a Chinese-Japanese expedition, that Wang told the story of his discovery of an "English dead" to an outsider, the Japanese climber Hasegawa Yoshinori. Says Hasegawa of the exchange, "He said to me, '8,100 metre Engleese' and he made a gesture to sleep. . . . Then Wang opened his mouth, pointed his finger to his cheek, [and] pecked it slightly with his finger. . . ."[4] The cheek, Wang was suggesting, had been pecked at by birds. That was all Hasegawa learned; an avalanche swept Wang to his death the next day. Years later, however, Everest expert Tom Holzel tracked down Zhang Junyan, and he corroborated Wang's story.[5] (See "A Brown Paper Bag—The Mysterious Chinese 'Present' on the 1979 Snow in Motion Symposium" in Appendix 1, Everest North Side: Resolved and Unresolved Mysteries.)

Whatever the validity of the other clues amassed over the years, it was clear to Hemmleb that this one was preeminent.

The challenge was straightforward: locate the site of the 1975 Chinese Camp VI and search an area with a radius that could be covered in a twenty-minute round trip (or more, to be safe). Pinpointing the camp, however, was no easy task.

The Chinese had released little documentation of the 1975 climb. At the time Wang found the body, their Camp VI had been located at 26,900 feet (8,200 m), though it was later moved, but there was no indication of whether it had been placed on Everest's North Ridge or the North Face. "I found one picture of the Chinese Camp VI that showed some background features,"[6] Hemmleb says, "and I wondered whether from this picture we could delineate the exact location for that camp and therefore narrow down the search area." When he compared the Chinese picture with pictures taken at other expeditions' Camp VIs, he soon realized that each was on a different site and the pictures had different backgrounds. "So the next question," he recalls, "was whether there was a way to delineate the exact locations of these different camps from the background that was visible. Was there a universal technique to delineate the location from which any photograph had been taken of Everest's North Face? And there was."

There is one distinctive reference point in every photograph taken from the upper North Ridge looking toward the summit: a triangular snowfield that, in fact, marks the high point reached by Geoffrey Bruce and George Finch during the 1922 British expedition. The photographer's position on any photograph of this area of the mountain can be determined by taking a back-bearing after vertically aligning features on the skyline with this distinctive reference point. "In the Chinese photo," Hemmleb explains, "the snow triangle is in vertical alignment with the summit ridge immediately beyond the so-called 'Third Step.' If you connect these same points horizontally on an aerial orthophotograph of the ridge, you can figure out a line on which the camp sits. To get the precise spot, you need a second back-bearing, which you get by vertically aligning two other features on the Chinese photo, a ledge on the First Step and a tongue of snow at the foot of the Yellow Band." In this way, Hemmleb was able to predict that the 1975 Chinese Camp VI would be found on an ill-defined rib of rock that bisects the snow terrace—a site too far off today's beaten path to the summit for anyone to have noticed it. "Forget the ice ax," says Hemmleb. "Find the camp and you'll find Irvine."

At 3:00 A.M. on May 1, 1999, six climbers from the Mallory & Irvine Research Expedition stirred themselves in their wind-battered tents at Camp V and began preparations to do just that. They had left Base Camp below the Rongbuk Glacier a week earlier and had gotten pinned down by high winds at Advance Base Camp for several days.

On April 29, the wind relented and the search team—Simonson, Hahn, Politz, Anker, Richards, Norton, and Pollard—climbed to the North Col. The next day they ascended to Camp V, though Simonson, who had not had the opportunity to acclimatize at higher altitudes, felt unwell and decided to descend rather than jeopardize the search. Simonson explains: "I went on this expedition planning to participate in the search climb, but I had to spend so much time handling administrative duties—juggling things with the film crews, the Chinese officials, the yak drivers, and the trekking expedition that followed us in—that I didn't get high enough soon enough to acclimatize. I could feel it as soon as we left Camp IV."

On the 30th, the remaining six climbers reached Camp V. Now, at 5:00 A.M., they were ready to go, guided by Hemmleb's search directions. "Once we'd gotten all our gear on and attached our oxygen masks," Dave Hahn recalls, "I realized we'd become as separate from one another as deep-sea divers. Without a word, we began working up the ridge."[7]

Hahn describes the climb to Camp VI: "As we left Camp V, there was a steady 25-mile-per-hour wind blowing—not enough to move you around, but enough to make taking care of yourself in the cold morning air a bit more stressful. Actual air temperature is almost irrelevant at this altitude; it feels much colder than it is because the body can't heat itself very efficiently when there's so little oxygen. It's like any fire: you need more than fuel and a spark; you need oxygen too."

Once they got moving and got out of the wind, though, Jake Norton recalls, "It seemed surprisingly warm; it was going to be a beautiful day." Groping along in the dimness of the shadow cast by the North Ridge, the team began the traverse toward the North Face. "The footing was uncomfortable with so little snow," Hahn says. "It was a mix of loose rock, rock frozen in place, and bedrock here and there, all of which was steeply pitched and none of which felt too good when you're walking on the points of your crampons. Eventually, you follow a traversing ledge that takes you around a corner and out on to the North Face proper. It's pretty exposed; if you look down off the edge of the ledge, you see all the way down to the main Rongbuk far below." It was at about this point that Thom

Pollard, complaining of problems with his oxygen set, decided to turn around.

Then, Jake Norton made a discovery. "This was my first trip on this route, and the exposure was pretty extreme; it doesn't encourage you to look down," Norton recalls, "but at one point I did, and saw something out of place: a piece of wood in a landscape that was nothing but rock and snow. I climbed down and discovered it was a very old wood-handled piton hammer."[8] Norton picked up the hammer and put it in his pack. Later, it would prove to be an important clue to the history of the old camp Andy Politz had found on the East Rongbuk Glacier.

While four of the climbers continued across the traverse, Politz decided to take a direct line up the North Ridge itself because that was understood to be the route that Mallory and Irvine had taken. Politz had another purpose as well. "I wanted to get to the area where Odell had seen Mallory and Irvine early that afternoon in 1924. There's been so much controversy over the last seventy-five years about what he did or did not see that I wanted to see the mountain from his perspective. No one had ever done that before and, given how vital his observations were to the question of how high [Mallory and Irvine] got, I figured it was time somebody checked out that view."

When he reached the area where Odell had stood, the result was dramatic: "The First, Second, and Third Steps were each clearly separated; you had no trouble distinguishing them. You are really close to them at that point. From the area where Odell stood, there was only one place that anyone could see as being 'a very short distance from the base of the final pyramid,' and that was the Third Step. The First Step is out of the question; the Second is also too far away to fit Odell's description. I took slide photos, digital stills, and video and, afterward, it was really obvious you couldn't confuse one with another, even in bad weather."

After about five hours of climbing, the remaining four climbers reached the area today used as Camp VI. "We hadn't yet established a Camp VI for our expedition," says Norton, "but we were carrying a tent and a few supplies, which we left at what seemed a good site, and then waited for Andy to rejoin us. We could see his red parka coming across from the North Ridge, though he had to climb almost as high as the Yellow Band to find a safe route across."

"We were all pretty excited," Hahn remembers, "and we were optimistic. The ground conditions were excellent, we had Jochen's guidance, and the weather was good. It had taken us a month and a half to get to this point, and now it was time to go to work at last. It was also a bit of a thrill to know we would be going away from known terrain into some new and sporty parts of the mountain."

At 10:30 A.M., after a half-hour rest, the five climbers headed west across the sharply tilted North Face toward the "ill-defined rib" identified in Hemmleb's search instructions. Within only fifteen minutes, Jake Norton hit pay dirt again. He radioed Base Camp that he'd found a distinctively painted, bright blue 1975 Chinese oxygen cylinder, proof that they were near the vicinity of the old Chinese camp, which they estimated to be higher up the sloping rib.

Hemmleb had laid out four possible search routes; they began with the first, fanning out vertically and horizontally along the North Face and walking west. "The plan was simply to keep each other in sight and keep the radios on," Politz says. "From there on we knew the terrain would tell us the plan." Hemmleb agrees: "Once they reached that spot, my job was over; they had to decide what was right from the landscape they found there."

"The idea that this was a 'snow terrace' quickly became a joke," Hahn remembers. "This wasn't like a bunch of guys fanning out across a field. Beyond the rib, the North Face was a consistent 30-degree-plus slope of loose scree and discontinuous ledges and walls, all of it wildly exposed to a long fall to the glacier below. And the area we were trying to cover was immense, maybe the size of twelve crazily tilted football fields."

Politz adds, "Maybe at sea level it wasn't that big an area, but at 8,000 meters, when your heart is working at jogging pace but your feet are working at a crawling pace and you're taking three breaths per step, it's a huge area." Climbing higher than he'd ever been before, Jake Norton was also taking great care: "Walking around looking for bodies is kind of an eerie job, especially when you're on slopes where a slight misstep could turn you into another victim."[9]

As they fanned out, each of the climbers was guided by his own private sense of what might have happened to Andrew Irvine. "I was looking for someplace hidden that he might have either fetched up against or sheltered in," says Hahn. Politz confesses, "I wanted Mallory and Irvine to have climbed down, run out of light and strength, sat down, and died of exposure. So I was looking up the mountain to see what route I might have chosen to come down." Politz also quickly realized that looking uphill was impractical; the slope was too steep and stair-stepped to be able to see much; it was better to be looking downslope. He climbed high, partway into the Yellow Band, to get a better downhill view. "I was also trying to pick a line where the Chinese climber, Wang, might reasonably have 'gone for a stroll' for ten or twenty minutes. I thought I'd read that he was a geologist and I figured the Yellow Band was the most geologically interesting part of the surrounding terrain, so that's where I went."

Anker took the opposite extreme and ranged far down the slope, quite near the point where the "terrace" ended in the long drop to the central Rongbuk Glacier. "I couldn't figure out what Conrad's logic was," Politz said later. "It seemed to me that anything that had fallen that far would have just kept on going."

Norton was roughly midway between them: "I had looked at the face of the Yellow Band and just picked an area down on the terrace where I thought a falling body that had picked up a good bit of speed might come to rest. It had always been assumed Irvine had fallen from the point where the ice ax had been found in 1933, so I traced a line down from there and started looking, like I had with the piton hammer, for anything that didn't belong there."

Only a half hour into the search, Richards, Anker, and Norton stumbled into a virtual graveyard of mangled, frozen bodies. "We found ourselves in a kind of collection zone for fallen climbers," Richards recalls. "We'd radio Jochen down in Base Camp and describe what we'd found, and he would immediately know who it was and when they'd died. It was pretty amazing how Jochen had all this information filed away. He could just about tell you what kind of socks that person would have been wearing on that day. I wasn't eager to get close to these bodies; besides, once I saw colorful Gore-Tex or plastic boots I knew it was neither Mallory nor Irvine. Death is like a fog that looms in the air over the North Face of Everest; it hit me really hard. Seeing those first few bodies was eerie, grim, and humbling."

In all, they found the bodies of a half dozen climbers, all relatively contemporary. The bodies troubled Dave Hahn: "I had chosen to believe that most of the fatalities on Everest had come about as exhausted climbers simply sat down to die. I was convinced that falls were rare. It was clear I had miscalculated."

They shook Jake Norton too. "Just seeing these twisted, broken bodies was a pretty stark reminder of our own mortality. I knew that in just a few days, we'd be up on that Northeast Ridge walking along the same route these climbers had fallen from. It was obvious from the contorted condition of their bodies that these climbers had suffered long and terrible falls."

Aware that other expeditions would be listening in to their radio transmissions and concerned about protecting anything they found from the curious, the search team had agreed on a series of code words if they found something from the 1924 expedition. "A boulder would mean either Mallory or Irvine," explains Richards, "and a gorak on a boulder meant a camera. But the truth is that, in the heat of the search, most of us forgot all about that."

Like Hahn, Andy Politz had stopped paying attention to his radio and had stuffed it into a chest pocket in his down suit. "The airways were full of cell phone calls, voice mail messages, answering machine recordings, and other babble," he recalls, "so I just turned the radio way down and kept searching. I vaguely heard Conrad saying something about Snickers and paid no attention. Then I heard 'Mandatory group meeting!'

and started looking around. Farther down the face, I could see the other guys already converging on Conrad."

Down at Base Camp, his eye glued to a telescope, Jochen Hemmleb could see them too. "When I saw Andy climbing down hundreds of feet from his high point," Hemmleb remembers, "I knew he wasn't climbing down just for tea and Snickers. No one at that altitude would climb down so far for that; it was too much effort. Something was up."

Something was indeed up.

Conrad Anker had been going on intuition, and his intuition had told him to look low. He had climbed down to the lower edge of the terrace, the point where it dropped away some 6,600 feet (2,000 m) to the main Rongbuk Glacier, and had started zigzagging back up the slope when he saw "a patch of white that was whiter than the rock around it and whiter than the snow." Climbing toward it, he realized the patch of white was another body. But this one was different: " . . . this wasn't a body from recent times; it was something that had been there for quite a while."[10]

Norton was the first to reach Anker. "I'm afraid I wasn't very eloquent," he recalls. "I just sat down on a rock next to Conrad, looked at this perfect alabaster body, and said to myself, 'Holy shit!' I had harbored no hope that we'd find anything this first day. We just expected to do a reconnaissance of the area. It was just amazing."

As Dave Hahn approached the site and saw the body, he recalls: "There was absolutely no question in my mind that we were looking at a man who had been clinging to the mountain for seventy-five years. The clothing was blasted from most of his body, and his skin was bleached white. I felt like I was viewing a Greek or Roman marble statue."

There was no exultation when the climbers all reached the site, no "high fives" signaling that, only an hour and a half into a search of a vast section of the North Face of Mount Everest, they had found their man. Instead, the five modern climbers stood or kneeled around the ancient body, speechless.

The body itself did the speaking. For here was a body unlike the others crumpled in crannies elsewhere on the terrace. This body was lying fully extended, facedown and pointing uphill, frozen in a position of self-arrest, as if the fall had happened only moments earlier. The head and upper torso were frozen into the rubble that had gathered around them over the decades, but the arms, powerfully muscular still, extended above the head to strong hands that gripped the mountainside, flexed fingertips dug deep into the frozen gravel. The legs were extended downhill. One was broken and the other had been gently crossed over it for protection. Here too, the musculature was still pronounced and powerful. The entire body had about it the strength and grace of a dancer. This body, this man, had once been a splendid specimen of humankind.

"We weren't just looking at a body," Hahn explains, "we were looking at an era, one we'd only known through books. The natural-fiber clothes, the fur-lined leather helmet, the kind of rope that was around him were all so eloquent. As we stood there, this mute but strangely peaceful body was telling us answers to questions that everyone had wondered about for three-quarters of a century: the fact that a rope had been involved; the fact that the hands and forearms were much darker than the rest of the body; the nature and extent of the broken leg and what wasn't broken, and what that said about this person's last moments; the fact that there was no oxygen apparatus."

The hobnail boot, of course, was the giveaway. No westerner was permitted on Everest from 1949 until 1979; Tibet, the "Forbidden Kingdom," was forbidden to outsiders. No one had died at this altitude on Everest between 1924 and 1938, and hobnailed boots had given way to crampons and more advanced boot construction by World War II. The body had to be Andrew Comyn Irvine. Jake Norton went so far as to begin scratching out a memorial stone with the words, "Andrew Irvine: 1902–1924."

"This isn't him," Andy Politz said to the rest of the climbers when he arrived at the spot where the others waited.

The rest of the team looked at Politz as if he were daft.

"Oh, I think so," Anker said.

"I don't know what made me say it," Politz now says. "Here was this very old body, perfectly preserved, with very old clothing and the hobnailed boots. I knew it had to be Irvine; Irvine was who we were looking for, and that's who it had to be."

But it wasn't.

Tap Richards, who had training in archeology, and Jake Norton began gently separating the ragged layers of clothing that were left around the protected edges of the body: several layers of cotton and silk underwear, a flannel shirt, woolen pullover and trousers, a canvaslike outer garment. Near the nape of the neck, Norton turned over a piece of shirt collar and revealed a fragment of laundry label: G. Mallory.

The climbers looked at each other dumbly for a moment, and finally someone said out loud what everyone else was thinking: "Why would Irvine be wearing Mallory's shirt?" Then they found another name tag: G. Leigh Ma[llory]. Then a third.

"Maybe it was the altitude and the fact that we'd all put aside our oxygen gear, but it took a while for reality to sink in," says Hahn. "Then it finally hit us: we had not found Andrew Irvine. We had not rediscovered Wang Hongbao's 'English dead.' We were in the presence of George Mallory himself . . . the man whose boldness and drive we'd grown up in awe of."[11]

"Now I realized why I had said it wasn't Irvine," Politz explained later. "It was the position of the body. Somewhere back in my subconscious, my intuition remembered that Wang had found a body that had been in a position where his mouth was agape and his cheek was exposed to the goraks. But this body was facedown. The head was almost entirely covered, and it had not been moved. What's more, it was too far from the 1975 Chinese Camp VI to have ever been found on a short walk. I just sat down. My knees literally got weak. My jaw dropped. Next to me, Dave was saying, 'Oh my God, it's George. Oh my God.'"

It had been an article of faith that if anyone had fallen, it would have been the inexperienced Andrew Irvine. "Throughout the seventy-five years since they disappeared," explains Jake Norton, "it had been understood that George Mallory was infallible, he didn't fall, he couldn't fall. It was a shock to discover that he was fallible, he did fall. We couldn't quite get used to the idea."

Meanwhile, however, time was passing. The climbers had a responsibility to document as professionally as possible what they had found, search for artifacts, provide Mallory a proper burial, and perform a Church of England committal service provided by the Anglican Bishop of Bristol, England. After that, they still had a two- to three-hour descent to Camp V to negotiate safely. "It would have been nice to have been able to leave the work for another day," says Hahn, "but on Everest, there are no guaranteed second chances; the monsoon could start tomorrow."

There was another issue as well: "We knew we were going to have to disturb him to do our job," Hahn explains, "and we only wanted to disturb him once. Then we wanted to leave him in peace. We knew if we did not do a thorough search for the camera and other artifacts, people would keep coming back and disturbing him again."

The first thing the climbers had done when they discovered the body—before they touched it, before they discovered who it was—was to document photographically both the site and the body. Then they discussed what to do next. "It came down to trying to decide what Mallory himself would have wanted," explains Politz. "In the end, Dave put it best: 'If we can find some evidence of what he accomplished, especially whether he and Irvine had made it to the summit, I think he'd want the world to know.'" As they stood around this man, this icon of Everest itself, the others agreed, and it was time to go to work.

Their main objective, of course, was to find the famous camera, the collapsible Kodak Vestpocket camera that Howard Somervell had lent Mallory for the summit attempt—the mechanism that would answer, it was hoped, the question of whether Mount Everest had been summited in 1924, more than a quarter century before Edmund Hillary and Tenzing Norgay did it by another route in 1953. In the cold, dry air of the mountain, Kodak officials had said, there was every reason to believe the film, if intact, would still be able to be developed.

The camera was not beside George Mallory's body and it seemed reasonable to assume that, if he had it, it would be in a pocket or around his neck—neither of which were immediately accessible, as Mallory was effectively locked in the icy embrace of the North Face.

The task before them was formidable. "It was immediately apparent," Hahn says, "that this was going to be neither simple, easy, or quick." Politz elaborates, "If you took a one-pound ice ax and started chopping concrete with it, you'd get the same effect as what it was like to try to chip away at the frozen gravel and rock that encased roughly half of George Mallory on that slope," Politz explains. "It was just brutally hard work."

It was also dangerous. The ground was uneven and very steeply sloped and, says Hahn, "a single misstep could easily send you down the slope and over the edge. When you got up off your knees, you wanted to be very sure where your feet were going to be. To keep things interesting, every once in a while a rock would go whizzing past our heads."

Progress was slow and, since the climbers had taken off their oxygen sets in order to work, exhausting. The advantage of this pace was that it gave them plenty of time to study Mallory carefully. The tibia and fibula of his right leg were broken above the top of his boot, and his right elbow was either broken or dislocated. There were a number of still-visible cuts, abrasions, and bruises along his right side as well, and the climbing rope in which he was tangled had compressed his rib cage and tugged at his skin. The rope had been passed twice around his waist and the frayed trailing ends were wrapped around his leg and upper body. Though the body was remarkably intact, Everest's goraks had pecked at it and damaged one leg, his buttocks, and the abdominal cavity.

As they worked on the ice, the climbers could not get used to how little Mallory had been wearing during his attempt to reach the highest point on earth. "We're standing there in down suits so thick that I couldn't even see the climbing harness around my waist," Hahn explains. "In our packs we had food, water, electronic gear, and extra mittens, and here was this man before us who was wearing what maybe added up to the equivalent of two layers of fleece. Hell, I walk out on the street in Seattle with more clothing than he had on at 28,000 feet on Everest! Clearly they were tough climbers, but there wasn't any room for anything to go wrong for these guys, no margin at all."[12]

After an hour of chipping at the ice and rock with their axes, the climbers, working in shifts in the thin air, first were able to free one jacket pocket, in which they found an altimeter, good to 30,000 feet; its crystal was broken and the hands were missing. Soon afterward, they removed enough of the frozen gravel around Mallory's torso to be able to free his right shoulder. Jake Norton, doing the delicate excavating with a penknife, reached underneath and discovered that Mallory had a pouch hanging from his neck. Norton looked up at the other climbers: "There's something hard and metallic in here." Carefully, he cut open the bottom of the pouch with his knife: "I just knew it was the camera."

In fact, it was a tin of "Brand's & Co.'s Savoury Meat

Lozenges" (a kind of bouillon cube). Next, a pair of nail scissors in a leather case emerged. Then, most astonishing of all, a letter in an envelope, perfectly preserved, the ink script crisp and clear, not the slightest bit faded or smudged, as if it had just been written.

Other items emerged from a pouch on Mallory's right side and from various pockets: a beautiful handkerchief with a burgundy, blue, and green foulard pattern, monogrammed G.L.M., carefully wrapped around another group of letters; a second monogrammed handkerchief in a red, blue, and yellow pattern; a white handkerchief wrapped around a tube of petroleum jelly; a single fingerless glove; a pocket knife with an antler handle; an undamaged box of matches, still useable; an assortment of boot laces and straps; adjustable webbing straps attached to a metal spring clip (to hold an oxygen mask to the flying helmet); a note from fellow expedition member Geoffrey Bruce; scraps of paper with gear checklists penciled in; and, deep in one pocket, a pair of sun goggles, intact. One by one, the artifacts, including samples of each layer of clothing, were placed in resealable plastic bags and put in Andy Politz's pack.

The climbers barely spoke to each other. "There was this intense feeling of reverence," Politz remembers. "At one point, I thought about how proud I was of my partners. We were walking a very fine line, trying to do a responsible job archeologically while still treating the body itself with the dignity it deserved. This was one of our great heroes, after all, and in an odd sense we felt we were working with Mallory the person, not Mallory the body. It was humbling."

"At one point, I just stood back," says Tap Richards, "and thought: here we are at 27,000 feet on the north side of Everest and no one else in the world knows anything about this but the five of us. Now we would be able to help George Mallory do something I knew he would have wanted: write a new chapter in the story of his life. I was also thinking about Jochen, down at Base Camp, and how much he must be wondering what was going on."

Wondering indeed. As the hours passed, Jochen Hemmleb was winding tighter and tighter. As if the radio silence were not enough, a haze had drifted across the mountain, and visibility from Base Camp had gotten poorer and poorer. At 1:45 P.M., Hemmleb called Eric Simonson at ABC to ask what he thought was happening. Simonson's cryptic reply was: "No news is good news."

"I knew they'd found something important and I was surprised at how quickly the radio had gone silent," Simonson confesses. "But we had a good search plan, we knew what we were looking for and where to look, we had five healthy climbers and excellent working conditions. Now all I had to do was wait and hope they didn't have any accidents."

Before the expedition had begun, BBC's Peter Firstbrook reported that he had spoken to the families of both Mallory and Irvine and received their support for the search and for photographing what was found. In addition, he said, the families had asked that the climbers take a DNA sample of whomever they found. Accordingly, the last thing the search team did was take a small skin sample from Mallory's forearm for the DNA analysis.

Then they began the arduous process of burying a legend, of drawing a protective cloak of stone over George Leigh Mallory.

"And that," Politz recalls, "turned out to be quite a project.

The idea was to gather rocks and cover the body with them, but rocks turned out to be hard to come by. Any loose rocks had obviously tended to avalanche down the slope and over the edge, and everything else was frozen solid. So we were ranging all over the slope to find, pry up, and haul rocks. Finally we got enough to be sure that Mallory wouldn't be bothered by the birds ever again."

The burial took nearly forty-five minutes. Then Andy Politz read the committal ceremony, and afterward the climbers gathered their gear. "It seems an odd thing to say," said Norton later, "but I don't think any of us wanted to leave him. We were very comfortable being with 'George.' We wanted to spend more time with him; he was so impressive to be with, even in death."

Finally, they shrugged on their backpacks and, at about 3:00 P.M., began working their way east across the terrace toward the North Ridge. "And as we were walking away," Politz recalls, "I was thinking to myself, 'Right; if George isn't happy with that ceremony, guess who's the first one who's going to get it?'" The climbers were both physically and emotionally spent, a dangerous combination on a mountain where most accidents happen on the descent. "I was picking a route across this slope," Politz continues, "and every step of the way I was conscious that I have two kids and a wife back at home, and every step matters here. Plus I've got Mallory's stuff in my pack!"

By 5:30 P.M., all five climbers had reached the relative safety of Camp V. "The last twenty minutes to the camp were rugged," Norton remembers. "I was beat anyway, and we were battling 50-mile-per-hour winds that tried to knock us over with every step. I finally crawled into the tent that Conrad, Tap, and I were sharing, and we just sat there for awhile, exhausted, talking about what had happened. Then Tap and I tried to go to sleep, but it was almost impossible; our minds were whirring."

In the other tent, Dave Hahn and Andy Politz radioed Base Camp to say that they had arrived and were fine. Then, choosing words carefully so that they would have meaning only for the expedition members, Hahn said, "Jochen, you will be a happy man now."

The next morning, May 2, they descended from Camp V, continued past Camp IV on the North Col, and walked into ABC at about 3:00 P.M. "Eric came out to greet us and we all just smiled and said, 'You're not going to believe this,'" Norton remembers. They walked straight to the expedition's big "Weatherport" tent, zipped the tent flaps closed, and began pulling artifacts out to show Simonson.

"He didn't know whether we'd found a body, a camera, or what," says Norton, "so the first thing we gave him was the envelope and letter addressed to 'Mr. George Leigh Mallory,' and he just looked up and smiled a very big smile."

CHAPTER 7

THE FINAL PYRAMID

The adventure seems more desperate than ever . . .
GEORGE MALLORY

The last stage of the 1999 expedition began with tragedy. For some weeks the team had been sharing the mountain with a group of Ukrainian climbers led by Mistisláv Gorbenko, an Everest veteran who had been on the Soviet team in the 1990 International Peace Climb led by American mountaineering legend Jim Whittaker. Simonson had met five of the other Ukrainian climbers on Cho Oyu in 1997, and they had become friends.

Tough and professional, the Ukrainian team was climbing in a style common among Eastern Europeans: get high fast, and travel light and, in this case, without oxygen. On the night of May 7, in marginal weather, three members of their expedition reached their High Camp at 27,230 feet (8,300 m). The next morning, despite steadily increasing wind and deteriorating weather, they headed for the summit, reaching it early that afternoon. Soon after they began their descent, however, the weather worsened further: it began snowing hard; the wind, already high, rose higher; and visibility dropped sharply.

Picking their way back down through nearly a mile of broken ledges and traverses, the climbers, exhausted and oxygenless, became separated. In the gathering darkness, one of the climbers, Viacheslav "Slava" Terseul, struggled down through the Yellow Band and made it to the High Camp. The other two, Vladimir "Vova" Gorbach and Vasily Kopytko, spent the night somewhere in the vicinity of 28,000 feet (8,500 m) on the upper Northeast Ridge, unprotected from the wind, snow, and cold. Later that night, when Slava realized his summit mates had not returned, he called for help from the rest of the Ukrainian team below, then, amazingly, climbed back up toward the First Step, still without oxygen, in search of the other two. Early the next morning, he found Gorbach, immobile but alive. Kopytko had vanished. Then he climbed back down through the Yellow Band, met the rescuers, and ascended yet again to lead them to Gorbach and back to Camp VI.

When a climber near the summit of Mount Everest reaches a stage of exhaustion and oxygen starvation so severe that he can no longer move on his own initiative, he is typically left to die. It is simply impossible for one climber to descend such treacherous terrain carrying or dragging the inert body of another. The mountain is littered with the bodies of climbers who have simply sat down and died of exposure. This time, however, because of the backup capacity of other team members lower on the mountain, the Ukrainians were able to send additional climbers to help Slava rescue his snow-blind, half-frozen comrade and carry him down to Camp VI. After another miserable night at 27,230 feet (8,300 m), they began lowering him down the mountain toward the North Col on May 10.

The night before, the summit team of the Mallory & Irvine

Research Expedition had arrived from Base Camp. The climbers, Americans and Sherpa alike, had taken a long rest after their return from discovering George Mallory's body. The period had been anything but restful, however, for Eric Simonson. For weeks, WGBH/NOVA producer Liesl Clark had been posting information-packed dispatches about the expedition's progress on NOVA's website. In the same fashion, she posted a dispatch about the expedition's May 1 discovery— as seen and heard that day from Base Camp. Although she did not state explicitly that the search team had found a body, the dispatch left little doubt that this was what had happened. Simonson first heard of this not from Clark but through an e-mail from his Ashford, Washington, office, and he was furious. Not only had he wanted to keep information about discoveries quiet until the expedition had completed its work on the mountain, but he felt Clark's dispatch compromised an exclusive contract the expedition had with MountainZone.com for news.

Feeling that his hand had been forced by Clark, Simonson sent a voice dispatch to MountainZone.com announcing that George Leigh Mallory had been found at last. The next morning, the news was on BBC World Service radio, and all the expeditions at Advance Base Camp knew about their find. That evening, when the team returned to Base Camp, Simonson found the communications tent swamped with literally hundreds of messages and interview requests from media outlets around the world. When he and the climbers left for their summit climb a week later, he was glad to be escaping the media frenzy. But they soon discovered that they were just walking into another crisis.

By midday on May 10, climbers at Advance Base Camp had learned some of the details of the Ukrainian epic and knew they were bringing down a badly frostbitten climber. There were at this point a dozen expedition teams of various sizes and strengths camped at ABC. Incredibly, many would have nothing to do with the Ukrainian emergency. Others sought payment to participate in a rescue. The rest—Simonson's Mallory & Irvine Research Expedition team; a group headed by Simonson's friend and fellow commercial expedition leader, Russell Brice; as well as several other climbers and Sherpa— attended a meeting called by Brice, and began pooling their resources. With the injured climber due to arrive at Camp IV at about 10:00 P.M., Conrad Anker, Jake Norton, Tap Richards, and Andy Politz, helped by a member of an Italian expedition who had rescue experience, climbed up to the North Col and began rigging up a system of anchors and ropes by which to lower a stretcher they carried up with them. When Vova Gorbach was brought to Camp IV, he was close to death, and Simonson's team administered intramuscular dexamethazone (a steroid that jump-starts the respiratory and circulatory systems). Then, with the badly frostbitten Ukrainian wrapped tightly into the stretcher, they lowered the litter in 200-meter stages down the steep walls of the col, with two of the climbers accompanying it as it descended.

Thom Pollard and Dave Hahn were waiting at the bottom, along with a small crowd of Sherpa, cooks, and other expedition members who would help ferry the stretcher over the difficult footing of the moraine to ABC. Pollard was stunned to see Roman Koval, a member of the Ukrainian team who by now had been working on his colleague's rescue at high altitude for more than forty-eight hours, climbing down with his injured colleague. Recalls Pollard, "[He] was covered in frost, and his eyes contained the blank stare of someone in need of rest and warmth. Despite his condition, he refused to let me take his pack, and wanted only to get on with the rescue. . . . At one point, I looked back and noticed he had taken one of the carrying positions on the sled. Of course, his pack was still on. Something very powerful was obviously driving him."[1] When they finally reached Advance Base Camp and medical assistance, it was nearly 2:30 A.M.

Gorbach survived, but during the next week, as the Mallory & Irvine Research Expedition's climbing team made their own summit attempt, they would have cause to remember the lesson of the Ukrainian climbers.

It was 11:00 A.M. on May 12—only a day and a half later—when Simonson's summit and search team—Conrad Anker, Dave Hahn, Jake Norton, Andy Politz, Thom Pollard, and Tap Richards—began climbing up the ice wall to the North Col again to make their summit bid and, in the process, answer more questions about Mallory and Irvine's last climb. The day was overcast and there was light snow that afternoon, but the climb was otherwise uneventful. The team spent the evening together in a crowded dome tent at Camp IV, talking and melting water for the next day's climb, then retired to their two-person tents.

Seventy-five years earlier, on June 4, 1924, Mallory and Irvine had done the same thing, but under a brilliantly clear sky. As they left their Camp III, expedition photographer Noel was concerned that Mallory did not appear to be at his physical best, but was nonetheless awestruck by his determination: "It was his spirit that was sending him again to the attack. He had his teeth in the job and he meant business. He was throwing his last ounce of strength into this fight."[2] They had a splendid day for climbing and, using oxygen for the first time, they reached the North Col in record time. Wrote Irvine in his diary, "We took exactly three hours going up . . . I breathed oxygen all the last half of the way and found that it slowed breathing down at least three times (using 1½litre/min.). George and I both arrived at the Camp very surprisingly fresh."[3]

By the time they settled into Camp IV, the temperature in the sun was 105 degrees Fahrenheit, though the temperature in the shade hadn't risen above freezing. Still, they had to get through the night at Camp IV, and an uncomfortable night it would be: "Snow may be delightful for a temporary siesta," Odell later wrote, " . . . but it is remarkable how soon it congeals to the consistency of the hardest rock, and how difficult it is to smooth out the relief of one's anatomy first impressed upon it."[4]

On May 12, 1999, Simonson's team would have heartily agreed: "We all spent a lousy night at Camp IV," Dave Hahn remembers. "The ice under the tents had melted in the previous weeks to conform to the shapes of Sherpa who had slept there, and it was clear their shapes didn't conform to ours." When they dragged themselves out of their tents, grumbling, the next morning, it was cloudy and light snow had begun to fall. "The weather was unstable," Hahn recalls, "but we didn't have a sense that it was serious in any way, and Eric's weather reports predicted an improving trend."

In contrast, the weather had been fine the morning of June

6, 1924, when Noel Odell photographed George Mallory and Andrew Irvine shouldering their oxygen packs a few moments before they turned up the slope toward Camp V. Now, separated by three-quarters of a century, another team of climbers began the long, steep march up the snowcrest of the North Col to the broken, bare ground of the North Ridge, heading for Camp V and later, they hoped, more answers.

Camp V exists for one reason only: it is the point at which most climbers run out of steam and daylight on the climb up from Camp IV toward the Northeast Ridge. Only someone who was too exhausted to care about comfort or safety would even consider calling it a "camp." It sits in an extremely exposed position, perched on a series of small, jagged, tilted rock ledges at the very edge of the North Ridge, with steep drop-offs in every direction but up. The ground is broken, uneven, and tilted, and the wind is vicious almost all of the time: "Not the kind of place where you wander around making social calls," Hahn quips.

That afternoon, in rising wind and dropping temperatures, Simonson's climbers crawled into securely anchored tents on tiny, crooked, and decidedly uncomfortable ledges and called it a night. Down below, most of the expedition's Sherpa had climbed from ABC to Camp IV carrying supplies for the summit team. The Sherpa don't like Camp V and planned to push all the way to Camp VI the next morning, meeting the summit team as they ascended from Camp V to VI. As the night came on, however, the wind rose to a gale and it began snowing hard. Down at ABC, expedition leader Simonson was philosophical: "On the North Ridge, sometimes you have to push up in marginal conditions so you can be in position to take advantage of better weather later." That was the hope, at least.

"The next morning, I knew without even looking outside that we wouldn't be climbing that day," Hahn recalls. "The wind was just hammering us—35 miles per hour gusting to somewhere above 60—and the tent was making that incredible roaring noise fabric makes when it's beaten by gusts. It was a nasty day; clouds were funneling through the North Col below us and the wind was just screaming over the ridgeline. It would snow hard one minute and then there would be a sun break the next. I had a feeling that the worst of it might be yet to come."

The climbers remained in their tents and the day passed as a series of sleepless resting periods on oxygen alternating with oxygenless working periods of melting snow or cooking and talking. Separated by several dozen yards and the white noise of the wind, they could communicate with each other only by radio. It was even hard to talk inside the tents: "You know the weather's bad when you have to yell to the guy sitting 3 feet from you," Pollard explained by radio.[5]

As darkness fell once again, the wind rose even higher. Hahn and Politz spent the night sitting up with their backs against the windward wall of their tent trying to stabilize it, being pummeled continuously. On the second morning at Camp V the wind was, if anything, stronger—Politz estimated it at 80 miles per hour—and the summit bid was put off again. Down at the North Col, the Sherpa, having also spent a bad two nights, began talking about returning to ABC. Their Sirdar, Danuru "Dawa" Sherpa seemed unable to dissuade them. "Dawa has been a Sirdar for me several times," Simonson later explained. "I'm fond of him, he's incredibly strong, and the other Sherpa like him, but he can be a bit too democratic. There are times when I'd like him to be a stronger leader and decision maker." In the end, only Dawa and Ang Pasang remained on the col.

"Now," Hahn says, "we had to face two realities: we had far fewer Sherpa to carry supplies up to Camp VI, assuming the weather improved, and we would soon run out of food at Camp V." The team spent several hours discussing strategies and consulting with Simonson below at ABC. Hahn, the summit team leader, knew they would not have enough supplies now to permit the full complement of six climbers and two Sherpa to reach the summit. After several hours of conversation by radio, Andy Politz finally decided that he and Thom Pollard would carry to Camp VI, but not go higher. Instead, they would spend the balance of the day in the vicinity of Mallory's body searching with a metal detector for other artifacts—and perhaps the camera. In fact, the team had two high-altitude film cameramen—Hahn, under contract to the BBC, and Pollard, working for PBS/NOVA. Of the two, Hahn had by far the most experience at altitude. In the end, Hahn decided it was his responsibility to do the high-altitude filming and help the climbing effort, and he agreed to Politz's plan. "I know Thom was disappointed, and I think he may have been capable of summiting, but he accepted the decision with grace."

On the third night at Camp V, the wind finally began moderating and the morning of May 16 dawned clear and calm at last. At 8:00 A.M., the entire team set off for Camp VI, beneath the Northeast Ridge, following the same route they had taken at the start of the search climb.

After nearly six hours of steady slogging, the climbers, who now included Dawa and Ang Pasang, reached their Camp VI, about an hour below the base of the Yellow Band. While the climbing team and Sherpa worked to hack additional tent platforms out of the snow and ice, Andy Politz and Thom Pollard, who carried supplies up to support the climbing team, returned to the site of Mallory's body.

. In 1924, Mallory and Irvine had sent their support personnel down as well; their remaining four porters carried the now-famous notes for both Odell, who was one camp behind them, and Noel, who was down at Camp III on the East Rongbuk Glacier. Mallory had previously discussed with Captain Noel that he planned to climb directly to the Northeast Ridge (rather than following Norton and Somervell's slanting ascent), and now he told Noel to watch for them there early the next morning.[6]

Seventy-five years later, Simonson's team of summit climbers had a short night. After melting snow and cooking dinner, they settled in for a brief rest, stirring themselves again at midnight to prepare for the final summit push at 2:00 A.M. It was Hahn's opinion that they could leave no earlier, because they needed daylight to film their efforts to negotiate the technically difficult climbs atop the Northeast Ridge, and no later and still be assured of returning before darkness once again descended. "To put it simply," Hahn explains, "it's a whole lot better to be going up in the dark when you're strong than coming down in it when you're exhausted."

Mallory, too, had signaled that he planned an early start in his note to Noel the previous day, but the concept of nighttime departures is a practice that became common on Everest only in the mid-1980s. It seems clear that Mallory and Irvine did not leave until first light; they had left their lever torches and magnesium flares behind at Camp VI and would have had no way of finding the route in the dark.[7]

As Simonson's climbers readied themselves for their own departure, it was with the knowledge that they had more to do than make a sprint for the summit. The team had two essential research tasks to complete to further resolve the Mallory and Irvine mystery. The first was to locate an old oxygen bottle that Eric Simonson remembered having seen during a 1991 climb he had led. Simonson had a mental image of at least one oxygen bottle tucked beneath a boulder somewhere below the First Step that he thought might have been old enough to have been used by one of the prewar British expeditions. Finding it and determining whether it was indeed from 1924 could help define how far Mallory and Irvine had traveled on their summit day and how fast they were moving, since the 1924 bottles were known to last no more than four hours at maximum flow (2.2 liters per minute).

The second task was even more critical, and it had been on rock climber Conrad Anker's mind ever since he had reached the mountain. The Second Step, a roughly 100-foot barrier to the summit that an earlier expedition had described as like "the sharp bow of a battle cruiser," has a vertical headwall at its upper reaches that climbers have surmounted by means of a rickety 15-foot aluminum ladder ever since it was installed by the Chinese in 1975. In the absence of a ladder, using only the hand- and footholds the rock had to offer, would the Second Step have been climbable by Mallory and Irvine in 1924? If it was, how difficult was the climb and how quickly could it be done? Could it be scaled by an accomplished climber "with considerable alacrity," the words Odell used to describe the movements of Mallory and Irvine when he last saw them on the afternoon of June 8, 1924? It was Anker's job to find out; he would attempt to free-climb the Second Step without the assistance of either the ladder or the kind of mechanical aids climbers use today. If it was, and if there was sufficient time left in the day, the climbers would continue to the summit itself.

Climbing through the dark from Camp VI, the first challenge that faced the team was finding a gully that rises up through the Yellow Band toward the ridge. "The entrance to the gully is by no means obvious in the dark, even for someone who's been there before," Hahn explains. Locating it by headlamp at about 3:00 A.M., the team readied itself for the first major technical climb of the ascent. Conrad Anker immediately took the lead, climbing up through the gully and installing new fixed rope for the others to clip in to. Progress was slow, however, both because new snow had fallen and because for safety the team didn't want more than one person on the rope at a time.

At 4:30 A.M., about halfway up through the Yellow Band, the team stopped for a break at a small terrace and noticed a piece of metal and some fabric protruding from the snow. Later, on their descent, Norton and Richards explored the site further, discovering a wooden tent pole and length of rope, a pack frame, a piece of old brown sleeping bag, and tent fabric. When expedition historian Jochen Hemmleb heard this inventory later, he smiled and told them, "This is exactly the same list of items the Chinese reported finding in 1960; it is the remains of the unsuccessful 1933 British expedition's highest camp." (See "The Rope and Tent Pole Mystery" and "The 'Mystery Tent'—A Camp Too High" in Appendix 1.)

Resuming their climb, the team angled to the right and followed one of several slanting branch gullies, reaching the top of the Northeast Ridge at 6:00 A.M. But as the sky brightened, the mood darkened; it had been intensely cold through the early morning hours and now the climbers could see a thick layer of cloud approaching from the southwest. In addition, a lens-shaped (lenticular) cloud seemed to be forming above the summit—almost always a sign of worsening weather. "There were clouds below and above us and the lenticular told us what the weather was likely to be a couple of hours later on—and we were guessing it wasn't going to be very nice," Hahn remembers. The situation was, in fact, ambiguous; when a cloud forms above the summit, it is a more serious warning than if the cloud forms on the lee, or eastern side of the mountain. The latter is an effect of the compression and subsequent expansion of the air streaming past the ridge, which fosters condensation and cloud formation, but does not necessarily signal a storm.

The climbers discussed the situation for a while and decided to go ahead at least as far as the First Step. "Between the top of the gully and the face of the step there would be time to watch the weather, and we wouldn't be making an irreversible commitment by continuing that far, so that's what we decided to do," says Hahn. They radioed their plan to ABC and Simonson agreed, partly because he already had decided this would be the last climb to altitude; it was, he believed, time to draw the expedition to a close. His climbers had been too high for too long and, with the discovery of Mallory, at too great an intensity to continue for much longer.

The climbers set off along the ridge toward the First Step. It was a deceptively easy-looking walk. A smooth snowfield stretched out to the left, a perfect route except for the fact that it actually was a thin, wind-carved cornice overhanging the infamous Kangshung or East Face of the mountain; one step too far to the left and it was a 10,000-foot drop to forever. A bit farther ahead, Simonson's team traversed to the right, away from the ridge crest across a fairly steep section of the North Face to the base of the First Step. Anker led the ascent, climbing first up a gully, then following a crack off to the right to the top of the wall. He installed new fixed rope as he climbed and, as before in the Yellow Band, the rest of the climbers bunched up at the bottom, each waiting his turn. The climbers judged the route to be relatively easy but with a high degree of exposure: "You don't want to spend much time looking over your shoulder there," Hahn jokes.

It is not at all certain that Mallory and Irvine would have taken this traverse. Mallory was known to prefer ascending by ridge crests. "He could have reached and surmounted the First Step by sticking to the ridge crest," Hahn reports, "but it would have been more time-consuming; there are a lot of landscape features there they would have had to climb around or over along that route. But it is definitely doable." In fact, Mallory could well have led up the ridge crest initially, but the most obvious thing to do at that point is to pick up the extreme left end of the ledge beneath the final tower of the First Step and follow it around to the right, thus joining the route Anker had led.

Could the time it took to surmount the First Step by the ridge route have accounted for the lateness of the hour when Odell saw Mallory and Irvine at 12:50 P.M.? Were they climbing the First Step when Odell saw them "going strong for the top," as he later wrote? Hemmleb and Andy Politz are convinced they were not: "The view of them that Odell describes is simply not the view you would have seen had they been ascending the First Step by the ridge. Odell describes them as 'silhouetted on a small snow-crest beneath the rock-step.' No snow crest exists in that position. Then he says they emerged at the top, but that's not the case either. You emerge, if that is even the proper term, on the ledge that leads away to the right. Then, in the account he wrote many months later, he changed the words 'snow-crest' to 'snow slope.' But photographs taken in 1924 show there was only a tiny patch of snow beneath the step that no one would describe as either a 'crest' or a 'slope.' Odell could not have seen them on the First Step."

As they cleared the First Step, the sun hit Simonson's climbers and they became more optimistic about conditions. The wind was still calm, the cloud cover was decreasing, and the lenticular cap above the summit had grown smaller. "It wasn't so good that it was a full-on green light," recalls Hahn. "It was more a case of 'Can we get away with this? Yeah, I think we can.' So we kept going."

The ridge line between the First and Second Step is, in the vocabulary of climbers, "pretty sporty"—which is to say terrifying, especially when the wind is screaming past. The ridge narrows to an uneven series of rocks and snow crests that form a fin only wide enough for one foot at a time. "I'd gone that way once before and wasn't sorry to be missing it this time," says Hahn. There was an alternate route. The vertical ridge wall drops down to the right from the knife-edge and then shallows out slightly, creating a traverse line that is somewhat safer than the crest.

But this route, too, has its "sporty" moments. In one spot in particular, the climbers had to make a tricky blind move around a bulge in the rock face. As Hahn explains, "You have to swing around basically on the hope that there's going to be something on the other side to step or hold on to." Earlier expeditions had left some fixed rope through these spots, but the rope was ancient, its sheath completely worn away in places. Nevertheless, each climber clipped the carabiner that was attached to his waist harness on to this rope, in the process breaking every rule they had ever been taught about using old rope. "You clip in anyway because it's better to clip in than not clip in," explains Hahn, "but it's a huge leap of faith to believe it would ever hold you if you fell."

No one had to test the strength of the rope; the team cleared the traverse uneventfully. Ahead, Anker had already arrived at a formation called the "Mushroom Rock," the site of a no-longer-used Camp VII.[8] "You've been crawling across the side of this mountain along rock that's slanted at the weirdest angles," Hahn explains, "and then there's this sort of patio of snow about 8 feet by 12 feet in the middle of all this geological craziness, backed by a bizarre rock shaped like a mushroom. It's strange, but welcome." Here the climbers and Sherpa regrouped. The sun was shining and it was warm enough to rest, have something to eat and drink, even remove their gloves. But it was also 10:00 A.M. and they had yet to scale the daunting Second Step, now straight ahead.

In 1996, eight climbers lost their lives on Everest in part because they reached the summit far too late in the day to be able to return safely. "Turn-around time"—that moment when an Everest climber must turn around and descend, whether the summit has been reached or not—has been a controversial issue ever since. Now, on the snow platform beneath Mushroom Rock, the climbers and Sherpa discussed their situation. Looking out across the torn clouds racing above the serrated landscape that surrounded them, it was clear that the weather, while currently pleasant, was by no means settled. The Kangshung Face was shrouded in cloud and neither Lhotse nor Makalu, the nearest peaks, was visible. Ahead of the climbers lay the most intimidating section of the entire summit route: another traverse to the right on to the North Face of the mountain over rough ledges of brittle, downsloping shale with yawning exposure to a drop of several thousand feet, and finally the barrier of the Second Step itself. A check of their oxygen supply made it clear that, at the rate the team was climbing, they would run out of oxygen at some point during their descent if they climbed higher.

Making their own personal calculations of risk and reward, and concluding that "the vibes just didn't feel right," Richards and Norton each decided that, for them at least, it was time to turn around. "The toughest part of making that decision was the fact that I felt strong. I think Jake also felt strong," Richards recalls. "It wasn't like some other days, when you just feel like hell and turning around is simply in your best interest. My mind was all over the place on that day; I couldn't help but think about the bodies we had seen in the basin below a couple of weeks earlier. At the age of twenty-five, I was pretty sure I hadn't done everything in life that I wanted."

It was a remarkably level-headed decision for two young climbers who might easily have been swept up by "summit fever" at this point. They radioed their decision to ABC and

Simonson told them what he had learned himself over the years: "You guys are young; you'll get another chance." Reflecting on their call later, Simonson would explain, "When you're a young climber who never thought he'd ever get to the Himalaya, being so close to the summit of Everest and having to turn around is really wrenching; you keep thinking it's your only chance. It took me several tries to make it, and each time it gets harder to turn around even though your rational mind tells you that you should." It was the kind of situation that George Mallory, who had been rebuffed by the mountain repeatedly, would have understood completely.

Down at Camp V, however, Andy Politz received this news with dismay. He had given up his place on the summit team to give the chance to the younger climbers, even though he had the strength to summit, knew the route, and could have provided backup camera work and a critical belay for Anker while Hahn filmed.

With Richards and Norton watching from the platform at Camp VII, Hahn and Anker set off again, followed by Dawa and Ang Pasang. "You could tell that even though both Sherpa were highly experienced climbers, they were intimidated by this traverse," says Hahn. The route crosses a series of broken, gravel-strewn slabs for about 300 feet (90 m) that tilt downward at an angle in excess of 35 degrees, ending in a short cliff that would launch a slipping climber down the entire North Face of the mountain. "It is really hairy, the rope is lousy, you're walking on the points of your crampons, and the drop-off below you actually steepens the farther down you look. It's a very scary spot."

Almost immediately, Ang Pasang stopped and called out that

he too was turning around. Dawa continued behind Hahn across the traverse to the bottom of the Second Step, then radioed the message to ABC that he too had decided he didn't want to go any farther.

Both Dawa and Ang Pasang had summited Everest before, but by the southern approach through Nepal pioneered by the successful 1953 British expedition that put Edmund Hillary and Tenzing Norgay on the summit—the route the vast majority of expeditions have taken over the years, including the ill-fated commercial expeditions of 1996. As Hahn explains, "I could tell they were worried about the time and, given what they knew from their own experience, it made sense. Ten o'clock is late to be so far from the summit if you're on the south side. There's no good reason to still be so low if you're on that route and, therefore, every reason to turn around. But from my point of view, the north side is different; the early part of the climb is difficult and time-consuming, and I knew the worst was almost behind us. We would almost certainly be descending in the dark, but I'd done that the last time I'd summited from the north, and I knew it would be okay."

Still, the climbers should have been higher. They had left Camp VI late, in part to be able to film the climb to the Northeast Ridge. And they had spent a great deal of time debating the weather and whether to continue. There was no question that they were pushing beyond a prudent safety margin.

With Richards, Norton, Dawa, and Ang Pasang watching before they began their descent, Hahn and Anker approached the Second Step. To complicate matters, now, as they approached the crux of the climb, Hahn's BBC video camera seized up. The camera had been a bone of contention between Hahn and the BBC producer from the start. Rented by the BBC at the last minute, untested in the conditions at which it would have to perform, delivered to Hahn without even a case, Hahn had been skeptical of its utility all along. Now his worst fears were being realized, and he was furious. "Here we were on this spectacular pitch, with Conrad ready to start up the [Second] Step and address one of the main questions of the Mallory mystery, and the damn camera didn't work!" After fiddling with it for awhile, Hahn realized he had better pay attention to his footing or they would be without a cameraman as well as a camera.

The Second Step—a 100-foot- (30-m-) thick band of dark limestone harder than the layers above and below it—is actually composed of three distinct pitches, only one of which is actually a vertical wall. Immediately above the base of the step, Hahn, who now led, had to climb up a narrow groove between the cliff face and a huge boulder and then step out, unprotected, on to the top of the boulder, with the entire North Face of Everest dropping away beneath him. With typical understatement, Hahn says, "It's kind of a committing move. It's a secure platform and not that difficult to get to, but in terms of exposure it's really out there."

From here Hahn led again, climbing a short, steep, cone-shaped snow slope to the foot of the vertical headwall near the top of the step. Anker followed while Hahn, having gotten the camera working again, filmed him coming up the slope. Ideally, someone else would have done the work of breaking trail through the snow so that Hahn could focus his attention, and his camera, on Anker alone. But they no longer had this luxury.

At last Anker was face to face with the technical climb he'd been itching to do ever since they'd arrived. While Hahn anchored himself to the old ladder from the 1975 Chinese expedition and tinkered with the balky camera, Anker scanned the headwall for ascent routes. Two were immediately apparent. To the right of the ladder, in the sun, was a right-slanting crack that looked like the preferred route, but after only a few feet, he abandoned it. "The rock was really loose and rotten, with bad fall potential," he reported.[9] Hahn had checked the same route on a previous climb, and had also found the rock crumbly. Repeatedly frozen and thawed, the rock was simply breaking up.

Immediately, Anker turned his attention to the second route, an off-width crack (one too wide for a fist and too narrow for a body) that lay in permanent shadow just to the left of the ladder. Before Hahn was even able to unclip from the ladder, turn 180 degrees, reclip to the ladder, and ready the camera, Anker was already near the top of the off-width crack. He had jammed his elbow and shoulder into the crack in an arm lock, and a foot and leg into it below, and had lifted himself up through the crack quickly and efficiently. Hahn was amazed; he hadn't even had time to arrange a belay (and, of course, had no one to do the belaying for him) before Anker's head was even with the top of the ladder. At the top of the crack, Anker needed to move to the right, around an overhang. There was a perfectly positioned narrow edge to make this move possible, but one of the ladder rungs was in the way. Anker later described the move: "I was able to knee-bar to the top . . . and got a size three Friend [a metal, spring-loaded cam device] at the top of it, and then got a hand jam into the crack I got the [cam] in, and then

I had to step out."[10] Reaching to the right and getting a firm handhold on the rock face, he pulled across, placing his foot on the rung where the edge was, and in only a few moments was at the top of the Second Step.

Although Anker had placed protection (rope anchoring devices) in two places near the top of the step, it was clear to both him and Hahn that they were superfluous, a matter of good practice rather than necessity. He hadn't used them to climb. What is more, the only reason Anker stepped on the ladder rung was because it was in the way of a perfectly good foothold that would have served the same purpose as he crossed the face to the right. "The ladder was more of a hindrance than a help," Hahn commented. Could Mallory have scaled the headwall? Says Anker, "That one crack is the only one that isn't rotten . . . he probably would have just knee-barred up that off-width and then just pulled over. It's not that long, but it certainly winds you."[11] Anker had climbed the headwall without oxygen.

Hahn agrees: "There is no question in my mind that an accomplished climber could have climbed that headwall with no aids, and we know Mallory was an accomplished climber." Still, he has some reservations: "I think it might have been at the limit of what he could have done, but it was certainly within his limit. The last part of the step is not that big; it's doable. But what I wonder about is the combination of factors. The headwall is at the top of a steep snow pitch that is not insignificant. The snow slope is at the top of the lower part of the step, the climbing of which is not insignificant, and the entire step is at the top of that exposed traverse from the old Camp VII, which is also not insignificant. Each of these things is doable, but could they have done it all? In 1924, when the route was unknown? I don't know."

Jochen Hemmleb takes a more coolly analytic approach to the question. The salient question, he believes, is not whether Mallory and Irvine were sufficiently skilled to surmount the step—Mallory, at least, certainly was, and just as certainly could have belayed Irvine up as well—but whether the geography of the Second Step fits with the details of the landscape Odell described when he says he saw the two climbers.

"The topography of the Second Step certainly fits Odell's description better than that of the First Step," Hemmleb says, "but the snow patch on the Second Step's face is only a couple of square meters and, due to its northern exposure, is in the shadows most of the day. It's not an easy place to spot two ascending climbers. Although Conrad's ascent proved that the headwall itself could be climbed with what Odell would have called 'considerable alacrity,' Mallory and Irvine wouldn't have emerged on the top of the step, as Odell suggests, but somewhere to the right of the top of the step, along the crest of the cliff. So the question is, is the Second Step really the spot that most closely resembles what Odell saw?" Hemmleb would soon learn that another alternative was possible.

If, like Anker and Hahn, Mallory and Irvine had been able to surmount the Second Step, would they then, given the late hour, have turned around? Mallory had, in the past, been capable of turning around when it was clear that it was foolhardy to continue, but he was also an impetuous climber and one clearly obsessed by this particular summit. In relating the story of his own climb on this day, Dave Hahn says something revealing: "I have a reputation as a cautious leader;

I've turned around on many, many climbs; but on that day, I too was impetuous. I was really focused on the summit and I didn't see anything from the Second Step onward that was going to get in the way of my going." Is there any reason to believe that George Mallory, on his fourth attempt in three years, and almost certainly the last opportunity of his life, would have responded any differently? The difficult technical climbing seemed clearly behind them. Ahead was a snow slope to the summit and some fairly benign features to surmount or circumvent. Then, the summit at last. In the end, it comes down to character. Said Geoffrey Winthrop Young, Mallory's longtime friend, climbing partner, and mentor, " . . . after nearly twenty years' knowledge of Mallory as a mountaineer, I can say . . . that difficult as it would have been for any mountaineer to turn back with the only difficulty passed—to Mallory it would have been an impossibility."[12]

So far as Young was concerned, there was no question: Mallory would have pressed ahead simply " . . . because Mallory was Mallory."[13]

At the time, Odell estimated that Mallory and Irvine were three hours from the summit when he saw them. Hahn's estimate was that he and Anker were two hours from the top, with "no serious obstacles ahead of us." Later he would add ruefully, "I made the same mistake in '94." In fact, Anker and Hahn were four difficult hours from the summit. Innocent enough at the time, it would prove a dangerous misjudgment. In the case of Mallory and Irvine, it may well have been the fatal misjudgment.

After a quick drink, a bite to eat, and a call to Simonson to let him know they'd cleared the Second Step, the two turned uphill again. Says Hahn, "The climb from the Second Step to the base of the Third Step is about the only place all day where you don't have to worry about falling off."

The climbers picked their way across a vast, boulder-strewn plateau, a landscape of stark black rocks and white snow patches. Above them, the clouds were lowering and the atmosphere began to get misty. "It was obvious that it was likely to snow or that we'd be enveloped in clouds," Hahn recalls, "but there was no wind to speak of and the sun was still bouncing around within these clouds and heating us up."

Soon the climbers were ascending a snow slope to the foot of yet another barrier, the broken bastion of rock at 28,550 feet (8,700 m) that has come to be called the Third Step.[14] Of this Third Step, Hahn says: "It has none of that airy, exposed feeling that the others do; it's more a scramble than a technical climb." It took less than fifteen minutes for the climbers to clear the Third Step.

Far below, on the moraine of the East Rongbuk Glacier above Advance Base Camp, Jochen Hemmleb was watching Anker and Hahn through a 600 mm camera lens, and was amazed by what he saw: "It was a step-by-step 'instant replay' of what Odell had reported as his last view of Mallory and Irvine: 'One tiny black spot silhouetted on a small snow-crest beneath a rock-step in the ridge; the black spot moved. Another black spot became apparent and moved up the snow to join the other on the crest. The first then approached the great rock-step and shortly emerged at the top; the second did likewise.' I was watching from almost exactly the same angle Odell had, though farther below. It was only after I'd snapped on a doubling lens and could see the color of their down suits that I could be sure

I hadn't simply stepped back in time seventy-five years! Now it seemed possible, perhaps even likely, that Odell had seen Mallory and Irvine at the Third Step, not the Second."

High above, Anker and Hahn headed for the summit. Snow began falling and quickly became heavy. Visibility dropped to about 100 feet. When they reached the Summit Snowfield, their progress slowed to a crawl. "We found ourselves knee-deep in unconsolidated snow and on an incline that began at about 45 degrees and then steepened to perhaps 55 degrees near the top," says Hahn. "What rope there was, left behind by other climbers, was buried deep in the snow." Anker took the lead, plodding up the steepening slope and yanking the rope out of the snow as he went—hard work under normal conditions, but grueling at nearly 29,000 feet. Fearing the possibility of an avalanche, Anker told Hahn to wait at the bottom so they wouldn't both be on the snowfield and the same rope at once.

"It was the right thing to do, but it was also very frustrating," Hahn recalls. "Conrad was up there doing all the work while I had to wait below. It was snowing like crazy and it was also taking a lot of time to make any progress."

For Anker, it was also unnerving. The snowfield is actually the very top of the Great Couloir, the massive gash in the North Face that drops all the way to the Central Rongbuk Glacier thousands of feet below. "It was clear that Conrad was uncomfortable up there. I got on the radio and told him that it had taken me a long time to come to terms with the same conditions here during my last climb to the summit. We also talked with Eric [Simonson] and Russell Brice down at ABC about ways of getting around the snowfield, and finally concluded that Conrad should cut to the right toward the North Face onto the rounded crest of the North Pillar, rather than climb to the tip of the snowfield." Soon the snow got harder and Anker was traversing to the right on his way around the Summit Tower, then up a steep ramp leading back up to the summit ridge. All Hahn had to do was follow him.

But Hahn was in trouble. Throughout the day he had not felt up to par. "I hadn't gotten enough rest at Base Camp before we left for our summit attempt and, of course, we spent most of the night we arrived at Advance Base [Camp] dealing with the Ukrainian rescue. That took a lot out of me, and I could tell that I wasn't at full strength." Far below, at ABC, Simonson was getting increasingly anxious. In contact with Anker by radio, they waited for news of Hahn's arrival. Ten minutes passed, then twenty, then a half hour. Had the snow slope avalanched, taking Hahn with it?

In fact, Hahn had cleared the snowfield, picked his way up a series of uneven, downsloping ledges beneath the Summit Tower, and gotten his crampons tangled in some old rope. Finally untangling himself, he labored along the 35-degree, badly exposed pitch to the ramp and slowly made his way up to the ridge and into sight. Anker radioed ABC: "Dave is about 25 yards away, catching up." Simonson relaxed and encouraged Anker to continue on to the summit, but Anker waited for his partner, saying "I wouldn't be on this mountain without Dave; we'll do this together."

By the time he reached Anker, Hahn was panting furiously. After a short rest, they turned and began climbing up the final crest. But after only a few steps up the ridge, Hahn was winded again. He stopped, tore off his oxygen mask, and asked Anker to check his regulator. Anker did . . . and discovered that

Hahn's oxygen bottle was empty. "This was sort of good news and bad news," Hahn says wryly. "The good news was that it helped explain why I had been climbing so slowly and breathing so hard—through a mask with no oxygen flowing. The bad news was I now had to complete the summit and descend without oxygen, and all I could think was, 'Oh boy, my problem list just got a lot longer'.

"I changed over to a full bottle at the foot of the Second Step, did a calculation, and decided to set it on full flow, estimating it would last me to the top," Hahn explains. "But when the climb up the summit pyramid took longer than I'd thought it would, I forgot to recalculate the oxygen and turn down the flow." Hahn is a professional; he should have been monitoring his oxygen periodically; that he didn't was only further evidence to him that he wasn't at his best that day. (It would later transpire that, due to a heretofore undiscovered intolerance to glutens, Dave Hahn was severely anemic throughout the expedition as well.)

Now, Anker and Hahn were only 300 feet (100 m) horizontally from the summit. Anker left his pack and oxygen at the spot where he had waited for Hahn, and the two of them started for the summit crest. Tired now, and climbing without oxygen, it took them three-quarters of an hour to cover that distance-taking a step, stopping to pant, then taking another. Finally, at 2:50 P.M., Anker's exuberant "Yeeeoooww!" came through the radio at ABC, signaling they could climb no higher. They had reached the top of the world. ABC rang with cheers of relief, but Simonson was worried about the exhausted sound of Hahn's voice and reminded the climbers that they had no time to sightsee. Shrouded in cloud anyway and with no view to

The 1999 Mallory & Irvine Research Expedition: (standing, from left) Lee Meyers, Conrad Anker, Andy Politz, Dave Hahn, Thom Pollard, Jake Norton, Tap Richards, Eric Simonson; (kneeling, front) Jochen Hemmleb

Graham Hoyland

Larry Johnson

The Sherpa team

'The trough' on the East Rongbuk Glacier, above Camp II

Rongbuk Base Camp, 1999

Puja ceremony at Base Camp

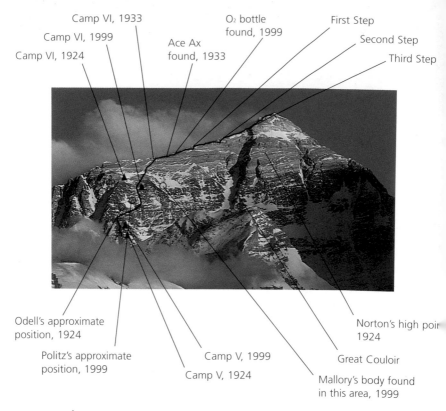

Camp VI, 1933

Camp VI, 1999

Camp VI, 1924

Ace Ax found, 1933

O₂ bottle found, 1999

First Step

Second Step

Third Step

Odell's approximate position, 1924

Politz's approximate position, 1999

Camp V, 1999

Camp V, 1924

Norton's high poir 1924

Great Couloir

Mallory's body found in this area, 1999

Above: 1999 summit route with critical features and sites

Below: Dave Hahn approaching the summit of Everest, May 17, 1999

Fallen Hero – George Mallory and the summit of Everest

Altimeter; matchbox and tin of meat lozenges;
Mallory's wristwatch; letter's and handkerchief, in
which they were wrapped; notes found in Mallory's
pocket; spare left glove and a section of climbing
rope; Mallory's pocketknife; Mallory's goggles

distract them, the two wasted little time. Hahn did some filming, took a few still photographs, and within five minutes, knowing full well that darkness would fall before they could return to the safety of Camp VI, they began descending.

Earlier that afternoon, as ABC monitored the descent of Richards and Norton from the First Step, Hemmleb was thinking about how tired and disappointed the two must be after failing to summit, when he overheard Simonson asking them to search the area for the old oxygen bottle he had seen in 1991. He was especially gratified when, despite the lateness of the day and the poor visibility, they obeyed. "When I thought about it later," Richards recalls, "it was pretty funny. Here was Eric describing a boulder he remembered as a landmark for the old bottle. It was snowing hard, the visibility was bad, and we were supposed to find this one particular boulder on a piece of real estate that is strewn with hundreds of similar-looking rocks. Yet not three minutes later, Jake and I were standing at a big brown boulder with an oxygen bottle wedged beneath it."

Hemmleb had already concluded that the most likely scenario was that the bottle Simonson remembered was either from the 1924 British expedition or the 1960 Chinese expedition. When, after a half hour of searching, Richards radioed ABC with the message, "I've found an old bottle that looks like the Chinese one from 1975, but without the blue paint," Hemmleb figured that clinched it.

Thus, he was totally unprepared when, the next day when the two arrived at ABC, Richards told Hemmleb he'd brought him "an interesting souvenir." He reached into his pack and pulled out an old, rusty, cigar-shaped cylinder. It took Hemmleb only seconds to recognize it: "It's a '24 bottle! You've found a '24 bottle!" Flabbergasted, eyes wide in disbelief, he held a piece of history in his hands, one that told him, more than any of their other finds so far, that Mallory and Irvine had actually been up there, climbing along that final ridge "going strong for the top," just as Odell had said. Another piece of the puzzle fell into place.

Back on the mountain, as Hahn and Anker descended from Everest's summit, Hahn knew he was struggling, and wrestled internally with the implications of his weakened condition. Anker, who clearly was the stronger of the two at this point, had selflessly given Hahn his own bottle of carefully husbanded oxygen as they moved downhill toward the Third and Second Steps. "I was at least as worried that I was creating a burden for Conrad and causing anxiety down at ABC as I was about my own situation. I knew the others were afraid for me. But I had been here before and knew I wasn't going to just sit down and die. What's more, Conrad and I had climbed together in Antarctica, and I knew that he knew I would keep going."

With the consequences of the Ukrainian team members having gotten separated from one another still fresh in his mind, Anker took pains to keep Hahn in sight and to wait for him to catch up from time to time. For his part, Hahn was immensely grateful: "I mean, think about it; here's Conrad, who's not using oxygen now and night is coming. With his great strength and climbing ability, he could have flown down that ridge. But he didn't."

Stumbling through the continuing snowfall and breathing hard, Hahn kept reassuring Anker that he was all right. True to his word, despite his slow pace, Hahn made it safely down to the Second Step, where Anker was working out their descent.

"There was one good length of rope there, and we decided that the most efficient descent of the Second Step would be to anchor the rope and then rappel down, rather than climb down the route we had ascended. The only question was whether the rope would reach all the way to the bottom."

It did. Even so, Hahn got his leg caught in a loop of old rope and the farther down he rappelled, the more he tipped upside down. "It's not like you're rock climbing in shorts and a tee shirt; with your pack on and your down suit and oxygen mask, you can't twist around and see what's going on." Ripping off his oxygen mask and holding himself in mid-rappel, Hahn finally untangled his boot and continued down to the base of the step where Anker waited. Anker fixed a rope to make their trip across the crazily tilted traverse below the step a little safer, and they moved quickly toward the old Camp VII platform.

Here, Hahn picked up the partial bottle of oxygen he'd left behind earlier and plugged into it. Anker continued the descent without oxygen. "Conrad was much stronger than me that day, but because technical rock climbing is his specialty, he was also much more comfortable on that terrain than I was. He would have been ahead of me even if I had been feeling at my strongest," Hahn admits.

Soon they were at the First Step. They rappelled down to the ridge and pressed on in gradually failing light. Anker called Simonson and suggested he ask Richards and Norton, who were resting at Camp VI, to come back up to help them through the Yellow Band in the darkness. "At that point I didn't think we needed to be 'rescued,' and I certainly didn't want to be," Hahn remembers, "but I could understand why Eric felt it was appropriate to send them, just in case. It was prudent and right, but I'm terribly sorry to have had to put the guys through that." Later, in the dark, the four would meet partway down the Yellow Band and, after seventeen hours of climbing, descend to Camp VI and safety.

The gullies leading down from the Northeast Ridge through the Yellow Band toward Camp VI are notoriously difficult to find on the descent, especially in the dark. Many expeditions have turned tragic at this point. On the right is the fatally attractive snow crest that overhangs the vertiginous Kangshung Face. A few hours before, when Norton and Richards passed this section, they had noticed a fresh hole in the cornice, "just the shape of a man with a rucksack on." It was all too easy to imagine the missing Ukrainian climber, coming down through the rocks in driving snow, exhausted and disoriented, wandering out on to the cornice and breaking through. From the cornice, it was a vertical drop of 100 feet and a steep, 2-mile slide into oblivion. Recalls Jake Norton, who descended with Tap Richards in somewhat similar conditions, "Had I not seen that fresh hole, I could easily have taken exactly the same route with exactly the same result."

To the left is an only slightly less dangerous prospect, the uneven terrain above the North Face and, somewhere, the entrance to the gullies. Hahn and Anker had marked the location on their way up and, with Hahn's previous experience of finding the route down in the dark, soon found the gully they sought.

"As we started down, ever so carefully," Hahn says, "I kept thinking about George Mallory. I knew now he was down there below me in the dark, and what kept flashing through my mind was, 'Where can you fall here? How does it happen?'"

CHAPTER 8

NOTES ON AN ENVELOPE

. . . some day you will hear a different story . . .
GEORGE MALLORY

When unraveling mysteries, it is wise to remember something Arthur Conan Doyle's Sherlock Holmes once said: "When you have eliminated what cannot be, whatever remains, no matter how improbable, is what must be." In good mysteries, hard evidence is hard to come by. The question of what happened to George Mallory and Andrew Irvine is a very good mystery indeed.

For seventy-five years, the absence of conclusive evidence has made it difficult to explain the events of June 8, 1924. But that has not been the only cause of the difficulty. A second cause is the confusion sown in the weeks and months immediately following their disappearance. The mystery captured both the interest and the imagination of many, and fueled speculation among mountaineers and laypeople alike throughout Britain and, indeed, the rest of the world. Theories were propounded by those who knew them and those who did not, by those who knew Everest and the vast majority who did not. Psychics provided answers from "the other side."

One has to pity poor Noel Odell. On the one hand, he faced naysayers who seemed convinced from the start that the mountain was unconquerable. On the other, he faced the friends of Mallory who asserted that, "because Mallory was Mallory," he would have forged ahead to the summit no matter what. Given Mallory's drive, argued these friends, he would charge to the summit from the Second Step; he didn't, apparently, so Odell must have been wrong about seeing him at the Second Step. Given the unconquerable nature of the mountain, crowed the naysayers, Mallory and Irvine could not possibly have climbed the Second Step "with alacrity," so Odell must be wrong, once again. Little wonder that he gradually changed his story to suggest that perhaps they had been at the First Step, rather than the Second, when he saw them.

The third cause of confusion is somewhat more recent and comes from the climbing establishment itself. There is a pervasive attitude, a sort of contemporary condescension bordering on arrogance, that while today's climbers might reach the summit with relative ease, "those poor blighters never had a chance." Look at them, these climbers seem to say: they were ill equipped by today's standards, their oxygen apparatus was primitive and unreliable, their clothing was appallingly inadequate, they knew little about acclimatization and virtually nothing about the dangers of dehydration. They ate badly, drank little, and were lucky to have survived as long as they did. Among some of today's best-known Everest climbers, there is an explicit and remarkably illogical attitude of "We did it, but they couldn't have."

Why not? Ultimately, success on Everest has less to do with either technical skill or modern equipment than it does with sheer brute strength, guts, and, not incidently, good fortune with the weather gods. Certainly the climbers in the 1920s British expeditions were ill equipped and ill informed about the dangers of high altitude, but a close reading of both the text and the technical notes of the formal expedition reports from that period reveals that these men climbed with remarkable speed, skill, and ease despite often dreadful conditions. They pioneered routes, established camps at sites still used today, and equaled or beat climbing rates considered normal even now—often without supplemental oxygen.[1] Furthermore, the climbers of this era had walked to Everest almost all the way from Darjeeling, India, much of the way at elevations in excess of 13,000 feet. By the time they reached Rongbuk Base Camp, they were a trail-hardened bunch, toughened considerably more than those who take today's rather plush bus and jeep trip to Rongbuk Base Camp.

The historical record does not prove them to be naïve and bumbling amateurs, but tough, able, and exceptionally strong mountaineers who succeeded repeatedly and often brilliantly in uncharted terrain with none of the modern conveniences that today's climbers have come to take for granted.

Before the 1999 Mallory & Irvine Research Expedition was mounted, the salient question was: Is there any evidence to suggest that Mallory and Irvine reached the summit of Everest in 1924? And the answer was: No. What seems to have escaped the attention of many observers, however, was that there was another equally salient question with an equally unequivocal answer: Is there any evidence to suggest that Mallory and Irvine did not reach the summit of Everest in 1924? The answer here too was: No.

Is it possible now, with the evidence collected by the Mallory & Irvine Research Expedition, to shift the balance in this stalemate? Or, to put the question as Sherlock Holmes might have, is it possible to eliminate some of what cannot be, so we have a better idea of what must be? The answer is, yes—at least to an extent.

To understand what happened to Mallory and Irvine on June 8, 1924, we need to know more about the amount of oxygen they carried, about the physical topography of the Northeast Ridge from the point where Odell saw them, about departure times and climbing rates, and about daylight and nightfall.

The Mallory & Irvine Research Expedition collected new and in some cases startling evidence in each of these areas. Ironically, however, in the weeks following the discovery of Mallory's body, some of the apparently important clues collected by the expedition have proven unimportant, and items of no apparent value have proven critical.

Consider, for example, the wristwatch. On May 16, 1999, as the rest of their colleagues were preparing for the summit climb, Andy Politz and WGBH/NOVA's Thom Pollard returned to George Mallory's body for one last search for the missing camera, this time with a metal detector.

After relocating Mallory's body—no simple task after a light snowfall—Politz spent a moment on his knees, in prayer. "Even now, two weeks after we'd found him," he remembers, "it was still incredibly moving to be with him. It's hard to explain." Then, carefully, he and Pollard moved some of the rocks with which Mallory had been covered and set them aside, a task which reminded them again just how steep the slope was, as the rocks did not want to stay put.

To their surprise, the first sweep immediately set off the metal detector. The first few items were unimportant: a rivet in Mallory's leather motorcycle helmet, a couple of buckles. But then, in a previously unexplored pocket, they found a wristwatch. Its crystal was missing, as was the minute hand, though neither the hand nor broken glass were in the pocket.

There was nothing more to be found. There was no camera in the vicinity. Just before they recommitted Mallory, Thom Pollard carefully examined Mallory's face. It was the first time anyone had. There was whisker stubble on the chin. Mallory's eyes were closed. And there was one more thing: a desperately critical puncture trauma in his forehead, fragments of the skull protruding. They lay George Mallory gently down again and quietly re-covered him, repeated the committal service, and left him well concealed and, at last, in peace.

Later, back at Base Camp, the expedition members noted that there were two distinctive rust marks on the face of the wristwatch: one directly beneath the hour hand, the other (the expedition members decided later) where the minute hand had once been.[2] Now, they concluded, at least we know when the accident occurred: at either 1:25 P.M. or A.M. This was hard evidence at last.

But it was not. Three points of ambiguity emerged. The first and most obvious was that, since the crystal was not in Mallory's pocket, it was just as likely—perhaps more likely—that it had been broken or lost sometime before Mallory had fallen, not during the fall.[3] Second, weeks later, using magnification, a watch expert noted that the stump of the missing minute hand did not align with the rust stain. In fact it was pointed in precisely the opposite direction, to fifty-five minutes after the hour, suggesting that the rust stain had bled downward from the stem, rather than being formed underneath the minute hand. Third, subsequent Xrays of the watch movement revealed that the mainspring of the watch was largely, though not completely, unwound. Had the watch been stopped by an impact, its balance shaft would have been broken. But when the watch face was removed and the works examined, the watch was found to be in working order. The wristwatch, which had seemed to hold such promise, told the researchers little of value.

Other items, however, turned out to speak volumes.

On July 11, 1999, weeks after the research expedition members had returned home from Tibet, Jochen Hemmleb and Seattle-based archeologist Rick Reanier sat in a basement room in the Washington State Historical Society Research Center in Tacoma, Washington, where the artifacts found with Mallory had been archived temporarily. Among the items the research expedition had found were a number of perfectly preserved letters and a few scribbled notes. The letters were from Mallory's brother Trafford, sister Mary, and a friend, unknown to the climbers, named Stella.[4] The dates of the letters suggested that they were the most recent, and last, mail Mallory had received before embarking upon the final summit climb. At the time they were first found, the scribbled notes—apparently random lists of gear—seemed simply proof that the reportedly forgetful Mallory had a habit of stuffing his pockets full of superfluous bits of paper. The research expedition members were much more interested in the beautifully preserved letters and, not incidentally, on speculating about who the mysterious "Stella" might have been.

But now Hemmleb and Reanier made a startling discovery: the envelope containing the letter from Stella, addressed in ink, also had several cryptic pencil notations on the front: a column of numbers—100, 110, 110, 110, and 110—and, opposite them, No. 33, No. 35, No. 10, No. 9, and No. 15, respectively. The two men looked at each other and, almost simultaneously, realized what the numbers meant. The second column was a list of numbered oxygen cylinders; the first, the bottle pressure of each. It was an inventory list of some of the oxygen cylinders that Mallory and Irvine took with them on the summit climb, recorded on the envelope when Mallory had nothing else to write upon. Indeed, one of the bottles, No. 9, corresponded to the number painted on the 1924 bottle that Tap Richards found on the Northeast Ridge on May 17. It was a splendid irony; it wasn't the letter from the mysterious Stella that was important, it was the envelope!

A few days later, in the same basement room, Hemmleb and Reanier turned to the notes that had been in Mallory's pockets and quickly realized that they were not random bits of paper at all. They were detailed provision lists for Mallory and Irvine's summit climb. The lists, in Mallory's distinctive handwriting, included food, fuel, and supplies. That these notes were written at Camp IV as checklists of items to take to Camps V and VI is spelled out in the notes. In addition, the notes contain a reminder to take up a section of tent pole to replace the one Somervell had taken from Camp VI some days earlier to use in place of the ice ax he had dropped, something Mallory could

have learned no earlier than June 5. But all of this new information paled in comparison with one item on the list: the
inclusion of six spare oxygen cylinders—three pairs at 16
pounds each.

Hemmleb was stunned. No one had ever known before the
details of Mallory and Irvine's preparations for the final summit
climb. Now the stage was set anew. It now seemed clear that in
addition to the cylinders each of the climbers had in their
oxygen packs the morning they left Camp IV, there were six
others on the provisions inventory. That fact alone had the
potential for rewriting the entire story of Mallory and Irvine's
final day.

Hemmleb went back to the expedition record and reread
Edward Norton's account of the last days of the 1924 expedition. As Norton, the expedition leader, lay in his tent suffering
from the early symptoms of snow blindness following his own
unsuccessful summit attempt, Mallory sat with him and laid
out his plan for a final attempt: " . . . he explained that . . . he
was determined to make one more attempt, this time with
oxygen, and how he had been down to Camp III with Bruce
and collected sufficient porters to enable the attempt to be
staged."[5] But how many cylinders had they used to get to Camp
VI? How many would have been available for the final summit
attempt?

Hemmleb noticed that Norton's sentence was footnoted,
and looked at the bottom of the page. There was the answer:
"It may be asked how it came that sufficient porters were now
available for an attempt with oxygen, seeing that we had
decided against an oxygen attempt at Camp I on grounds of
inadequate transport [porters]. Mallory and Irvine *decided to use*

practically no oxygen up to Camp VI. . . . And, lastly, Camp VI having been established with tents and bedding by Somervell and me, *nearly every available porter could now be used for carrying oxygen cylinders."* (emphasis added)

With this new oxygen information and the additional findings of the 1999 Mallory & Irvine Research Expedition, the story of Mallory and Irvine's last days, like Odell's vision of them high on the mountain on June 8, 1924, began to clear.

Mallory is often characterized as hopelessly forgetful and occasionally impetuous. Both may well be accurate, but on June 6, 1924, as he and Andrew Irvine left Camp IV on the North Col and headed up the North Ridge toward Camp V, he was neither. He had planned the ascent in detail. He knew, for example, that Norton and Somervell had left most of their gear behind at the higher camps, and that meant he and Irvine would need to carry relatively little. He also had plenty of food to choose from. According to a note found with Mallory's body, Geoffrey Bruce had sent a number of provisions up from Camp III the day before Mallory and Irvine departed: two tins of Bully Beef (canned, pressed corned beef); two tins of Bovril (a dried bouillon/brewers' yeast blend, also available as a paste); one tin each of biscuits, beef tongue, and foie gras; and tins of both a petrol/oil mixture and solid fuel for the Unna cookers used at higher camps. In addition, Mallory's notes make clear that he and Irvine would take with them from Camp V to Camp VI a variety of high-energy foods (raisins, prunes, biscuits, chocolate, Kendall's mint cake—not a cake in the traditional sense, but a very sweet mint candy—butterscotch, and ginger nuts), as well as food for supper the night before their summit attempt and breakfast the next morning (tea, milk, macaroni, and sliced ham and tongue).

It is curious that, over the years, no one has wondered why Mallory and Irvine needed eight porters to accompany them to Camp V, when they began climbing on June 6, 1924. Their provision-carrying requirements were limited; their supplies could have fit easily into one, or perhaps two, backpacks. We now know the reason: they were carrying a lot of oxygen cylinders. Mallory and Irvine had brought oxygen cylinders and apparatus up from Camp III two days before they left Camp IV for the summit.[6] And from his note to Mallory, we now know that Geoffrey Bruce sent additional oxygen cylinders up from Camp III the following day. We can readily deduce that the cylinders Mallory and Irvine carried themselves were not from the stock of six Mallory listed in his provisions list because, again, they would not have needed eight porters to carry just two or three spares. Thus there were, at a minimum, six reserved cylinders.

Mallory, Irvine, and their eight porters did not make rapid progress from Camp IV to Camp V; they barely matched Norton and Somervell's climbing rate without oxygen a few days earlier.[7] Why were they climbing so slowly? With the boost they would have received from the oxygen they were using, they should have been moving faster.

The answer is obvious: they were moving slowly precisely because they were not climbing with the benefit of oxygen. They were carrying the cylinders and apparatus on their backs, but, just as Norton had stated in his footnote in the expedition report, they "had decided to use practically no oxygen up to Camp VI." Indeed, as the famous "last photograph" taken at the moment the two were about to leave Camp IV illustrates, there were two cylinders on Irvine's carrying frame, but apparently only one on Mallory's—clearly, he was serious about using very little oxygen to Camp VI. In the photograph, two other cylinders lie discarded in the snow behind Mallory— probably the half-spent cylinders they used to climb from Camp III to Camp IV.[8]

By 5:00 P.M., four of Mallory and Irvine's eight porters were back down at Camp IV bearing the note to Norton that there was, remarkably, no wind at Camp V and that "things look hopeful." The next morning Mallory, Irvine, and the remaining four porters pushed on to Camp VI.

Once they had reached Camp VI, Mallory sent the last four porters back down to Camp IV and gave them a note to give to Noel Odell (who was climbing a day behind them in support), whom they passed at Camp V. "In Mallory's note to Odell," Hemmleb points out, "we have the confirmation that they had indeed used very little oxygen on their two-day climb to Camp VI. Mallory reports that they had climbed 'to here on 90 atmospheres for the 2 days.' A full cylinder includes 120 atmospheres. Thus, they had used only three-quarters of a bottle each to reach Camp VI from Camp IV." Mallory's note actually tells us even more than this: it demonstrates that the two climbers climbed to Camp VI without using oxygen at all for part of the climb; had they been using oxygen continuously, even at the lowest flow rate possible, the bottles would have been empty long before they reached Camp VI. Put differently, at 1.5 liters per minute (the flow rate they used when they climbed up from Camp III to Camp IV a few days earlier), the 90 atmospheres they used to Camp VI would have lasted only four and a half hours. It had taken ten hours of climbing to reach Camp VI.

Once they had reached Camp VI, the critical question is, how many full or nearly full oxygen cylinders did Mallory and Irvine have left as they prepared for their summit bid? It now seems likely they left the North Col with a minimum of nine, although more are possible. They had used the better part of two on the way up; seven were left. It is possible that from Camp V to Camp VI both Mallory and Irvine carried two cylinders each and their four porters carried the remaining five; this would explain how Mallory knew, as he said in his note to Odell, that two cylinders in the carrying packs (the packs had a carrying capacity of three cylinders) were "a bloody load for climbing." (Actually, the total weight of the apparatus with three cylinders, as modified by Irvine, was twenty-seven or twenty-eight pounds, and eight pounds less with two cylinders.)[9]

Mallory's note to Odell also apologized for the fact that they had managed to let their Unna cooker (the solid-fuel stove) roll down the slope just before they left Camp V for Camp VI. Some analysts have pointed to this event as potentially disastrous for Mallory and Irvine. Without a stove to take to Camp VI, they would have been unable to melt snow for food and drink. Indeed, it would have been foolhardy to continue the ascent at all. Here again, however, only the opposite conclusion—that they had means to melt snow—is logical, and Odell himself proves this is the case. In his own recounting of the last climb, he writes that the loss of the stove " . . . was an occurrence which meant cold supper and breakfast for me!"[10] In saying so, Odell makes it clear that he had expected the stove to be waiting for him and, thus, had not carried one up for himself. Clearly it had never been planned that the Unna cooker would go up to Camp VI with Mallory and Irvine; that is why Mallory knew Odell would be annoyed and sent his note of apology. The reason Mallory had not been concerned for himself and Irvine was that there was already an Unna cooker at Camp VI, left behind by Norton and Somervell a few days earlier, along with the rest of their gear. All Mallory needed to do was to take up Meta (solid) fuel for it, which the notes found on his body indicate is exactly what he did.

Mallory had also sent a note from Camp VI to John Noel, the photographer, saying, "We'll probably start early to-morrow (8th) in order to have clear weather." But how early? Mallory was known to be "a habitual early riser";[11] on this day, "early" had to have meant no earlier than daybreak, as Mallory and Irvine had left behind most, if not all, of their lighting gear.[12] On June 8, 1924, at that altitude on the mountain, dawn broke just before 4:00 A.M. and the sun rose at 5:15 A.M.[13] Given Mallory's announced plan and natural inclination, there is every reason to believe the two could have begun their summit bid by 5:30 A.M., as Norton and Somervell would have done four days earlier, had they not been delayed by a spilled thermos bottle.

"A number of people in the past have argued that Mallory and Irvine made a later start than this," Hemmleb notes. "They point to the rather late hour at which Odell saw them on the summit ridge, and the fact that Odell found parts of the oxygen apparatus at Camp VI, as evidence that Mallory and Irvine were delayed by trouble with their oxygen sets." Once again, however, there is little to support this conclusion. When Odell arrived at the small two-man tent at Camp VI on the afternoon of June 8, he reported, " . . . within were a rather mixed assortment of spare clothes, scraps of food, their two sleeping bags, oxygen cylinders and parts of the apparatus; outside were more parts of the latter and of the duralumin carriers."[14] From this, Odell says, "it might be supposed that these were undoubted signs of reconstruction and probable difficulties with the oxygen outfit."[15] The former conclusion may well be valid; the latter almost certainly is not, as Odell himself explains: "Nothing would have amused [Irvine] more . . . than to have spent the previous evening on a job of work of some kind or other in connection with the oxygen apparatus, or to have invented some problem to be solved even if it never really had turned up . . . and here to 27,000 feet he had been faithful to himself and carried his usual traits. . . ."[16]

There is no evidence that the equipment was giving them difficulty. Indeed, the oxygen sets Mallory and Irvine were using had performed flawlessly ever since they had picked them up at Camp III, days earlier. Certainly Mallory, the inveterate note-writer, made no suggestion in his notes to either Odell or Noel that there was anything wrong with them.

At some point—perhaps at Camp IV, perhaps V, perhaps even VI—Mallory and Irvine tested the pressure of their unused oxygen bottles. We know this from the pencil notes on the envelope of the Stella letter. Five of them (Nos. 33, 35, 10, 9, and 5) had lost some pressure in the weeks between Calcutta, where they had been recharged, and Everest. It was important for Mallory and Irvine to determine what was in each bottle, since their lives might well end up depending upon a fairly precise knowledge of when any particular bottle would run out. These five were sufficiently below full capacity for Mallory and Irvine to note which held what quantity of oxygen.

The fact that the list on the Stella envelope identifies the pressure for only five cylinders raises a question: is it possible that Mallory and Irvine had only five cylinders when they left Camp IV? It is impossible. First, that would have left them with only three bottles altogether when they left Camp VI, in direct contradiction to Mallory's note to Odell saying he had at least four. Second, there would have been no need for eight porters if that had been the case.

Could this be all that the remaining four porters could carry from Camp V to Camp VI? Hardly; the average load for porters in the 1920s was only twenty pounds, but the four porters together would have had a carrying capacity of eighty pounds, enough to handle the forty-eight pounds that six oxygen cylinders weighed, with as much as thirty-two pounds left over for food for Mallory and Irvine—far more than they would have needed for one supper and a breakfast (tents, sleeping bags, and other gear were already at Camp VI).

Is it possible, then, that these are the only bottles Mallory and Irvine had left when they reached Camp VI? It would be, except for one critical fact: in his note from Camp VI to Odell down at Camp V, Mallory wrote, " . . . we'll probably go on two cylinders [to the summit]." Note that Mallory did not write, " . . . we'll have to go on two cylinders." By using the word "probably," Mallory signaled that he had a choice, and the only way he can have had a choice is if he had at least six full or nearly full cylinders in addition to the two they used on the way up. Mallory was a writer of significant talent; he used words with precision.

Odell's observations of the interior of the tent also provide some clues about how much oxygen Mallory and Irvine might have taken with them on summit day. He notes that there were oxygen cylinders inside, but doesn't say how many. We can be certain that there were at least two: the two nearly empty cylinders that Mallory and Irvine had used on their two-day ascent to Camp VI. Historian and climber Tom Holzel has suggested that Mallory and Irvine might have used oxygen during the night to help them rest and stay warm.[17] There is no evidence to support this conclusion, although it is possible that the apparatus parts Odell noticed in and around the tent at Camp VI reflect Irvine's having cobbled together a T-tube by which the two could share a cylinder for the night. If they did, they would first have finished the bottles they used to climb up to Camp VI and, perhaps, have emptied one more. Did Mallory and Irvine each use an additional new oxygen bottle during the night? This is even more unlikely, for two reasons. First, the small tent would have been extremely cramped if both climbers had oxygen bottles and regulators in the tent with them. Second, and more importantly, this would have left the climbers with only five full or nearly full bottles (unless they had left Camp IV with more than nine in the first place). With only five, we are squarely at odds, again, with Mallory's "probably." Only if Mallory and Irvine had a choice of going to the summit with either four or six cylinders does Mallory's "probably" make any sense.

Did they, perhaps, leave two full bottles behind in their tent in addition to the two nearly empty ones they had used coming up (and, possibly, one more that they had used at night) to use during their descent? Both seem unlikely, for two reasons. First, the cylinders themselves are not small. More than three of them, combined with the other gear Odell noted, would have packed the tiny tent tight, and he suggests no such thing. Indeed, he sheltered in the tent during the snow squall that blew up that afternoon. Second, none of the 1924 expedition members believed oxygen would be of value on the descent, so there would have been no reason to leave any behind. As Odell put it in the expedition report, " . . . descending [without oxygen] at high altitudes is little more fatiguing than at any other moderate altitudes. . . ."[18]

The principal reason that students of the Mallory and Irvine mystery have used to support the claim that they could not have succeeded in reaching the summit is that two cylinders would not have gotten them there. This is unquestionably true. But if we take Mallory at his word, he had the option to carry more. And, since he seems unlikely to have left his extra oxygen inventory behind, it is possible, perhaps even probable, that Mallory and Irvine were carrying a full load of three cylinders each when they left Camp VI on June 8, 1924—enough to last nearly twelve hours (some were at slightly less than full capacity) on full flow, and even longer on a lower flow. If this is true, it changes the picture of the next twenty-four hours dramatically, though unfortunately it does not change the eventual outcome.

What kind of progress did they make on that morning? In his note to photographer and cinematographer John Noel, Mallory wrote, "It won't be too early to start looking out for us either crossing the rock band under the pyramid or going up skyline at 8.0 P.M. [sic]." Odell and others have interpreted "crossing the rock band" as meaning surmounting the Second Step, high on the Northeast Ridge. When he saw them doing what he thought was just that, but at 12:50 P.M., Odell concluded that they were nearly five hours behind their schedule (which is also, no doubt, the genesis of his conclusion that they had started late due to oxygen apparatus problems).

But in fact there is nothing in Mallory's note to suggest that he meant to be at the Second Step at 8:00 A.M. What his note does suggest is that Mallory and Irvine were still uncertain as to whether they would choose Norton and Somervell's slanting ascent route through the Yellow Band, thus "crossing the rock band under the pyramid" as Norton had, or climb directly to the Northeast Ridge and follow its crest—"going up skyline." Moreover, given what he had learned both from his own climb to Camp VI and Norton and Somervell's summit attempt, Mallory would have had every reason to believe that they could achieve either one of these goals by 8:00 A.M.

And that appears to be almost exactly what he and Irvine did that morning: they climbed directly to the Northeast Ridge and were "going up skyline" only forty-five minutes to perhaps an hour later than they had estimated. We know this because of "No. 9," the spent 1924 oxygen bottle that Tap Richards retrieved from the Northeast Ridge. Mallory's notes show that No. 9 had 110 atmospheres of pressure, 10 atmospheres less than full capacity. At a flow rate of 2.2 liters per minute—the full flow rate—the bottle would have lasted three hours and forty minutes, twenty minutes less than a fully charged cylinder. If we accept that Mallory and Irvine did precisely what Mallory had said they would do—that is, make an early start sometime near sunrise, probably between 5:00 and 5:30 A.M.—oxygen cylinder No. 9 would have gotten him (or Irvine) to the crest of the ridge in the vicinity of 8:30 A.M. and some distance along its crest (where it was found) before the bottle ran out between 8:45 and 9:15 A.M.

Could cylinder No. 9 have been discarded not during their ascent but during their descent from the mountain? It is virtually impossible, for two reasons. First, under any plausible scenario Mallory and Irvine would have run out of oxygen completely much higher on the mountain and would certainly not have continued to descend carrying the heavy empty bottle and apparatus. Second, no oxygen apparatus was found with the bottle. Could the apparatus be somewhere in the area where No. 9 was found? Technically, yes. But why would the exhausted climbers go to the trouble of separating the empty oxygen cylinder from the now-useless carrying frame? Almost certainly they would have dropped the entire apparatus when the last bottle ran out. But only the cylinder was discarded. Thus, No. 9 was discarded when it ran out on the way up, not on the way down.

No. 9 also tells us that Mallory and Irvine were climbing strongly that morning. The difference in altitude between Camp VI and the spot where the cylinder was discovered is approximately 850 feet (260 m). Dividing that distance by the time the bottle lasted yields a perfectly respectable climbing rate of 230 feet (70 m) per hour, roughly the same rate as the 1999 research expedition climbers took to cover the same distance. Today's climbers are often slowed down by the task of setting fixed ropes. Mallory and Irvine climbed before the era of fixing ropes and would have moved together, and therefore more quickly, though they would have spent somewhat more time sniffing out the best route.

They had a good day to climb. The conditions on the morning of June 8, 1924, were nearly ideal. There was almost no snow, the weather was clear, and the wind was relatively still, though it was cold. As for the difficulties of climbing through the Yellow Band, the 1924 expedition climbers were almost dismissive: "absolutely easy and almost devoid of snow," Norton later wrote;[19] "a safe and easy route towards the summit ridge," said Somervell.[20] These are not surprising statements; the prewar climbers climbed with little more than a length of rope and, as a consequence, were more accustomed to moving quickly over steep terrain without protection.

At 8:00 A.M., as Mallory and Irvine approached the crest of the Northeast Ridge, Noel Odell left Camp V. He spent the next several hours with his nose to the ground, studying the geology of the mountain and searching for fossils. Sometime around noon, he spotted his fossils.[21] At 12:50 P.M., he spotted his colleagues, Mallory and Irvine.

But where? In his diary he wrote, "nearing the base of the final pyramide [sic]." His initial dispatch was similar: "the prominent rock-step at a very short distance from base of the final pyramid." In his second dispatch, he added a cryptic "[at] the last step but one" from the final pyramid. Then, a full year later in the expedition report, he began to change his story. His initial accounts, including his accounts in Britain's *Alpine Journal*, tell us that his view of the mountain was clear and unobscured; he says he saw "the whole summit ridge and final pyramid unveiled." He used virtually the same phrase in the expedition report, but then contradicted himself only a few sentences later: "Owing to the small portion of the summit ridge uncovered I could not be precisely certain at which of these two 'steps' they were, as in profile and from below they are very similar, but at the time I took it to be the 'second step.' However, I am a little doubtful now whether the latter would not be hidden by the projecting nearer ground from my position below on the face."

Here, clearly, Odell was trying to satisfy the disbelievers: his observation is topographically impossible; given the general tilt of the slope, the projecting ground obscures the First Step before the Second, not the other way around.

Which account, then, are we to believe, the clearly stated firsthand account or the much later, much fuzzier account so obviously affected by public debate? Odell was a scientist trained in careful observation. He was also the fittest and most well-acclimatized member of the entire expedition team on that day (both of which he would demonstrate only twenty-four hours later). And we now know, thanks to Andy Politz's observations of the summit ridge from Odell's viewpoint,[22] that Odell's doubts about what he saw, a year after the event, were unfounded. From where he had stood that morning, the First and Second Steps would have been clearly separate and distinct, as would the Third Step higher up the mountain.

Finally, cylinder No. 9 was found only 620 feet (190 m) away from the base of the First Step. If, as seems clear, Mallory or Irvine discarded No. 9 and switched to a fresh cylinder at sometime between 8:45 and 9:15 A.M., they would certainly not have been at the First Step when Odell saw them at 12:50

P.M.; they would have been much higher. The only way they could have been at the First Step at that time is if they had left Camp VI much later than 5:00 or 5:30 A.M. But there is absolutely no evidence to support this alternative, and it flies in the face of Mallory's stated intent. It is hardly likely that Mallory would have overslept on the most important day of his life. What is more, he knew from Norton and Somervell's attempt a few days earlier roughly how long it would take to cover the terrain above Camp VI, even with the assistance of oxygen. Finally, there is nothing to suggest they were having mechanical problems that morning that would have delayed them for nearly three hours.

Thus, we can only conclude that Odell was right the first time: he saw Mallory and Irvine at the Second Step . . . or very possibly higher . . . when he saw them at 12:50 P.M. Is there any other evidence to support this conclusion? There is. It is reasonable to expect Odell, a geologist, to be precise in describing the terrain the two climbers were traversing at the time he saw them, and indeed he was. In his original diary entry, Odell wrote that he "saw M[allory] & I[rvine] on ridge nearing base of final pyramide [sic]."[23] Under no circumstance can the First Step be thus described. Indeed, nothing in his topographical description fits any feature of the First Step.

Was he describing the Second Step? Perhaps, but here too the problem is that the topography Odell describes is not fully consistent with the topography at the Second Step either. Odell described a "snow crest" (later changed to "snow slope") "beneath a rock-step in the ridge." Both 1999 and 1924 were very dry years; in 1999, there was no snow crest (or slope) at the base of the Second Step. There was one beneath the Third Step.

Odell also said that first one, then the other climber "shortly emerged at the top" of the rock-step as he watched them (though he does not define "shortly"). The Second Step in its entirety cannot be surmounted in a period of time for which "shortly" would be an appropriate descriptor. The Third Step can. Further, when one climbs the Second Step, one does not "emerge at the top" but around to its right, indirectly. At the Third Step, one does indeed emerge at the top, etched against the skyline.

Did Odell see them at the Third Step, then? It is an exciting prospect, but one that is hard to accept. It is true that the Third Step conforms best to Odell's description, and Andy Politz, the one climber who stood where Odell had stood seventy-five years earlier, remains convinced that what Odell described can only be interpreted as the Third Step. "[T]hose three steps are definitely separated, from that perspective," he says. "I have no doubt that he saw them on the Third Step. I think it's very obvious. What he described is clearly easy to define, even when . . . you have just a few seconds of observation. And the summit pyramid is stacked right behind that [third] step these guys climbed."[24] Jochen Hemmleb, watching Anker and Hahn climb the Third Step through his telescope, found that what he saw matched perfectly Odell's description of his view of Mallory and Irvine.

But could they have made it to the Third Step by 12:50 P.M.? Bottle No. 9 tells us they were on the Northeast Ridge, still below the First Step, at about 9:00 A.M. It would have been extremely difficult (though not impossible) for them to have made it as far as the Third Step by 12:50 P.M. Says Eric Simonson: "Even today, using fixed ropes and the Chinese ladder to surmount the headwall at the top of the Second Step, you have to push pretty hard to make it to the Third Step in under five hours, and they had none of the advantages we have today."

The First Step is impossible and the Third Step seems unlikely. Is there another alternative? There may well be—indeed, it appears to be the only one possible, given what we know. It is an alternative first proposed by Tom Holzel in 1981.[25] The Second Step is climbed in three stages: a traverse to the right from its base to a short rock climb, a steep climb up a very small patch of snow, and an ascent of the relatively short vertical headwall near the top. It is entirely possible that Odell had seen the two climbers come up that small snow patch (neither a crest nor a slope), although the snow patch would have been in deep shadow when he saw them, and then scale the headwall at the top. If this is what Odell saw, the next question is, can the headwall be scaled in a period of time that can be described with the word "shortly"?

During the 1999 research expedition, Conrad Anker answered that question decisively: it most certainly can. He had knee-barred up the off-width crack in the face of the headwall so quickly—with such "alacrity," to borrow Odell's words—that his companion, Dave Hahn, had not even had time to adequately belay him. At the top, at 10:45 A.M., Anker called expedition leader Eric Simonson, who asked him the critical question: could Mallory have climbed the headwall? Anker's response was, "Yes, with a high level of commitment and risk, he could [have]."[26] Of the headwall climb, Anker said, "I would give it a 5.8 rating at sea level,[27] but up here it feels more like 5.10."[28]

Whether they were at the Second or Third Step when Odell saw them later, it is clear that Mallory and Irvine had made excellent progress earlier that morning as they moved along the Northeast Ridge and surmounted the First Step. Other expeditions since 1924 have spent a lot of time negotiating this ridge section, notably the inexperienced Chinese expedition in 1960. The 1933 British expedition's Wager and Wyn-Harris chose to go around the First Step, rather than scale it. After moving laterally along the upper edge of the Yellow Band for three hours, they found it impossible to find a route up to the ridge crest again (later expeditions have, but only under conditions of heavy snow cover). Mallory was known to have preferred the ridge-crest route and was exceptionally skilled at routefinding. David Pye, his friend, climbing partner, and, eventually, biographer, commented: "I remember being repeatedly impressed by his genius for picking out a complicated route, both from a distance, and in detail when it came to close quarters."[29]

As research expedition member Dave Hahn has pointed out, Mallory and Irvine could have topped the First Step either by a direct route up the ridge crest or by the now common traverse around to the right. The former would have taken more time, but both are possible.

Their next hurdle was, of course, the Second Step. In 1960, the Chinese expedition first considered climbing directly up the terminal prow of the Second Step, but abandoned that alternative in favor of a traverse around to the right, in roughly the same manner by which one turns the First Step. It is the obvious line of least resistance—though, as Hahn would later say, "it definitely had its sporty bits."

Whichever route Mallory and Irvine took, what certainly is

clear from Odell's account is that by 12:50 P.M., they had successfully scaled the Second Step. Whether Odell saw them at the Second or Third Step is, in effect, immaterial, at least in this regard. They were demonstrably not at the First Step; they were high on the mountain.

But now there were three new issues they had to deal with: weather, oxygen, and time. As for the weather, it is possible, but not at all certain, that conditions could have deteriorated during the next three hours. A snow squall hit Odell at about 2:00 P.M., just after he reached Camp VI, but it does not necessarily follow that it also hit Mallory and Irvine high up on the mountain. Even if it did, it is clear from Odell's description, and his own actions, that the squall did not create whiteout conditions; he proved to be perfectly capable of clambering higher, whistling and calling as the snow swirled around him. Under similar conditions, Mallory and Irvine would have had relatively little trouble continuing their climb, especially since they had already cleared the most dangerous stretch, the Second Step.

As for oxygen and time, we are squarely in the realm of Holmsian detective work. That is, we can only determine what might have happened by eliminating what could not have happened. If either Mallory or Irvine emptied oxygen cylinder No. 9 at between 8:45 and 9:15 A.M., as seems the case, the next cylinder would have been empty by sometime between 12:45 and 1:15 P.M. (assuming it had full capacity and was set at full flow), the very point at which Odell saw them climbing "with considerable alacrity." That they were still climbing strongly can be explained three ways; either they were unbelievably strong despite having run out of oxygen, they had been climbing with their second cylinders at less than full flow (in which case they had not yet run out of oxygen), or they had switched to a third, fresh oxygen cylinder.

If the climbers had carried only two cylinders each, they would now be faced with a terrible dilemma: either abandon the summit, turn around, and descend immediately to safety, or continue climbing toward the summit without supplemental oxygen. If they chose the latter, and climbed at a rate roughly similar to Norton's during his last hour of oxygenless climbing (125 feet per hour) a few days earlier, Mallory and Irvine would not have reached the summit until 7:00 P.M., just as the sun was about to set. (In the unlikely event that Odell had actually seen them at the Third Step at 12:50 P.M., they could have reached the summit an hour and a half earlier, at 5:30 P.M.) Even if they turned around immediately at 7:00 P.M., the two climbers would have not had enough time, in the remaining one and a half hours of dusk, to descend the summit pyramid after dark, much less climb back down the difficult Second Step. Having left virtually all of their lighting gear at Camp VI, the two climbers would have had to rely upon moon- and starlight to see anything. And although it was a clear night, the moon disappeared beneath the horizon early on June 8, 1924, at 11:25 P.M. Could they have climbed down the Second Step in the dark? Everest veterans, including Eric Simonson, say it is impossible.

But of course we know that Mallory (and presumably Irvine as well) did climb down the Second Step successfully; his body was found below the Yellow Band, north of the First Step, not the Second. If it is impossible to climb down the Second Step in the dark, then the only conclusion one can draw is that they

191

climbed down the Second Step in daylight or dusk. There are only two ways by which this might have happened. Either Mallory and Irvine turned around when their second cylinder of oxygen ran out, just after they surmounted the Second Step, and descended immediately (or fairly soon thereafter), or they kept going, with a third oxygen cylinder, and climbed down the Second Step in twilight.

If they turned around, they would have been back at Camp VI sometime later that afternoon, while it was still daylight. But if Mallory was descending in broad daylight when he fell, why were his sun goggles in his pocket, when he had seen his own expedition leader struck snow-blind by such an error just two days before? There are only two possible conclusions: either Mallory was both clumsy and stupid, which he manifestly was not, or he and Irvine did not turn back when their second bottles ran out. And there is only one conclusion we can reach if this is what they did: they each had a third oxygen cylinder to help speed them toward the summit . . . or at least some distance toward it.

Driven on by the realization that the summit was at last within their reach, and no doubt climbing more slowly than they had earlier in the day, Mallory and Irvine could have reached the summit of Mount Everest by about 3:30 P.M., before their third oxygen cylinders ran out. By this scenario, they would have had just enough time to summit and descend through the Second and First Steps with sufficient, albeit waning, daylight and a degree of safety, and have ended up in the Yellow Band in darkness. (If Odell had seen them at the Third Step that afternoon at 12:50 P.M., their margin of safety would have been at least an hour greater.)

Did they reach the summit? The plain truth is that there is still no definitive answer. Even though 1924 was a dry year, it may be that when the two climbers reached the summit snowfield, above the Third Step, the snow was too deep or too avalanche-prone to continue. Odell had, in fact, reported seeing "a considerable quantity of new snow."[30]

Eventually, the oxygen cylinders may tell us more, though even this is not certain. What we do know with some certainty is that they did run out of oxygen high on the mountain and jettisoned their apparatus there. They did not have it on when they fell; the straps that held Mallory's mask to his face were tucked away in one of his pockets. If someone finds empty 1924 oxygen bottles still strapped into their apparatus somewhere between the Second and Third Steps, we will be able to say with some degree of certainty that they turned around at that point—largely because they could not have pressed ahead, oxygenless, to the summit and have descended safely all the way through the Second and First Steps to the Yellow Band in the darkness. If someone finds only empty 1924 bottles between the Second and Third Steps (without the apparatus), we may be able to speculate with some certainty that they each had changed to a third cylinder and had gone on toward the summit. Ultimately, however, without a definitive snapshot from the famous Kodak Vestpocket camera, we will never know with certainty whether they reached their goal.

There is one especially tantalizing, if indirect, clue that they may well have made it. It is known that Mallory had intended to place a photograph of his wife, Ruth, on the summit if he reached it.[31] When Mallory's body was found, there were several letters in the pouch around his neck. None was from his wife, and no photograph of her was found on his body. Forget-ful as he might have been, it is virtually unthinkable that he would have forgotten the photograph, or at least a letter from his beloved Ruth, with whom he corresponded regularly throughout the expedition. Where are they, if not at the summit?

While Mallory and Irvine were still high on the mountain, Noel Odell was descending, as Mallory had instructed him to do. He began his descent from Camp VI sometime after 4:00 P.M., when the snow squall ended, and arrived at the North Col camp at 6:45 P.M.[32] From time to time during his solitary descent, he turned to scan the summit ridge, but saw no sign of the climbers. Later, after he reached the North Col at 6:45 P.M., Odell and Hazard (who had been manning Camp IV) kept a watch on the mountain in the gathering twilight, but by that time it is likely that Mallory and Irvine's descent would have been obscured by the curvature of the slope between the base of the Third Step and the Second Step. Odell would later write, "The evening was a clear one, and we watched till late that night for some signs of Mallory and Irvine's return, or even an indication by flare of distress. The feeble glow that after sunset pervaded the great dark mountain face above us was later lost in filtered moonlight reflected from the high summits of the West Rongbuk."[33] Soon, however, even this faint light was gone.

And somewhere in the dark they fell.

They did not fall far. They did not fall from the dangerous Northeast Ridge, as had the many badly twisted bodies frozen in agonized death in the great catch-basin of the "snow terrace." George Leigh Mallory has told us that himself, by the way in which he died and the repose in which he lay when the 1999 research expedition climbers found him. And, as Jochen Hemmleb had suspected all along, his fall was unrelated to the ice ax that Percy Wyn-Harris found sixty-six years ago on a rock slab atop the ridge.[34] The two have nothing to do with each other.

George Mallory fell to his death from a spot well down the face of the Yellow Band, tantalizingly close to Camp VI and safety; his injuries are too mild, his body too unmarred, for there to be any other explanation. And he did not fall alone; at the critical moment, he appears to have been roped to his partner, Andrew Irvine. That Irvine fell too and was injured, though not as profoundly as Mallory, is suggested by the fact that the body found by Wang Hongbao, clearly Irvine's and not Mallory's, was within perhaps a half hour from the 1924 Camp VI.

This is what seems to have happened. The two mountaineers were in the final stretch of a historic day. Whether they actually reached the summit or not, they had climbed higher on Mount Everest than had anyone before them, much higher. Now, exhausted, dehydrated, and oxygenless, they groped down through the Yellow Band in the dark, with neither moonlight nor their own lanterns or torches to light the way. They probably were following the route by which they ascended, but to avoid the steep gullies along that route, they may also have descended into the Yellow Band earlier, right after the First Step, following the route that Norton had taken a few days earlier.[35] We may never know which.

At some point in the Yellow Band, they encountered a nearly vertical segment. Perhaps both men were moving down together, the rope between them. Mallory, as is usually the case with the more experienced climber, was bringing up the rear as Irvine picked his way down through the fractured limestone of the band.

Suddenly, a misstep: Mallory loses his footing and, in seconds, is plummeting down the face past Irvine's position. Or perhaps Irvine slips and pulls Mallory after him. The extra coils of rope in Mallory's hand unravel and then, after what seems like an eternity but is only a matter of seconds, there is a sharp jerk. The rope catches on an outcropping, Mallory smashes into the cliff face with his right side and dislocates his right elbow, the rope digs into his left side, and the jolt breaks ribs. For a millisecond, Mallory thinks he is saved. But the moment ends in a heartbeat as the shock-loaded rope snaps and he continues falling. Almost immediately, he lands on one foot on a section of steep slope. As the downward force of the fall meets the sudden stop of his body, the tibia and fibula of his right leg snap just above the top of his boot.

But he does not stop. The slope is too steep, his momentum already too great. He is sliding into the darkness of the great North Face, plummeting toward the final drop-off to the Central Rongbuk Glacier thousands of feet below. He is in agony, but he is not dead and he has not given up. He swings his down-racing body into self-arrest and digs his fingers into the frozen scree, scrabbles at each passing rock. But he is sliding so fast and the ground is so rough that it rips off his gloves. It is as if he is being dragged behind a runaway locomotive and he is trying to brake the speeding engine by the sheer strength of his arms and fingers. Just at the point at which he thinks he may be slowing, however, he hits a tilted slab, flies up, and, when gravity takes over again, hits the slope hard, his forehead smashing into a viciously sharp shard of rock. Slowing now, he slides off another ledge and finally stops.

His fingers still claw the slope. He is face down in the rock. His head injury is severe. He is losing consciousness. In his last act—it may not even be conscious—he crosses the good leg over the broken one protectively. Then almost immediately his agony, and his life, end.

He can no longer hear Irvine, who, also injured but alive, is calling him in the darkness. After a while, Irvine stops calling and begins, instinctively, to drag himself eastward toward Camp VI, which is some 400 yards away. He doesn't make it. At some point exhaustion, his injuries, or some combination of the two stop him, ten minutes from an ill-defined rib in the center of the snow terrace and another thirty minutes from his camp. He sits down and, in the desperate cold at 27,000 feet, Andrew Comyn Irvine, twenty-two years old, yields to the mountain, closes his eyes, and slips into a darkness for which there will be no dawn.

BECAUSE IT'S THERE

*. . . a purer air surrounds it, a white clarity envelops it
and the Gods there taste of a happiness which lasts as long
as their eternal lives.*

HOMER

Mount Olympus, Mount Sinai, Mount Fuji, Mount Kilimanjaro, Mount Everest: the magic of mountains seized the imagination of mankind long before man seized the mountains' summits. Where mountains did not exist to assuage this apparently primeval need, man created them: the Tower of Babel in Babylon, the ziggurats of ancient Mesopotamia, the stepped temples of the Maya in the Yucatan, the pyramids of the Nile Valley.

As if the Himalaya were not enough, the sacred scriptures of the Hindi of northern India imagined Mount Meru, the 84,000-mile-high home of their gods, the core of their cosmos, the center of their earth. Buddhism later adopted Mount Meru and built replicas—stupas—in front of every temple and monastery: square at the bottom, round at the top, and white, like the snowcapped Himalaya. Even at the foot of Everest itself, there is a stupa in front of the Rongbuk Monastery.

*

"Because it's there," Mallory is alleged to have replied to a *New York Times* reporter when asked, for what must have been the hundredth time, why he wanted to climb Mount Everest. This sounds much more like a snappy New York newspaperman's quip than it does Mallory himself.[1] Mallory was both a pedant and a romantic, and neither nature is given to such crisp locution. On another occasion, a newspaper reported a reply that is much more characteristic of George Mallory:

> If one should ask me what "use" there was in climbing, or attempting to climb the world's highest peak, I would be compelled to answer "none." There is no scientific end to be served; simply the gratification of the impulse of achievement, the indomitable desire to see what lies beyond that ever beats within the heart of man. With both poles conquered, the mighty peak of the Himalayas remains as the greatest conquest available to the explorer.[2]

It is this "indomitable desire" that distinguishes Mallory, Irvine, and the other Everest pioneers from the rest of humanity, a level of passion and determination that astonishes us yet today. It is the fierceness of that desire that lies at the heart of the fascination with George Mallory and that draws us to him and his last days so powerfully three-quarters of a century after he disappeared. There is something about Mallory that we want to believe about ourselves, something having to do with purity of purpose, unwavering commitment, and, in an odd way, invincibility.

Some years ago, writing about her own search for Mallory, Everest historian Audrey Salkeld wrote, "Whoever dares to tamper with myth is moving in a realm beyond the reach of reason."[3] But George Mallory is neither a myth nor beyond the reach of reason. Indeed, it is his vivid, almost luminous reality that is part of his enduring attraction.

George Leigh Mallory and Andrew Comyn Irvine were knowable. They had characters and histories, though Irvine's history was tragically short. We can know that Irvine was strong, handsome, earnest, and a born engineer. We can know that George Mallory was a brilliant and graceful climber and a man torn between the demands of family and career and his obsession with Everest. We can speculate about the extent to which that obsession was capable of driving him. We know from his colleagues that it created within him immense reservoirs of energy and determination, gave him the strength to press ahead where other, more mortal men might resign themselves to failure—or at least to self-preservation.

The notes found in Mallory's pockets are not myth either. Oxygen cylinder No. 9, waiting for seventy-five years to be retrieved from the Northeast Ridge, is not a myth. Noel Odell's sighting of Mallory and Irvine on the mountain, described initially in crisp detail, was not a myth—until he appears to have felt pressured to turn it into one. The length of time an oxygen bottle will last, the level of technical difficulty of a given pitch, the distance from one hurdle on the mountain to another—none of these things is mythical. Each is knowable, each discoverable.

The 1999 Mallory & Irvine Research Expedition set out, in part at least, to answer the question, Did they make it? In two months, the expedition gathered more information than has been known about their summit attempt for more than seven decades. A dispassionate analysis of that information suggests that it is more likely than had previously been thought that they did make it—but it is still far from certain. Other analysts may examine this new information and come to different conclusions. We encourage them to do so. A fully conclusive unraveling of the mystery will take minds as relentless in the pursuit of truth as Mallory and Irvine themselves were in pursuit of the summit of the world's highest mountain.

Finally, some who examine the new evidence and this analysis of it will choose to hold fast to their own versions of the story regardless, in the process revealing more about themselves, perhaps, than about Mallory and Irvine. This is significant, for the story of Mallory and Irvine has captured the public imagination not simply because it is a good mystery but because it has meaning—and a different meaning—for each of us. Each of these individual "stories" is a mix of fact and personal philosophy—about achievement and failure, about free will and fate, about mortality and immortality.

In the end, the answer to the question Did they make it? may well be another question: Does it matter? Surely what matters, what warrants our attention and our awe, is the scale of their achievement given the resources available to them, their astonishing strength and grit, the indomitability of their desire.

And this—not whether they summited the world's highest mountain, on June 8, 1924—is what matters in the story of George Leigh Mallory and Andrew Comyn Irvine.

NOTES

PROLOGUE

1. E. F. Norton, *et al.*, *The Fight for Everest* 1924 (London: Edward Arnold and Company, 1925), 125.

2. There is some confusion in the literature about the location and precise altitude of Camp VI; analysis of aerial orthophotographs and comparison with contemporary accounts suggest 27,000 feet is the accurate altitude of Camp VI.

3. Letter from George Mallory to Ruth Mallory, in Dudley Green, *Mallory of Everest* (Burnley, England: Faust Publishing Company, 1990), 96.

4. There is considerable uncertainty about the altitude this party had reached. Their aneroid had read 26,800 feet (8,170 m), but later theodolite measurements corrected this figure to 26,985 feet (8,225 m). Recent photogrammetric surveys by Jochen Hemmleb indicate that the highest picture by this party was taken from c. 26,600 to 26,700 feet (8,100 to 8,130 m).

5. Here again, the official figure can now be corrected. George Finch, the leader of this attempt, gives only a general description of the exact location of the high point: "We were standing inside

the bend of a conspicuous inverted v of snow, immediately below the great belt of reddish-yellow granite." A comparison of a photograph from that expedition and the actual topography of the area makes it clear that, in fact, the high point was no lower than 27,460 feet (8,370 m) and probably as high as 27,560 feet (8,400 m).

6. Norton, *Fight for Everest*, 125.
7. Tom Holzel and Audrey Salkeld, in *First on Everest: The Mystery of Mallory and Irvine* (New York: Henry Holt and Company, 1986), 222, suggest that the particular apparatus Odell used on at least two occasions was, in fact, defective.
8. J. Noel, *Through Tibet to Everest* (London: Edward Arnold and Company, 1927), Kingfisher Library Edition, 1931, photo of letter, facing page 220.
9. Norton, *Fight for Everest*, 128.
10. Ibid., 129.
11. Odell's report in "The Mount Everest Dispatches," *Alpine Journal* (vol. 36, no. 229, November 1924), 223.
12. Norton, *Fight for Everest*, 134.
13. Ibid., 136.
14. Ibid., 137.
15. Ibid., 138.
16. "Mount Everest Tragedy," *The Times*, June 21, 1924.

CHAPTER 1
1. The book was Tom Holzel and Audrey Salkeld's *First on Everest*.
2. Geoffrey Young, quoted in David Robertson, *George Mallory* (London: Faber and Faber, 1969), 84.
3. Ibid., 74.
4. Sir Francis Younghusband, *The Epic of Mount Everest* (London: Edward Arnold and Company, 1926), Longman's Green and Company edition, 27.

5. Ibid., 27 and 29.
6. Little has been written about Andrew Comyn Irvine's tragically short life. A slim book by Herbert Carr, *The Irvine Diaries: Andrew Irvine and the Enigma of Everest 1924*, was published in 1979 by Gastons-West Col Publications.
7. Ibid.
8. Robertson, *George Mallory*, 17.
9. Ibid., 29.
10. Ibid., 71.
11. Jon Tinker was the expedition leader for the 1993 commercial expedition to the Northeast Ridge of Everest organized by Out There Trekking of Sheffield, England, and the first Englishman to successfully climb the classic North Col route. His "OTT deviation" completed the route first attempted, unsuccessfully, by Finch and Bruce in 1922; linked up with the traverse along the Yellow Band pioneered by Norton and Somervell in 1924; but then cut directly up to the Second Step instead of continuing to the Great Couloir.
12. Letter from Hiroyuki Suzuki, Foreign Secretary of the Japanese Alpine Club, to Tom Holzel, February 7, 1980, as quoted in Holzel and Salkeld, *First on Everest*, 2–3.

CHAPTER 2

1. A figure, in fact, substantially higher than Brice actually charges.
2. Peter Gillman, ed., *Everest: The Best Writing and Pictures From Seventy Years of Human Endeavour* (New York: Little, Brown and Company, 1993), 10.
3. Holzel and Salkeld, *First on Everest*, 29.
4. Matt Dickinson, *The Other Side of Everest* (New York: Times Books, 1999), 21. Originally published in the United Kingdom as *The Death Zone*.
5. Faxed letter from Peter Firstbrook, BBC Travel and Adventure

Features series editor, to Eric Simonson, Mallory & Irvine Research Expedition leader, October 21, 1998; expedition files.

6. W. Unsworth, *Everest* (London: Allen Lane, 1981), 33.

7. Younghusband in Norton, *Fight for Everest*, 1.

8. Holzel and Salkeld, *First on Everest*, 178.

9. Ibid., 53–5, provides details.

10. Letter from George Mallory to A. R. Hinks, quoted in Unsworth, *Everest*, 40.

11. Odell's report in "The Mount Everest Dispatches," *Alpine Journal* (vol. 36, no. 229, November 1924), 245.

12. Holzel and Salkeld, *First on Everest*, 142.

13. *Alpine Journal*, op. cit., p. 246.

14. Younghusband, *Epic of Everest*, 176–7.

15. Robertson, *George Mallory*, 221.

16. Geoffrey Keynes's recollection is quoted in Holzel and Salkeld, *First on Everest*, 169–70.

CHAPTER 3

1. Lieutenant-Colonel C. K. Howard-Bury, *Mount Everest: The Reconnaissance*, 1921 (London: Edward Arnold and Company, 1922), 24.

2. Younghusband, *Epic of Everest*, 37.

3. Dave Hahn, "The Kathmandu Duffel Shuffle," *Mallory & Irvine Research Expedition Dispatches*, March 20, 1999, MountainZone (www.mountainzone.com).

4. Ibid.

5. Showell Styles, *Mallory of Everest* (New York: The Macmillan Company, 1967), 42.

6. Unsworth, *Everest*, 106.

7. Younghusband, *Epic of Everest*, 181.

8. Carr, *Irvine Diaries*, 67.

9. Bruce in Norton, *Fight for Everest*, 24.

10. Unsworth, *Everest*, 47.
11. Ibid., 25.
12. Ibid.
13. Norton, *Fight for Everest*, 31–3.
14. Unsworth, *Everest*, 47.
15. Younghusband, *Epic of Everest*, 190.
16. Letter to Geoffrey Winthrop Young, June 9, 1921, quoted in Holzel and Salkeld, *First on Everest*, 66.
17. Howard-Bury, *Mount Everest*, 166.
18. Norton has this backward; in fact the panorama he describes is from right to left.
19. Norton, *Fight for Everest*, 48.
20. Ibid.
21. Dave Hahn, "Motorcycles and Bureaucrats," *Mallory & Irvine Research Expedition Daily Dispatches*, March 24, 1999, MountainZone (www.mountainzone.com).
22. Dave Hahn, "Portable Mountain Chunks Above, River Below," *Mallory & Irvine Research Expedition Daily Dispatches*, March 26, 1999, MountainZone (www.mountainzone.com).
23. Dave Hahn, "Like from Winnemucca to Elko," *Mallory & Irvine Research Expedition Daily Dispatches*, March 30, 1999, MountainZone (www.mountainzone.com).
24. Graham Hoyland, "The Finding of George Mallory," unpublished paper.
25. Norton, *Fight for Everest*, 49-50.

CHAPTER 4
1. A Hindi word meaning a plan of action, arrangement, or settlement of details; literally, "tying and binding."
2. Dave Hahn, "Mountain Buddhism," *Mallory & Irvine Research Expedition Daily Dispatches*, April 2, 1999, MountainZone (www.mountainzone.com).

3. Ibid.
4. In fact, they were flaked and rusted galvanized steel.
5. This expedition was controversial because for many years, western climbers doubted the Chinese had reached the summit; a doubt that has since been abandoned. Jochen Hemmleb's analysis of photographic evidence from the 1960 climb proved conclusively that the Chinese had indeed cleared the Second Step.
6. From the original site of the 1960 Chinese camp to the site where the remnants were found in 1999, they had traveled just over 0.5 mile (1 km) in thirty-nine years, indicating that this part of the East Rongbuk Glacier has been moving at an average rate of 80 feet (25 m) per year—¼ inch (0.7 cm) per day.

CHAPTER 5

1. Norton, *Fight for Everest*, 51.
2. Carr, *Irvine Diaries*, 91.
3. Ibid.
4. "In Memoriam," *Alpine Journal*, (vol. 36, no. 229, November 1924), 387.
5. Carr, *Irvine Diaries*, 69.
6. Ibid., 81.
7. Ibid., 87.
8. Younghusband, *Epic of Everest*, 191–2.
9. Norton, *Fight for Everest*, 52.
10. Noel, *Through Tibet*, 222.
11. Bruce in Norton, *Fight for Everest*, 62–3.
12. Ibid., 66.
13. Noel, *Through Tibet*, 227.
14. Norton, *Fight for Everest*, 103.
15. Holzel and Salkeld, *First on Everest*, 62.
16. Noel, *Through Tibet*, 223.

17. Robertson, *George Mallory*, 199.
18. Ibid., 245.
19. Norton, *Fight for Everest*, 74.
20. Ibid., 77–8.
21. Ibid., 237.
22. Ibid., 86–7.
23. Ibid., 91.
24. Norton's expedition report (drawn from expedition dispatches) dates this climb at June 1, but is in error, as is a note found on Mallory's body. From Somervell's account of his and Norton's June 2 departure from the North Col to Camp V, during which he meets the descending Mallory, it is clear that the real date Mallory left Camp III was May 31. Norton corrects his error in one of the two accounts of this period in *Alpine Journal*, op. cit., 261, and the May 31 date is corroborated in Andrew Irvine's diary (Carr, *Irvine Diaries*, 108).
25. Norton, *Fight for Everest*, 96.
26. Holzel and Salkeld, *First on Everest*, 205.
27. T. Howard Somervell, *After Everest: The Experiences of a Mountaineer and Medical Missionary* (London: Hodder and Stoughton, 1936), 126.
28. Norton gives the altitude of this camp as 26,800 feet (8,170 m), but the topographic features described when the 1924 high camp was discovered by the 1933 British expedition, when matched with orthophotographs, make it clear that the actual location of the camp was at 27,000 feet (8,230 m).
29. Norton is in error here. In no place is the ridge crest more than about 400 feet (120 m) above Norton's traverse line along the Yellow Band.
30. Norton, *Fight for Everest*, 112.
31. Somervell, *After Everest*, 129.
32. Norton, *Fight for Everest*, 112–13.

33. Somervell, *After Everest*, 130–1.
34. Ibid.
35. Norton, *Fight for Everest*, 116.
36. Odell in Norton, ibid., 123.
37. Noel, *Through Tibet*, 262.

CHAPTER 6
1. Indeed, an expedition was mounted in 1986 on this premise. Initiated by historians Tom Holzel and Audrey Salkeld, it was turned back by bad weather and a fatal accident before ever reaching its intended search area.
2. Noel Odell, letter, *Alpine Journal* (vol. 46, no. 249, November 1934), 448.
3. Tom Holzel, "Mallory & Irvine: The First to the Top of Everest?" *Summit* (September–October 1987), 20–7.
4. Audrey Salkeld, *People in High Places: Approaches to Tibet* (London: Jonathan Cape, 1991), 130.
5. Ibid., 133.
6. In *Another Ascent of the World's Highest Peak—Qomolangma* (Beijing: Foreign Languages Press, 1975), 73.
7. Dave Hahn, "The Search at 27,000 Feet," *Mallory & Irvine Research Expedition Daily Dispatches*, May 4, 1999, MountainZone (www.mountainzone.com).
8. It was this hammer that Jochen Hemmleb ultimately identified as having been carried by one of the climbers in the 1960 Chinese expedition.
9. Jake Norton, "Kind of an Eerie Job," *Mallory & Irvine Research Expedition Daily Dispatches*, May 3, 1999, MountainZone (www.mountainzone.com).
10. Conrad Anker, "A Patch of White," *Mallory & Irvine Research Expedition Daily Dispatches*, May 3, 1999, MountainZone (www.mountainzone.com).

11. Dave Hahn, "The Find After 75 Years," *Mallory & Irvine Research Expedition Daily Dispatches*, May 4, 1999, MountainZone (www.mountainzone.com).

12. George Finch had created for himself a down-filled coat for the 1922 expedition, but the fashion apparently hadn't caught on.

CHAPTER 7

1. Thom Pollard, "The Rescue," *PBS/NOVA Online Adventure*, May 11, 1999, dispatch (www.pbs.org).

2. Noel, *Through Tibet*, 258.

3. Carr, *Irvine Diaries*, 111.

4. Norton, *Fight for Everest*, 120.

5. "Pinned in at Camp V," *Mallory & Irvine Research Expedition Daily Dispatches*, May 14, 1999, MountainZone (www.mountainzone.com).

6. Noel, *Through Tibet*, 261.

7. See Norton, *Fight for Everest*, 141, and Hugh Ruttledge, *Everest 1933* (London: Hodder and Stoughton, 1934), 132–3.

8. The only climbers who have used this site as a high camp have been the Chinese in 1975, the Chinese/Japanese/Nepalese expedition in 1988, and the 1990 International Peace Climb; 1990 expedition leader Jim Whittaker had the Russian, Chinese, and American climbers use the site to ensure that all three nation's climbers would make the summit on summit day. Expedition veterans now generally believe Camp VII forces climbers to spend too much time at too high an altitude.

9. Liesl Clark, "On Top of the World," *PBS/NOVA Online Adventure*, May 17, 1999, dispatch (www.pbs.org).

10. Ibid.

11. Ibid.

12. Letter to D. W. Freshfield, quoted in Holzel and Salkeld, *First on Everest*, 243.

13. Ibid.

14. The well-known Everest historian Audrey Salkeld was the first to put a name to the Third Step and discuss it specifically as a possible location for Odell's sighting in *People in High Places*, 133–5.

CHAPTER 8

1. E. F. Norton, "The Problem of Mt. Everest," *Alpine Journal* (vol. 37, no. 230, May 1925), 2. Norton presents a table of climbing times and distances that documents climbing times of 5:10 and 4:50 hours for climbs from Camp IV to V and Camp V to VI, respectively—in fact, shorter times than many current climbs have achieved, including the 1999 Mallory & Irvine Research Expedition.

2. The hour hand was subsequently lost, but expedition archive photos document its position.

3. Indeed, subsequent examination by an archeologist and a watch specialist demonstrated that the bezel of the watch opened with just the slightest effort; a tap against some hard object could easily have opened it, releasing the crystal.

4. Thought to be Stella Gibbons, a British journalist.

5. Norton, *Fight for Everest*, 116.

6. In addition, one of their porters also carried a third oxygen set, which Mallory carried up to the descending Norton and Somervell that night after the latter's unsuccessful summit attempt. Norton had roared, "We don't want the damned oxygen, we want drink!" They left the extra apparatus there, and Odell picked it up the day before Mallory and Irvine's summit attempt and carried it up to Camp V, in case Mallory and Irvine needed it if they were still alive.

7. Based upon the time when four of the porters returned to Camp IV.

8. The expedition reports indicate that Mallory and Irvine climbed up the North Col with their oxygen flow at only 1.5 liters per minute, and in his diary Irvine writes that he used no oxygen at all until the upper segment of the climb.

9. Norton, *Fight for Everest*, 331.

10. N. E. Odell, "The Last Climb," *Alpine Journal* (vol. 36, no. 229, 1924), 266.

11. Holzel and Salkeld, *First on Everest*, 217.

12. Odell found that they had left their magnesium flares behind (Norton, *Fight for Everest*, 141). The 1933 British Expedition found both their folding candle lantern and lever torch in the remains of the 1924 high camp, as noted in Hugh Ruttledge's *Everest 1933* (London: Hodder and Stoughton, 1934), 133.

13. Data provided by Harry Hett, using Xephem 3.2.2, and Thomas Wetter, using Redshift (both astronomical computing software). The figures used are for Everest at an altitude of 28,900 feet (8,800 m).

14. Odell writing in Norton, *Fight for Everest*, 131.

15. Ibid.

16. Ibid.

17. Holzel and Salkeld, *First on Everest*, 226–7.

18. Norton, *Fight for Everest*, 133.

19. E. F. Norton, "The Climb with Mr. Somervell to 28,000 Feet," *Alpine Journal* (vol. 36, no. 229, November 1924), 264.

20. E. F. Norton, "Mr. Somervell's Story," *Alpine Journal* (vol. 36, no. 229, November 1924), 213.

21. Later proven not to be fossils after all (Unsworth, *Everest*, 654.)

22. Odell said that he was at 26,000 feet when he saw Mallory and Irvine, and that he then climbed to Camp VI (27,000 feet) in an hour—a virtually impossible climbing rate of 1,000 feet per hour without oxygen. It is far more likely that he was at about 26,500 feet, and it is at roughly this point that Politz made his

observations as well. Indeed, had Odell been at 26,000 feet, the three steps would have been even more easy to distinguish.

23. Odell quoted in Tom Holzel and Audrey Salkeld, *The Mystery of Mallory and Irvine*, revised edition (London: Pimlico, 1996), 288.

24. Politz quoted in Liesl Clark, "Pieces of the Puzzle," *NOVA Online*, May 6, 1999 (www.pbs.org/wgbh/nova/everest).

25. Tom Holzel, "The Search for Mallory & Irvine," *Summit* (September–October 1981), 11.

26. Since then, Anker has changed his opinion and no longer believes that Mallory and Irvine could have climbed the Second Step headwall, though the rating he gives the pitch is not consistent with this conclusion.

27. Under the Yosemite Decimal System, a Class 5 climb typically involves the use of ropes, belays, and mechanical or natural protection against falls. A 5.8 climb is defined as within the range of the average weekend climber; a 5.10 as at the upper end of difficulty for a dedicated weekend climber. The range of 5.11 to 5.14 indicates a level of difficulty best left to trained experts. Ratings description from Don Graydon and Kurt Hanson, eds., *Mountaineering: Freedom of the Hills*, 6th ed. (Seattle: The Mountaineers, 1997), 510–13.

28. "Anker Free-Climbs Second Step," *Mallory & Irvine Research Expedition Daily Dispatches*, May 17, 1999, MountainZone (www.mountainzone.com).

29. David Pye, *George Leigh Mallory: A Memoir* (London: Oxford University Press/Humphrey Milford, 1927), 105.

30. Odell, "Last Climb," 268.

31. Holzel and Salkeld, *First on Everest*, 1996 revised edition, 293, and information from Clare Millikan.

32. Norton, *Fight for Everest*, 133.

33. Odell writing in Norton, *Fight for Everest*, 134.

34. It is possible that the ice ax was placed, not dropped, by either Mallory or Irvine on the descent. They had passed the areas where an ice ax would be critical and may have needed both hands free. But there is no question that Mallory did not fall from the very top of the Northeast Ridge; his injuries are too modest for such a brutally long fall.

35. This theory was first expressed by Frank Smythe in *Camp Six* (London: Hodder and Stoughton, 1937), 306–7.

EPILOGUE

1. Holzel and Salkeld made this argument in *First on Everest*, 295.

2. Ibid., 298.

3. Salkeld, *People in High Places*, 27.

APPENDIX 1

EVEREST NORTH SIDE: RESOLVED AND UNRESOLVED MYSTERIES

NO MATTER OF DOUBT—THE 1960
CHINESE ASCENT OF THE NORTH RIDGE

For years, the West doubted the validity of the Chinese claim that they had scaled the Second Step, much less summited Everest, in 1960. The doubts were based in part on a viewing of the Chinese expedition film, *Conquering the World's Highest Peak*, at the Alpine Club in London in October 1962, of which it was noted:

> The climbing sequences in the film undoubtedly took the ascent up to the old 1933 Camp V. . . . The commentary then continues with a number of supporting shots past "8,100 meters" to a point where it claims: "We are now at 8,500 meters." Except for long-focus shots from about this point up the face toward the summit, no higher picture than this was identifiable in the film.

But the shots are not, in fact, "long-focus." With the help of the BBC's Graham Hoyland and Everest historian Audrey Salkeld, Jochen Hemmleb obtained a video copy of the Chinese film. "The crucial footage is in two parts," explains Hemmleb. "A still from the first sequence, an eleven-second panorama covering about 30 degrees of the view to the northeast, had been analyzed by Basil Goodfellow, Lawrence Wager, and Hugh Merrick in the early 1960s. Although the former two demonstrated that the picture could indeed have been taken from above the Second Step, as the Chinese had claimed, Merrick believed it was taken from as low as the First Step. In 1985, Tom Holzel matched this photograph with a picture from the 1975 Chinese expedition taken on the plateau above the Second Step. Yet as the 1960 photograph lacks any foreground details, a degree of uncertainty remained."

Hemmleb then studied the second sequence, a ten-second panning shot of the summit pyramid, and discovered that during the last four seconds, rocks from the foot of the Third Step appear in the lower-left foreground. The very last frame of the sequence shows individual features of the Third Step, which are readily identifiable on another picture from the 1975 Chinese expedition, again taken from the plateau above the Second Step. The level of detail in the 1960 photograph could not have been obtained with a telephoto lens; the image is clear and fairly steady, and has too high a resolution for a telephoto.

"This single image," says Hemmleb, "the only image in the 1960 film showing topographic details of the mountain above 28,500 feet (8,700 m), is the direct visual evidence that on the morning of May 25, 1960, the photographer, Qu Yinhua (and presumably his three comrades), was standing on the plateau above the Second Step and had therefore overcome the crux of the way to the summit."

Did they reach the summit? Analysis of the two contemporary written accounts of the 1960 expedition, in the *Alpine Journal* and *Mountaincraft* (see Selected References), shows that they incorporate descriptions of topographical details of the final pyramid that could only have been obtained if the party had indeed reached the top. As

Tom Holzel wrote, "The Chinese 1960 climb of Mount Everest must now certainly be ranked among the most hard-fought ascents in Himalayan history. And it must be recognized as the first proven ascent of the north side of the mountain."

THE ROPE AND TENT POLE MYSTERY

There has been an interesting side note to the 1960 Chinese ascent: At a 1981 American Alpine Club meeting, the expedition leader, Shi Zhanchun, was understood to have said through an interpreter that a hank of manila rope and a short wooden pole were discovered above the Second Step during that ascent. Yet the altitudes and locations Shi gave were all below the First Step. A year later, American climber Nick Clinch interviewed Shi and reported that Shi had said that the pole and rope were found at 28,000 feet (8,500 m) on the slabs of the North Face below the Second Step.

Had Mallory and Irvine taken extra rope and a wooden pole to somehow assist them in their summit climb? Had the equipment been left after descending the Second Step? Some researchers, including Jochen Hemmleb, thought it possible. But in 1998, Hemmleb received an e-mail from Maohai Huang, a Chinese researcher living in Boston, Massachusetts, which put the issue to rest: Translating from a Chinese book, *History of Mountaineering in China* (see Selected References), he wrote, "At 8,300 meters (27,230 ft.) . . . Shi Zhanchun *et al.* found an old camp, a messed-up brown sleeping bag waving in the wind, and a piece of hemp rope (1 cm in diameter) close to the sleeping bag. At the corner of the camp stood a small wooden pole." Given the approximate altitude of the discovery and what is known about the route of the Chinese team, these were almost certainly the remnants of the 1933 British Camp VI, 27,490 feet (8,380 m), on the Yellow Band north of the First Step—which is, after all, in accordance with the information Shi Zhanchun originally gave.

When members of the Mallory & Irvine Research Expedition passed the site of the 1933 Camp VI on their way to the summit on May 17, 1999, they still saw remnants of the tent fabric, the brown sleeping bag, and the wooden pole sticking out of the snow. They also recovered a metal pack frame with perfectly preserved leather straps, identical to one seen in a photograph of the 1933 Camp VI (see page 141).

TWO TINY DOTS—WHAT DOES CAPTAIN NOEL'S FILM REALLY SHOW?

In mid-March 1999, Jay Budnick, who summited Everest from the north in 1995, told Mallory & Irvine Research Expedition coordinator Larry Johnson that he had an enhanced copy of Captain John Noel's film of the 1924 expedition, and in it he could see "two tiny dots" descending the summit snowfield. This was electrifying news—for it would have meant that proof that Mallory and Irvine had reached the summit had been in the record for seventy-five years, but escaped everyone's notice.

It seemed too good to be true . . . and was. WGBH/NOVA's producer Liesl Clark had stills from the original Noel film enhanced and e-mailed to Base Camp. When seeing the pictures for the first time, Jochen Hemmleb immediately had an uneasy feeling about the "two tiny dots." They seemed to be poised right on the edge of the summit snowfield, which is a route normally avoided by climbers due to the cornices overhanging the East Face. Even more revealing was Hemmleb's observation during a later hike to Advance Base Camp, when he happened to look up to the summit pyramid and could clearly see two dots in exactly the same place. Yet when Hemmleb and other expedition members watched the summit ridge through binoculars the next morning, the dots had disappeared. . . .

It was only after the expedition that the mystery was resolved: In Noel's book, *Through Tibet to Everest*, he describes how he obtained his "best picture" of the summit pyramid, which is almost certainly the sequence used in his film. And although Noel gives no date, it becomes clear from the context that he took this footage during Norton and Somervell's climb from the North Col to Camp V—six days before Mallory and Irvine's attempt. Moreover, a much more recent film, *Mount Everest, Summit of Dreams* (Bellingham, Wash.: Peak Media, 1995), shows the two dots again—as rocks. And finally, a picture from the 1996 Norwegian North Ridge expedition, looking down the summit snowfield, shows how the rocks stick out from behind the corniced ridge crest. All at once it becomes clear how they could be hidden from view by even the slightest snow drift and thus "disappear" overnight.

Mystery solved—but even knowing that we are looking at rocks, the image in Noel's film is still captivating: the majestic summit pyramid with its roaring plume, and on the final slope leading to the top of the world, two tiny dots . . . ghosts of Everest.

A BROWN PAPER BAG—THE MYSTERIOUS CHINESE "PRESENT" ON THE 1979 SNOW IN MOTION SYMPOSIUM

On April 28, 1999, the Mallory & Irvine Research Expedition received an e-mail from Doug Fesler at the Alaska Mountain Safety Center, containing a bombshell: Twenty years earlier, it stated, at an international avalanche conference in Colorado, three Chinese glaciologists had presented the conference chairman, Peter Martinelli, with a brown paper bag containing some remains—a boot, some scraps of cloth, and a small leather case. It was understood that these were the remains of George Mallory, found on a ledge on Everest's North Face. . . .

Could this have been true? The Mallory & Irvine Research Expedition itself provided a possible answer when they found Mallory's body with an intact right boot and the top part of the left boot. Could the Chinese then have confused their find with Maurice Wilson, the eccentric soloist who died below the North Col in 1934 and whose remains have regularly surfaced from the East Rongbuk Glacier? Again, most likely not, because he had not been wearing his boots when the British reconnaissance expedition of 1935 found him.

When expedition coordinator Larry Johnson returned from Everest, he immediately set about trying to locate the conference's participants to confirm the Chinese account. As for the remains in the brown paper bag, Peter Martinelli unfortunately had now no recollection of what became of these. A reply from Dr. Charles Obled, from Grenoble, France, eventually provided a promising lead:

> . . . the remains found were those of Dr. Keith Warburton, leader of the Batura Muztagh expedition, who was caught in an avalanche in 1959. The glacier released his remains in 1975 and 1978. These are described in two papers presented by the Chinese delegates, including some photographs. I remember well the oral presentation, where the assistant to the speaker suddenly took out of a bag a climbing shoe and a watch, among a few other things . . . and we understood, with some surprise, that the remains were found on a corpse!

Indeed, the inventory listed in the papers submitted by the Chinese match Fesler's information, as do the photographs. But Muztagh is in the Karakoram, not the Himalaya. If the remains are Warburton's, they could not have come from Everest. It seems almost certain that Fesler's information was based on a misunderstanding of the Chinese report—yet as this book goes to print, it still can't be ruled out completely that remains found on Everest were mentioned in a different context during the same conference. If so, where could they have come from? Could they have stemmed from the "English dead" found by Wang Hongbao in 1975? We know that Wang had told a few of his fellow climbers of his find after they had descended from the mountain. Could others have returned to the site later in the expedition to recover some artifacts? Unless further reports surface or more discoveries are made, there remains a very faint possibility.

THE "MYSTERY TENT"—A CAMP TOO HIGH

During the writing of this book, Jochen Hemmleb was contacted by a researcher from Seattle (anonymity respected), who submitted the following transcript of an interview done some fifteen years earlier with Gonbu, the Tibetan member of the 1960 Chinese summit team. In this, he reveals an astonishing find:

> At 8,500 meters (27,900 ft.), beyond the Yellow Band, we came upon a tent, one higher than another old tent, at about 8,300 meters (27,230 ft.). It was tied down with ropes. Inside, we found only a few articles of clothing . . . this was at 8,500 meters.

The tent at 27,230 feet (8,300 m) has since been identified as the 1933 Camp VI, and Chinese researcher Maohai Huang says that the book *History of Mountaineering in China* states explicitly that this was the highest camp found by the 1960 expedition. He assumes that Gonbu must either have confused the locations—or that his find is not in the official record. It is significant that Gonbu made the clear distinction between the two camps and, when questioned again by the interviewer, repeated that this second tent was above the Yellow Band.

There is no indication whatsoever that Mallory and Irvine could have carried a spare tent. They were the only party besides the 1933 expedition known to have passed the location before 1960, and neither of the 1933 team reported leaving or seeing a tent in the area. So if this "mystery tent" really existed, there is no conclusive answer as to who could have brought it up there. Except for the Soviets in 1952. . . .

It has constantly been denied by Russian climbing circles that this expedition ever took place. Yet the most recent denial, an article by Yevgeniy Gippenreiter in the *Alpine Journal*, contains surprising detail about the expedition members and events—quoted from a contemporary report in *The Times* of London. Although the time of the expedition seems wrong—a late post-monsoon attempt between mid-October and the end of December—it doesn't prove anything. And as one researcher put it, why repeat at such length details of an event that apparently had never happened? There is one statement in Gippenreiter's article that is of particular interest:

> From Camp VIII at 8,200 m (26,900 ft.), the leader radioed that the assault party, being in good condition, expected to reach the top within the next two days, weather permitting.

Unless the assault party had reason to suspect being halted by bad weather, "within the next two days" could indicate that they had intended to place one more camp during the summit assault. Could this account for the "mystery tent"? Its altitude, 27,900 feet (8,500 m), would place it at the foot of the First Step. The Chinese themselves had a camp there in 1960 and 1975, and the site was occasionally used by later expeditions.

It remains to be seen whether further information emerges from China to substantiate Gonbu's account. What becomes apparent, however, is that the early Chinese expeditions could have uncovered considerably more on Everest than is generally known—and that, therefore, some keys to the North Face mysteries are possibly still hidden in China.

MALLORY & IRVINE RESEARCH EXPEDITION STATISTICS

EXPEDITION MEMBERS (age as of June 1999, in parentheses)

Climbing Team/Support

Conrad Anker (36)	climber
Dave Hahn (37)	climber, high-altitude cameraman
Jake Norton (25)	climber
Andy Politz (39)	climber
Tap Richards (25)	climber
Eric Simonson (44)	expedition leader
Jochen Hemmleb (27)	researcher, support climber
Lee Meyers (52)	doctor
Larry Johnson (53)	expedition organizer
Dan Mann (46)	geologist/glaciologist
Michael Nelson Ntiyu (26)	support climber
Bernhard Rabus (33)	geophysicist
Schelleen Scott (32)	sponsor coordinator

BBC and PBS/NOVA Film Teams

Peter Firstbrook (48)	producer
Graham Hoyland (42)	associate producer

Ned Johnston (44)   cameraman
Liesl Clark (32)   producer
Thom Pollard (37)   high-altitude cameraman
Jyoti Rana (37)   sound recordist

Sherpas
Ang Chhiring (37)
Ang Pasang (34)
Ang Phinjo (46)
Da Nuru (21)
Danuru "Dawa" Sherpa (40)   Sirdar
Lakpa Gelje (28)
Lakpa Rita (27)
Pa Nuru (31)
Pasang Nuru (45)   cook
Pemba Tshiri (31)   cook
Tashi Dorje (29)

Trekking Team
Heidi Eichner (32)   guide
Heather Macdonald (29)   guide
Wayne Curtis (37)
Rene Contreras (56)
Horst Jung (65)
Vlad Langer (56)
Alice Norton (54)
Deborah Read (42)
Edward Smith (29)
Janette Sweasy (47)
Troy Walker (36)
Josef Wolfgruber (60)

SPONSORS

Financial and Product Contribution

Mountain Hardwear: high-altitude tents (Camps III—VI) and high-altitude down suits. Partnered with W.L. Gore and Associates for fabrics and Easton Technical Products for tent poles.

Lowe Alpine Systems: packs, fleece, and outerwear.

Vasque Outdoor Footwear: trekking boots and technical ice climbing boots.

Slumberjack: sleeping bags, sleeping pads, and camp furniture. Partnered with Dupont for bag fill/fiber.

Eureka!: low-altitude tents (Base Camp, Camps I and II).

Outdoor Research: gloves, mittens, gaiters, overboots, and hats.

Lincoln LS: MountainZone.com cybercast sponsor.

PowerBar: PowerBars and PowerGel.

Starbuck's: coffee.

Glazer's Camera: 35mm camera and Kodak slide film.

Product Contribution

Dupont Industrial Yarn Division and Pigeon Mountain Industries: Dupont donated the nylon fiber and PMI built the rope used on the mountain.

Smith Sport Optics: sunglasses and goggles.

Adventure Medical Kits: medical kits.

LEKI: trekking poles.

Outdoor Products: duffle bags.

Dermatone: sunscreen and lip protection.

Cascade Designs: Platypus hydration systems.

Thorlo: socks.

Special thanks to the following individuals: Jack Gilbert, Mike Wallenfels, and Jennifer Slaboda at Mountain Hardwear; Frank Hugelmeyer and Anna Schreiber at Lowe Alpine Systems; Bill Sweasy and Cindy Taube at Red Wing Shoe Company/Vasque Outdoor

Footwear; Ron Gregg and Jim Meyers at Outdoor Research; Joel Anderson and Karen Bridgeman at Slumberjack; Lee Wishau at Eureka!; Wendy Smith at PowerBar; and the whole team at Lincoln LS.

DIARY OF EVENTS

Base Camp (BC)	17,000 feet (5,200 m)
Intermediate Camp (IC)/	
Camp I (C I)	19,325 feet (5,890 m)
Camp II (C II)	20,000 feet (6,100 m)
Advance Base Camp (ABC)/	
Camp III (C III)	21,200 feet (6,460 m)
Camp IV (C IV)/North Col	23,200 feet (7,070 m)
Camp V (C V)	25,600 feet (7,800 m)
Camp VI (C VI)	26,900 feet (8,200 m)

March

18 Main party (Anker, Hahn, Meyers, Norton, Politz, Richards, and Simonson) arrives in Kathmandu

19 In Kathmandu; organization

20 Hemmleb arrives in Kathmandu

21 PBS/BBC team members (Clark, Johnston, and Pollard) arrive in Kathmandu

22 *Puja* ceremony in Kathmandu; remaining BBC members (Firstbrook and Hoyland) arrive in Kathmandu

23 Expedition leaves Kathmandu, driving to Kodari (Nepali-Tibetan border); spends night in Zhangmu, 7,550 feet (2,300 m)

24 In Zhangmu

25 Expedition drives from Zhangmu to Nyalam, 12,300 feet (3,750 m) via Bhote Kosi gorge

26 In Nyalam; acclimatization hikes

27 Expedition drives from Nyalam via Tsong La, 16,815 feet (5,125 m), to Tingri, 14,400 feet (4,390 m)

28 In Tingri; Sherpas and trucks leave for Base Camp (BC), 17,060 feet (5,200 m)
29 Hemmleb stays behind at Tingri due to illness; rest of team drives via Pang La, 16,800 feet (5,120 m), to BC
30 Establish BC
31 Hemmleb arrives at BC

April

1 *Puja* ceremony at Base Camp; Sherpas to Intermediate Camp (IC)/Camp I (C I), 19,325 feet (5,890 m); trekking team arrives in Kathmandu
2 Anker, Norton, Pollard, and Richards to IC; Sherpas to Advance Base Camp (ABC)/Camp III (C III), 21,200 feet (6,460 m); trekking team flies to Lhasa
3 Hahn joins climbing team at IC; Sherpas establish ABC
4 Anker, Hahn, Norton, Pollard, and Richards to ABC
5 Anker, Hahn, and Sherpas fix route third of way up to North Col; trekking team drives to Shigatse
6 Anker, Hahn, Norton, Pollard, Richards, and Sherpas fix route to about 160 feet (50 m) below North Col; Hemmleb, Hoyland, Meyers, Politz, and Simonson, plus film crew (Clark, Johnston, Rana, and Lakpa Gelje), to IC; trekking team drives to Tingri
7 Rest day at ABC; Richards descends to BC; Hemmleb, Hoyland, Meyers, Politz, and Simonson, plus film crew, to C II, 20,000 feet (6,100 m)
8 Anker, Norton, and Pollard complete route to North Col (C IV), 23,200 feet (7,070 m); Hemmleb and film crew to ABC and back; Hoyland, Politz, and Simonson stay at ABC; trekking team visits Xegar
9 Hoyland descends to BC with stroke symptoms, accompanied by Anker, Hahn, Meyers, Norton, and Pollard; Hemmleb, Politz,

Simonson, and film crew stay at C II; trekking team drives to Rongbuk

10 Hemmleb, Simonson, and film crew descend to BC; Politz up to ABC; trekking team arrives at BC

11 Rest day at BC; Politz to North Col and back, discovers remnants of 1960 Chinese campsite at c. 21,750 feet (6,630 m) on upper East Rongbuk Glacier

12 Hoyland leaves BC for Kathmandu; climbing team stays at BC; Politz to North Col and back

13 Anker to ABC; Norton, Pollard, and Richards to C II

14 Norton, Pollard, and Richards to ABC; Clark, Hahn, Hemmleb, Johnston, and Simonson from BC to C II; Rana and Lakpa Gelje from BC to ABC

15 Anker, Norton, Pollard, Richards, and Sherpas to North Col, Sherpas stay at North Col; Clark, Hahn, Hemmleb, Johnston, and Simonson to ABC; members of trekking team reach IC; Firstbrook is evacuated to BC with pulmonary edema

16 Sherpas fix route up North Ridge to c. 24,950 feet (7,600 m); Hahn, Hemmleb, Politz, Simonson, and film crew (Clark, Johnston, Rana, and Lakpa Gelje) investigate old campsite

17 Politz to BC; Anker, Norton, and Pollard to North Col for night; trekking team continues to C II

18 Norton to c. 24,950 feet (7,600 m); Anker and Pollard rest at C II; Hahn and Richards to North Col; Hemmleb to North Col and back; five members of trekking team reach ABC and return to C II

19 Anker and Sherpas fix route to C V, 25,600 feet (7,800 m); Richards carries to C V; Hahn and Pollard to c. 24,950 feet (7,600 m); Anker and Pollard descend to ABC; Hahn and Richards stay at North Col; Norton descends to BC; Hemmleb, Simonson, and film crew descend to BC; trekking team descends to BC

20 Hahn and Richards to ABC; in afternoon, whole climbing team descends to BC; trekkers leave BC
21 Rest day
22 Rest day
23 Rest day
24 Meyers, Politz, and Simonson to C II
25 Meyers, Politz, and Simonson from C II to ABC; Anker, Hahn, Norton, Pollard, and Richards from BC to ABC; Hemmleb solo to below junction of West Rongbuk Glacier, c. 18,400 feet (5,600 m)
26 Rest day at ABC; Hemmleb returns to BC
27 Rest day at ABC (high winds); Meyers descends to BC
28 Rest day at ABC
29 Anker, Hahn, Norton, Politz, Pollard, Richards, and Simonson to North Col
30 Anker, Hahn, Norton, Politz, Pollard, and Richards to C V; Simonson turns back at c. 24,950 feet (7,600 m) and descends to ABC

May

1   Anker, Hahn, Norton, Politz, and Richards to C VI and search area; Pollard turns back at c. 25,750 feet (7,850 m); at 11:45 A.M., Anker discovers body of George Mallory at c. 26,770 feet (8,160 m); search party spends three hours investigating and recovering artifacts, returns to C V at 5:30 P.M.
2   Search party to ABC
3   Search party to BC; Firstbrook leaves BC with DNA sample
4   Rest day
5   Rest day
6   Rest day
7   Rest day; Scott leaves BC with artifacts; Hemmleb and Meyers abandon hike to ABC below IC/C I

8   Rest day; team visits Rongbuk Monastery

9   Anker, Nelson, Norton, Politz, Pollard, and Richards to ABC; Hahn and Simonson to C II

10 Hahn and Simonson from C II to ABC; Clark and Johnston from BC to ABC; Hemmleb and Meyers to C II; nighttime rescue of Ukrainian from North Col

11 Rest day; Hemmleb and Meyers from C II to ABC

12 Summit team (Anker, Hahn, Norton, Politz, Pollard, Richards, Dawa, and Ang Pasang) to North Col

13 Summit team to C V; Johnston and Lakpa Gelje to North Col; Hemmleb and Meyers discover remains of Maurice Wilson on side moraine below ABC

14 Summit team at C V (high winds); Johnston and Lakpa Gelje at North Col

15 Summit team at C V (high winds); Johnston and Lakpa Gelje descend to ABC; Hemmleb abandons carry to North Col at c. 22,300 feet (6,800 m)

16 Summit team from C V to C VI, 26,900 feet (8,200 m); Danuru "Dawa" and Ang Pasang from North Col to C VI; Politz and Pollard reinvestigate Mallory site, return to C V at 9:00 P.M.

17 Summit team (Anker, Hahn, Norton, Richards, Dawa, and Ang Pasang) leaves C VI at 2:00 A.M.; Norton, Richards, and Sherpas turn back at C VII, c. 28,090 feet (8,560 m), at 10:30 A.M., recover 1924 oxygen bottle below First Step, arrive at C VI at 2:00 P.M.; Anker free-climbs Second Step; Hahn and Anker reach summit at 2:50 P.M., arrive back at C VI at 9:20 P.M.; Politz and Pollard descend to ABC

18 Summit team descends to ABC

19 Whole team descends to BC

20 Pack up BC

21 Pack up BC

22 Expedition leaves BC, spends night at Zhangmu

23 Expedition arrives back at Kathmandu
24 In Kathmandu; evening signing session at Rum Doodle Bar
25 In Kathmandu; press conference at Yak & Yeti Hotel
26 Hemmleb and Johnston leave Kathmandu
27 Remaining team leaves Kathmandu

SELECTED REFERENCES

The following list of resource material is by no means complete. It concentrates on the British prewar expeditions to Everest and the mystery of Mallory and Irvine. Later expeditions to the North Ridge have been included only if they provided new information related to the early attempts.

The Alpine Club and Royal Geographical Society in London host a vast collection of documentary material (reports, photographs, diaries, and letters) relating to the British prewar attempts. Where such material has been used for research, it is cited in the relevant works. Though a few citations may lack all the facts of publication, they include sufficient information to allow the interested reader to locate them.

The following booksellers have helped in acquiring the literature used for researching this book:

The Adventurous Traveler Bookstore, Burlington, Vermont, USA

Aree Greul-International Alpin-und Polarliteratur, Frankfurt, Germany

Chessler Books, Evergreen, Colorado, USA

Verandah Books, London, Great Britain

BOOKS

Anderson, J. R. L. *High Mountains and Cold Seas: A Biography of H. W. Tilman*. London: Victor Gollancz, 1980.

Blanch, C., and J. Masson. *El Everest, Historia de una Conquista*. Barcelona: Ediciones Peninsula, 1986.

Boustead, Sir H. *Wind of Morning*. London: Chatto and Windus, 1971.

Bruce, Brig. Gen. C. G., *et al*. *The Assault on Mount Everest 1922*. London: Edward Arnold and Company, 1923.

Calvert, H. *Smythe's Mountains: The Climbs of F. S. Smythe*. London: Victor Gollancz, 1985.

Carr, H. R. C. *The Irvine Diaries: Andrew Irvine and the Enigma of Everest, 1924*. Reading, England: Gastons-West Col Publications, 1979.

Clydesdale (Marquess), and D. F. M'Intyre. *The Pilot's Book of Everest*. Edinburgh: W. Hodge and Company, 1936.

Dickinson, M. *The Death Zone: Climbing Everest through the Killer Storm*. London: Hutchinson, 1997.

Fellowes, P. F. M., *et al*. *First Over Everest: The Houston-Mount Everest Expedition 1933*. London: John Lane/The Bodley Head, 1933.

Finch, G. I. *The Making of a Mountaineer*. London: Arrowsmith, 1924. 2d ed. (London: Arrowsmith, 1988), includes new page viii and a new 116-page memoir, 'George Finch—The Mountaineer' by Scott Russell

— . *Der Kampf um den Everest*. Leipzig: Brockhaus, 1925.

— . *Climbing Mount Everest*. London: G. Philip, 1930.

Gangdal, J. *Til topps på Mount Everest*. Kolsås, Norway: Arneberg Forlag, 1996.

Gillman, P., ed. *Everest, the Best Writing and Pictures from 70 Years of Human Endeavour*. London: Little, Brown and Company, 1993.

Green, D. *Mallory of Everest*. Burnley: Faust Publishing, 1990.

Greene, R. *Moments of Being: Random Recollections.* London: Heinemann, 1974.

Hargreaves, J., comp. *L. R. Wager—A Life 1904–1965.* Oxford: privately printed, 1991.

Herligkoffer, K. M. *Mount Everest, Thron der Götter.* Munich: Langen-Müller, 1982.

Holzel, T., and A. Salkeld. *The Mystery of Mallory and Irvine.* London: Jonathan Cape, 1986. Revised edition, London: Pimlico, 1996.

Howard-Bury, C. K., *et al. Mount Everest: The Reconnaissance 1921.* London: Edward Arnold and Company, 1922.

Howard-Bury, C. K., and G. L. Mallory. *Everest Reconnaissance, The First Expedition of 1921.* New edition of *Mount Everest: The Reconnaissance 1921*, includes new biographical material by Marian Keaney and extracts of Howard-Bury's 1921 diaries. London: Hodder and Stoughton, 1991.

Longstaff, T. G. *This My Voyage.* London: Murray, 1950.

Madge, T. *The Last Hero—Bill Tilman: A Biography of the Explorer.* London: Hodder and Stoughton, 1995.

Mantovani, R. *Everest, the History of the Himalayan Giant.* Vercelli: White Star, 1997.

Messner, R. *Der gläserne Horizont: Durch Tibet zum Mount Everest.* Munich: BLV Verlags-Gesellschaft, 1982.

Morshead, I. *The Life and Murder of Henry Morshead: A True Story from the Days of the Raj.* Cambridge: Oleander, 1982.

Noel, Capt. J. B. L. *Through Tibet to Everest.* London: Edward Arnold and Company, 1927.

Norton, E. F., *et al. The Fight for Everest 1924.* London: Edward Arnold and Company, 1925.

People's Republic of China. *Another Ascent of the World's Highest Peak—Qomolangma.* Beijing: Foreign Languages Press, 1975.

People's Republic of China. *A Photographic Record of the Mount Jolmo*

Lungma Scientific Expedition 1966–1968. Beijing: Chinese Academy of Science/Science Press, 1974.

People's Republic of China. *High Mountain Peaks in China—Newly Opened to Foreigners*. Beijing: CMA, and The People's Sports Publishing House of China/Tokyo: Shimbun Publishing, 1981.

People's Republic of China. *Mountaineering in China*. Beijing: Foreign Languages Press, 1965.

Pye, D. *George Leigh Mallory, a Memoir*. London: Oxford University Press, 1927.

Roberts, D. *I'll Climb Mount Everest Alone: The Story of Maurice Wilson*. London: Hale, 1957.

Robertson, D. *George Mallory*. London: Faber and Faber, 1969.

Ruttledge, H. *Everest 1933*. London: Hodder and Stoughton, 1934.

—. *Everest, the Unfinished Adventure*. London: Hodder and Stoughton, 1937.

Salkeld, A. *People in High Places*. London: Jonathan Cape, 1991.

Sayre, W. W. *Four Against Everest*. Englewood Cliffs, N.J.: Prentice-Hall, 1964.

Shipton, E. E. *Upon that Mountain*. London: Hodder and Stoughton, 1943.

—. *That Untravelled World: An Autobiography*. London: Hodder and Stoughton, 1969.

Siggins, L. *Everest Calling*. Edinburgh: Mainstream Publishing Company, 1994.

Smythe, F. S. *Camp Six: An Account of the 1933 Mount Everest Expedition*. London: Hodder and Stoughton, 1937.

—. *The Adventures of a Mountaineer*. London: Dent, 1940.

Somervell, T. H. *After Everest: The Experiences of a Mountaineer and Medical Missionary*. London: Hodder and Stoughton, 1936.

Steele, P. *Eric Shipton: Everest and Beyond*. London: Constable and Company, 1998.

Styles, S. *Mallory of Everest*. New York: The Macmillan Company, 1967.

Tenzing Norgay (with J. R. Ullman). *Tiger of the Snows: The Autobiography of Tenzing of Everest*. New York: Putnam, 1955.

Tilman, H. W. *Mount Everest 1938*. Cambridge: Cambridge University Press, 1948.

Unsworth, W. *Everest*. London: Allen Lane, 1981. 2d ed., revised and enlarged, Sparkford: Oxford Illustrated Press, 1989.

Watanabe, H./Japanese Alpine Club. *Chomolangma—Tibet: Official Account of the Japanese Alpine Club Chomolangma Expedition*. Tokyo: Kodan-sha, 1981.

[*Yomiuri* Newspaper]. *Stood on the Summit of Chomolangma*. Tokyo: Yomiuri, 1980.

Younghusband, Sir F. E. *The Epic of Mount Everest*. London: Edward Arnold and Company, 1926.

Zhang, Caizhen, ed. *History of Mountaineering in China*. Han Kou: Wuhan Publishing House, 1993.

Zhou Zhen and Liu Zhenkai. *Footprints on the Peaks: Mountaineering in China*. Seattle: The Mountaineers Books, 1995.

PERIODICALS

A.J. Alpine Journal

A.A.J. American Alpine Journal

G.J. Geographical Journal

H.J. Himalayan Journal

Adler, J. "Ghost of Everest" (Mallory found). *Newsweek*, 17 May 1999, 72–4.

Alpine Journal. Obituary of J. de Vere Hazard, in *A.J.*, 1969, 350.

Astorg, P., and Marmier, J. C. "Echec au Qomolangma." *La Montagne* 3, 1981, 143–5.

"The Battle with Everest." *A.J.* 36, no. 229, 1924, 277–81.

Beauman, R. Greene, and H. Ruttledge. Obituary of F. S. Smythe, in *A.J.*, pp. 102–4; *H.J.*, 1949, 230–5.

Blacker, L. V. S. "The Mount Everest Flights." *H.J.*, 1934, 53–6.

Blakeney, T. S. "A. R. Hinks and the First Everest Expedition, 1921." *H.J.*, 1971, 3–18.

— . "The First Steps towards Mount Everest." *A.J.*, 1971, 43–69.

— . "Maurice Wilson and Everest." *A.J.* 70, pp. 269–72.

— . Obituary of J. G. Bruce, in *A.J.*, 1973, 283.

— . Obituary of R. W. Hingston, in *A.J.* 71, p. 347.

Blakeney, T. S., and N. E. Odell. Obituary of E. O. Shebbeare, in *A.J.* 69, pp. 327–8.

Blakeney, T. S., T. A. H. Peacocke, and B. R. Goodfellow. Obituary of G. I. Finch, in *A.J.*, 1972, 287–90.

Bruce, Brig. Gen. C. G. "The Organisation and Start of the Expedition." *A.J.* 36, no. 229, 1924, 241–4.

Bruce, Capt. J. G. "The Journey through Tibet and the Establishment of the High Camps." *A.J.* 36, no. 229, 1924, 251–60.

Bueler, W. M. "New Information on Chinese Ascents of Everest." *Off Belay*, April 1980, 35–9.

Bullock, G. H. "The Everest Expedition, 1921—Diary of G. H. Bullock." *A.J.* 67, pp. 130–49, 291–309.

Child, G. "The Big Easy—Everest the Weird Way." *Climbing* 155, September–November 1995, 82–8, 149–51.

Collie, J. N. "A Short Summary of Mountaineering in the Himalaya, with a Note on the Approaches to Everest." *A.J.* 33, no. 222, 1921, 295–303.

— . "The Mount Everest Expedition." *A.J.* 34, no. 224, 1922, 114–17.

Crawford, C. G. "Extracts from the Everest Diary (1933) of C. G. Crawford." *A.J.* 46, 1934, 111–29.

Farrar, J. P. "The Everest Expeditions; Conclusions." *A.J.* 34, no. 225, 1922, 452–6.

Faux, R. "Mallory's Grandson Fulfils Family's Everest Dream." *The Times* (London), 23 May 1995.

Fiedler, T. "Der Marmor-Mann" (Mallory found). *Stern* 20, 12 May 1999.

Finch, G. I. "The Second Attempt on Mt. Everest." *A.J.* 34, no. 225, 1922, 439–50.

— . "Equipment for High Altitude Mountaineering, with Special Reference to Climbing Mt. Everest." *A.J.* 35, no. 226, 1923, 68–74. Also appeared in *G.J.* 61, pp. 194–207.

— . "Oxygen and Mount Everest." *A.J.* 51.

Freshfield, D. W. "The Conquest of Mount Everest." *A.J.* 36, no. 228, 1924, 1–11.

— . "The Last Climb" (poem). *A.J.* 36, no. 229, 1924, 227.

Gippenreiter, Y. B. "Mount Everest and the Russians 1952 and 1958." *A.J.*, pp. 109–15.

Goodfellow, B. R. "Chinese Everest Expedition, 1960—A further commentary." *A.J.* 66, 1961, 313–15.

Harvard, A. C. "Everest Attempt" (note on 1986 Mallory & Irvine Research). *A.A.J.*, 1987, 300–1.

Hawley, E. "China and Everest." *OutThere*.

— . "Mount Everest: Ascents and Attempts during the Pre-Monsoon Season" (1995; notes on Alison Hargreaves' unsupported ascent of the Northeast Ridge). *A.A.J.*, 1996, 311–12.

Hemmleb, J. "Second Step—Unravelling the Mystery." Research paper. Author's collection, Frankfurt, Germany, 1994, pp. 1–7 and 4 appendices, pp. 8–16.

— . "Second Step—Update, Spring 1995." Research paper. Author's collection, Frankfurt, Germany, 1995, pp. 17–21.

— . "Second Step—Update, Spring 1998: Revising the Mystery." Research paper. Author's collection, Frankfurt, Germany, 1998, pp. 22–34.

— . "Second Step—Update, Autumn 1998: No Matter of Doubt—

The 1960 Chinese Ascent of the North Ridge." Research paper. Author's collection, Frankfurt, Germany, 1998, pp. 35-44.

— . "Second Step—Update, Winter 1998." Research paper. Author's collection, Frankfurt, Germany, 1998, pp. 45–53.

— . "Second Step—Update, Summer 1999: The Mystery Unravelled." Research paper. Author's collection, Frankfurt, Germany, 1999, pp. 54–72 and appendices/postscript, pp. 73–80.

— . "The Location of the 1975 Chinese Camp VI—A Possible Key to the Mystery." Special report (7 pps.) and addendum/appendices (10 pps.). Author's collection, Frankfurt, Germany, 1998.

Himalayan Club. "The Problem of Mount Everest." *H.J.*, 1937, 110–25.

Hingston, R. W. G. "Physiological Difficulties in the Ascent of Mount Everest." *A.J.* 37, no. 230, 1925, 22–38.

Hinks, A. R. "The Mount Everest Maps and Photographs." *A.J.* 34, no. 224, 1922, 228–35.

Hoelzgen, J. "Das phantastischste Rätsel des Jahrhunderts" (Mallory and Irvine). *Der Spiegel* 27, 1986, 140–52.

Holguin, N. "A Partner in Myself" (Messner solo ascent). *Mountain* 80, July–August 1981, 36–7.

Holzel, T. "The Mystery of Mallory and Irvine." *Mountain* 17, 1971, 30–5.

— . "The Mallory and Irvine Enigma" (letter). *Mountain* 26, 1972.

— . "The Search for Mallory & Irvine." *Summit*, September–October 1981, 8–13.

— . "Mallory & Irvine Second Step Clues" (note). *A.A.J.*, 1983.

— . "Oxygen Use on Mt. Everest." *Summit*, March–April 1985, 20–5.

— . "The Chinese 1960 Ascent of Mount Everest." *Mountain* 101, January–February 1985.

— . "Mystery on the Mountain." *Dartmouth Alumni Magazine*, September 1987, 33–6.

— . "Mallory and Irvine: First to the Top of Everest?" *Summit*, September–October 1987, 20–7.

Howard-Bury, Lt. Col. C. K. "The 1921 Mount Everest Expedition." *A.J.* 34, no. 224, 1922, 195–214.

Irving, R. L. G. Obituary of G. H. L. Mallory, in *A.J.* 36, no. 229, 1924, 381–5.

Lloyd, P. "Oxygen on Mount Everest, 1938." *A.J.* 51, pp. 85–90.

Lloyd, P., and H. Adams Carter. Obituary of N. E. Odell, in *A.J.*, 1988, 309–12.

Lloyd, P., and C. Putt, Obituary of H. W. Tilman, in *A.J.*, 1979, 132–5.

Longland, J. L. "Between the Wars 1919–1939." *A.J.* 62, pp. 83–97.

— . Obituary of L. R. Wager, in *A.J.* 71, pp. 349–55.

Longland, J. L., T. H. Somervell, and R. Wilson. Obituary of H. Ruttledge, in *A.J.* 67, pp. 393–9.

Longstaff, T. G. "Some Aspects of the Everest Problem." *A.J.* 35, no. 226, 1923, 57–68.

— . "Lessons from the Mount Everest Expedition of 1933." *A.J.* 46, 1934, 102–10.

Mallory, G. L. "Mount Everest: The Reconnaissance." *A.J.* 34, no. 224, 1922, 215–27.

— . "The Second Mount Everest Expedition." *A.J.* 34, no. 225, 1922, 425–39.

Mallory, G. "Summit Day on the Mallory Route." *OutThere* 8, 1995.

Marmier, J. C. "Experience Chinoise." *La Montagne*, 1980, 343–7.

Mason, K. "Some Observations on the Problem of Mount Everest." *H.J.*, 1939.

Merrick, H. "Everest: The Chinese Photograph." *A.J.* 67–8, 1962, 310–12; 1963, 48–9 and 359–60.

Messner, R. "I Climbed Everest Alone . . . at my Limit." *National Geographic*, October 1981, 552–66.

Millman, L. "Our Man in Everest" (Maurice Wilson). *Summit*, Winter 1992–3, 19–21.

Mountain. Obituary of P. Wyn-Harris, in *Mountain* 69, September–October 1979.

Nightingale, M. R. W., T. G. Longstaff, E. L. Strutt, and A. P. Harper. Obituary of C. G. Bruce, in *A.J.* 52, pp. 101–7.

Norton, Col. E. F. "The Mount Everest Dispatches." *A.J.* 36, no. 229, 1924, 196–241.

— . "The Personnel of the Expedition." *A.J.* 36, no. 229, 1924, 244–51.

— . "The Climb with Mr. Somervell to 28,000 ft." *A.J.* 36, no. 229, 1924, 260–5.

— . "The Problem of Mt. Everest." *A.J.* 37, no. 230, 1925, 1–22.

— . Obituary of H. T. Morshead, in *A.J.* 43, pp. 348–52.

Odell, N. E. "The Last Climb." *A.J.* 36, no. 229, 1924, 265–72.

— . Obituary of A. C. Irvine, in *A.J.* 36, no. 229, 1924, 386–8.

— . "Observations on the Rocks and Glaciers of Mount Everest." *G.J.* 66, no. 4, 1925, 289–315.

— . "The Ice Axe found on Everest." *A.J.* 46, no. 249, November 1934, 447–9.

— . "To the Editor" (Mallory and Irvine reference). *A.J.* 59, 1954.

— . "The Ice-Axe found on Everest in 1933." *A.J.*, 1963.

— . "Mallory and Irvine's last climb, 1924." *A.J.* 78, 1973.

Odell, N. E., and T. S. Blakeney. Obituary of T. H. Somervell, in *A.J.*, 1976, 272–4.

Paget, H. L. (Lord Bishop of Chester). "Memorial Services in Memory of the Men Killed on Everest." *A.J.* 36, no. 229, 1924, 273–7.

People's Republic of China. "Nine Who Climbed Qomolangma Feng." *Mountain* 46, November–December 1975, 20–4.

Perrin, J. "Capt. J. B. L. Noel." *Climber & Rambler*, January 1978, 20–3.

—. "H. W. Tilman." *Climber & Rambler*, April 1977, 20–4.

Pfau, P. "The Ghosts of Everest Past." *Rock & Ice* 86, 1998, 46–8.

"Russische Everest-Expedition" (note). *Der Bergsteiger* (Munich), April 1952.

"Russische Mount Everest—Expedition spurlos verschwunden?" (note). *Der Bergsteiger* (Munich), November 1953.

Ruttledge, H. "The Mount Everest Expedition, 1933." *A.J.* 45, 1934, 216–31.

—. "Mount Everest: The Sixth Expedition." *A.J.* 48, no. 253, November 1936, 221–33.

Salkeld, A. "Important Diaries Come to Light" (Irvine). *Mountain* 69.

—. "The Unquiet Ghost: The Strange Story of Maurice Wilson." *Mountain* 99, p. 46.

—. Obituary of J. B. L. Noel, in *Mountain* 127, pp. 42–3.

Sayre, W. W. "Commando Raid on Everest." *Life*, 22 March 1963, 62–72 and 76A–76B.

Schulz, M. "Marmormumie am Himalaja" (Mallory found). *Der Spiegel* 19, 1999, 230–2.

Seiner, D. D. "Everest: A Few More Words." *Summit*, July–August 1982, 28–30.

Shipton, E. E. "The Mount Everest Reconnaissance, 1935." *A.J.* 48, no. 252, May 1936, 1–14.

Shi Zhanchun [or Shih Chan-chun]. "The Conquest of Mount Everest by the Chinese Mountaineering Team" (extensively annotated by T. S. Blakeney). *A.J.* 66, 1961, 28–41.

Smythe, F. S. "The Accident on the S. Face of Mont Blanc" (ice-axe reference). *A.J.* 46, 1934, 414–19.

—. "Everest: The Final Problem" (letter). *A.J.* 46, 1934, 442–6.

Somervell, T. H., and T. G. Longstaff. Obituary of E. F. Norton, in *A.J.* 60, pp. 157–60.

Sors, A. "Everest" (note on 1985 Catalan ascent). *A.A.J.*, 1986, 297.

Spender, M. "Survey on the Mount Everest Reconnaissance, 1935." *H.J.*, 1937, 16–20.

Stelfox, D. "Everest North Side Story." *High*, September 1993, 44–8.

— . "Everest Calling." *A.J.*, 1995, 15–24.

Suzuki, H. "Bodies on Mount Everest" (note). *A.A.J.*, 1980, 658.

Tambe, S. "Mount Everest, Reconnaissance from the North" (note). *A.A.J.*, 1980, 3–17.

Tilman, H. W. "Mount Everest, 1938." *A.J.* 51. Also in *G.J.*, 1938, 481–98; and *H.J.*, 1939, 1–14.

Tinker, J. "Everest North Ridge." *High*, March 1994, 70–5.

— . "Climbing the North Ridge of Everest." *A.J.*, 1995, 25–9.

Unna, P. J. H. "The Oxygen Equipment of the 1922 Everest Expedition." *A.J.* 34, no. 224, 1922, 235–50.

— . "Everest Expedition, 1922; Notes on Illustrations." *A.J.* 34, no. 225, 1922, 450–2.

Ward, M. "The Exploration and Mapping of Everest." *A.J.*, 1994, 97–105.

— . "Northern Approaches: Everest 1918–22." *A.J.*, 1996, 213–17.

Wager, L. R. "Mount Everest: The Chinese Photograph." *A.J.* 68, 1963, 49–51 and 360.

Wang Fuzhou [or Wang Fu-chou], and Qu Yinhua [or Chu Yinhua]. "How We Climbed the World's Highest Peak." *Mountaincraft*, July–September 1961, 9–11.

Warren, Dr. C. B. "The Medical and Physiological Aspects of the Mount Everest Expeditions." *G.J.* 1937, 126–47.

— . Obituary of E. Shipton, in *A.J.*, 1978.

— . "Everest 1935: The Forgotten Adventure." *A.J.*, 1995, 3–14.

Watanabe, H. "The Chomolangma Project 1980—North Face and Northeast Ridge." *Sangaku* (Tokyo), 1980, 1–5.

Wyn-Harris, Sir P., and J. Paine. "What happened to Mallory & Irvine?" *Mountain* 21, 1972, 32–7.

"Zur Everest-Tragödie." *Mitteilungen des Deutschen und österreichischen Alpenvereins* (Munich), September 1926, 195.

MAPS AND GUIDEBOOKS

Howard-Bury, C. K., and G. L. Mallory. *Mount Everest: The Reconnaissance 1921*. London: Edward Arnold and Company, 1922, Preliminary Map of Mount Everest, 1:100,000, after E. O. Wheeler (1921).

Kielkowski, J. *Mount Everest Massif: Climbing Guide—Monograph—Chronicle*. Gliwice, Poland: Explo, 1993.

— . *Mount Everest Massif: Mountaineering Atlas*. Gliwice, Poland: Explo, 1993.

National Geographic Society and Boston's Museum of Science/Bradford Washburn. *Mount Everest, 1:50,000*. National Geographic Society and Boston's Museum of Science/Bradford Washburn, 1988; 2nd ed., 1991, with 1:25,000 enlargement of the main peak area.

Norton, Col. E. F., *et al. The Fight for Everest 1924*. London: Edward Arnold and Company, 1925, *Mount Everest and the Group of Chomo Lungma, 1:63,360*, after E. O. Wheeler (1921) and H. Singh (1924).

Royal Geographical Society/G. S. Holland. *Mount Everest Region, 1:100,000*. Royal Geographical Society/G. S. Holland, 1975.

Ruttledge, H. *Everest, the Unfinished Adventure*. London: Hodder and Stoughton, 1937, *The Northern Face of Mount Everest, 1:20,000*, after M. Spender (1935).

FILMS, VIDEOS, AND CD-ROMS

Breashears, D. *The Mystery of Mallory and Irvine*. Newton, Mass.: Arcturus Motion Picture Company/British Broadcasting Corporation, 1987. Investigates the Mallory and Irvine mystery in the context of the 1986 research expedition; includes interviews with Capt. J. B. L. Noel, N. E. Odell, J. L. Longland, Edmund Hillary, Chris Bonington, and T. Holzel.

Dickinson, M., A. Hinkes, K. 't Hooft, and N. Johnston. *Summit Fever*. Channel 4, 1996. Film (45 minutes) of 1996 ascent of the North Col route.

Ducroz, D., and J. P. Chaligne. *Sous l'oeil de Qomolangma*. 1981. Expedition film of French military expedition to North Col route.

Everest, Ten on Top—The 1991 American Expedition. AFFIMER, 1991. Video (50 minutes) of ascent of North Col route, led by Eric Simonson; summit footage by M. Whetu and B. Okida.

The Fatal Game. New Zealand. Film (45 minutes) of 1994 North Ridge tragedy and aftermath, from the perspective of survivor M. Whetu.

Kore Ga 'Chomolangma' Da! Tokyo: Nippon TV, 1980. Expedition film of Japanese ascent of Northeast Ridge and North Face.

Noel, Capt. J. B. L. *The Tragedy of Everest*. London, 1922. Expedition film. Also listed as *Climbing Mount Everest* in *Everest* by W. Unsworth (London: Allen Lane, 1981); unclear whether the film is known under two titles or two edited versions exist.

——. *Epic of Everest*. London: Explore Films, 1924. Expedition film.

Peet, S. *The Mystery of Mallory and Irvine*. London: British Broadcasting Corporation, 1974. "Yesterday's Witness" documentary, including footage from Capt. J. B. L. Noel's films, and interviews with Noel, N. E. Odell, and T. H. Somervell.

People's Republic of China. *Conquering the World's Highest Peak*. Beijing: China Newsreel and Documentary Film Studio, 1960. Expedition film of Chinese ascent from the north; filmed by Wang Hsi-mou and Mou Sheng (additional footage by Chu Yin-hua, Shi Ching, Wang Fu-chou, and Liu Chi-Ming).

People's Republic of China. *Another Ascent of the World's Highest Peak*. Beijing: China Newsreel and Documentary Film Studio,

1975. Expedition film of Chinese ascent; summit footage filmed by Kunga Pasang, Ngapo Khyen, Hou Shen-fu, and Sodnam Norbu.

Reneker, S. *The 1995 American Mount Everest Expedition.* S. Reneker, 1996. Video (50 minutes) of 1995 Everest "Commemorative Climb" by the North Col route; ascent by Mallory's grandson. Only still photographs of summit climb.

Three Flags over Everest. Pal Productions, 1990. Video (50 minutes) of 1990 USA-USSR-China "Peace Climb" ascent by the North Col route.

Whetu, M., and M. Perry. *Mount Everest, the Summit of Dreams.* Bellingham, Wash.: Peak Media, 1995. Video (45 minutes) of 1994 ascent of the North Col route and tragedy (additional footage by D. Hahn, C. Fawley, and R. Robert). The accompanying CD-ROM *Everest—Quest for the Summit of Dreams* has probably the most comprehensive collection of photographs of the North Col route, including the Steps of the summit ridge.

Wyn-Harris, P. *Climbing Mount Everest.* Privately produced, 1933. Expedition film; includes footage from near the ice-ax location. Also listed as *The Fourth Everest Expedition* in *Everest* by W. Unsworth (London: Allen Lane, 1981).

INDEX